5 de Mayo de 2018

Querido Michael:

Hoy en el día que recibiste tu primera comunión, te entrego este pequeño regalo. En sus lecturas encontrarás el alma de la sabiduría popular, que también pueden iluminar tu camino.

te quiere tu tío-abuelo

Guillermo

FOLK TALES
AND FABLES
OF THE WORLD

FOLK TALES AND FABLES OF THE WORLD

Europe page 5
Middle East page 75
Africa page 117
Asia page 147
Australasia page 191
The Americas page 239

Retold by BARBARA HAYES
Illustrated by ROBERT INGPEN

BARNES
&NOBLE
BOOKS
NEW YORK

About The Authors

Illustrator, ROBERT INGPEN, has brought wonder, excitement and beauty to the illustrations. Robert is already acclaimed as one of the world's leading illustrators of children's books and we are proud that his outstanding talent has gone into the making of the book.

Writer, BARBARA HAYES, has taken over a year to carefully collect the base material. Some stories had suffered badly in translation, so Barbara went back to source material. We believe this collection is as near the original as research can make it.

Often the work of an editor goes unnoticed, but a book of this nature needs a stand-off view, so we asked leading children's book editor, Anne Bower Ingram, to use her editorial skills to bring this collection to fruition.

The publishers also sincerely thank Sandra Step for the germ of an idea that grew into this book.

This edition published in 1995 by
Barnes & Noble, Inc.
by arrangement with David Bateman Ltd.
1995 Barnes & Noble Books
© David Bateman Ltd

First published in 1987 by David Bateman Ltd
32-34 View Road, Glenfield, Auckland, New Zealand
Editor Anne Bower Ingram

ISBN 1-56619-890-9

Typeset in Bembo by Graphic Type Limited, Hong Kong
Produced by Mandarin Offset
Printed and bound in Hong Kong

M 10 9 8 7 6 5 4 3 2 1

Europe

EUROPE

The Grey Palfrey   8

Beowulf   14

The Apples of Iduna   18

Aesop's Fables   23
  - Mercury and the Woodman - The Wolf and the Lamb - Belling the Cat
  - The Fox and the Grapes - The Goose that Laid the Golden Eggs
  - The Oak and the Reeds

The Pedlar of Swaffham   28

How Arthur Pulled the Sword from the Stone   30

The Lambton Worm   35

The Lost Islands   40

Lazy Jack   43

The Smith and the Little People   46

How Finn Found Bran   50

The Green Children   55

The Fisherman and the Rich Moor   58

St Mark and the Saving of Venice   59

The Best Teacher   62

The Lorelei   63

The Story of Perseus   66

The Grey Palfrey

Towards the end of the Middle Ages, life in Europe became a little less grim. The scourge of the Black Death had come and gone. Large national groupings were emerging to form the countries we know today. In the new security of a large kingdom, persistent local warfare suddenly seemed old-fashioned. At last there was time to think of more than basic survival. The young folk began to suggest there should be more to marriage than property contracts. There was talk of love and happiness. In France there began to be told the romantic tales which were the forerunners of our modern novels.

Long ago, in the Champagne region of France, there lived a handsome young knight. He was brave and strong, but he was not wealthy. He owned but a small manor house and a few fields that were set deep in a forest, away from the highways.

Poor though he was, the young knight had one possession which was the envy of the district. He owned a fine grey palfrey. This pretty riding horse was the finest-limbed and the best-trained creature ever seen in the realm. Many noblemen, richer than the young knight, offered to buy the grey palfrey, but he would not part with it.

"I trained it and it is mine to serve me and to be my friend," he said, with more truth than he realized.

Being of noble birth, the poor knight took part in the social gatherings at the great aristocratic houses of Champagne. Everyone knew and liked him, but as he was blessed with few of this world's goods, he was regarded as of no importance. At dinner he was seated far away from the grand folk at the head of the table. No mother put him on the list of desirable husbands for her daughter. However, the handsome face of the brave young knight caught the eye of the daughter of a great duke, she fell in love with him and he with her. They met in secret, but they knew their love was hopeless.

The maiden was aware that her father would arrange for her to marry a wealthy man. The brave knight knew that without rich property, he could never ask for the hand in marriage of the daughter of a duke.

Fortunately for the young couple, the home of the duke was in the forest not far from the young knight's manor house. Whenever he could, the knight rode through narrow forest paths, known only to him and came to the walls of the duke's great house. At a little barred grating hidden amongst bushes, he would wait for his beloved. Whenever she could, the maiden slipped away to talk to her knight, and he always waited. If the maiden came to him and whispered words of love and touched his hand through the opening in the wall, he rode home singing with happiness. If he waited at the wall in vain while the lovely maiden stayed in the house, unable to slip away to join him, then the poor knight rode back through the forest filled with misery. Tears would run down his cheeks, as he slumped in the saddle of the grey palfrey, scarcely noticing whither he went.

Several years passed in this manner, for the knight and the maiden were both young. The knight began to wonder if after all he might dare to ask the duke for the hand of his daughter.

The knight was brave and fearless, and as he grew to the full strength of his manhood he achieved more and more success at the great tournaments.

In those days all young men of noble blood were expected to learn to be skilful fighters. Mock battles called tournaments were regularly held, the winners of the combats taking the armour and horses of their opponents. These trophies could be of considerable value and after several victories, the young knight was able to set some coffers of gold in his strong room.

"I am not rich, but now I am not poor. My house and lands are small, but they feed me and cloth me, my family is of noble blood and I am a skilled soldier. Surely the duke could welcome me as a son-in-law," he thought.

Wearing his finest clothes, he rode the grey palfrey to the house of the duke and asked to speak to the great man. The duke agreed to see him, for the young knight had been known to him since boyhood.

The knight bowed.

"Your grace," he said, "you see before you a skilled soldier and an honest man able to manage men and estates. You see a man fit to be a member of your household. I have a request to ask of you."

The duke looked at the knight in astonishment. "Surely you are not asking for employment," he said. "Nobles do not work. They fight and live from the produce of their property. You know that."

The young knight smiled. "Indeed I do. I am not seeking employment, I am endeavouring to persuade you that I am a fit man to marry your daughter. Long have I loved her, long has she loved me. Our feelings will never change. Will you give me your daughter's hand in marriage?"

The duke laughed until the tears ran down his cheeks. "Have you taken leave of your senses?" he asked. "My daughter will inherit my vast property. She must marry a man equally rich. I will not waste her on a boy with a few bags of gold in his paltry manor house." Then the duke smiled at the young man in a kindly way, for he had known him since he had been a child.

"Go home and forget such foolish dreams," he said. "Busy yourself at your tournaments. One day you will find the daughter of another poor nobleman, living in a manor house the like of yours and she will suit you very well."

The young knight turned away with a heavy heart. He rode his grey palfrey home through the secret, narrow paths of the forest. The next day he set off for a tournament in a far part of France. "If I win enough tournaments then, one day, perhaps the duke might relent," he thought.

The young knight was away from Champagne for many weeks and during that time an old friend of the duke's came a-visiting. This man was as old and grey-haired as the duke himself, and both were avaricious by nature. The friend looked with envy at the fine home and rich lands of the duke, for although he had much he still wanted more.

The old comrades sat talking of days gone by, and of long dead men and women whose faces would never smile at them again.

"Ah, how I miss my wife," sighed the friend. "Being left a widower is a lonely fate."

Then the duke looked at his friend and said, "I am a wealthy man and you are a wealthy man. Joined together, we should be richer than anyone else in France. If you were to marry my daughter, we could manage our affairs to our mutual benefit. No one would be more powerful than we two combined."

His friend liked the duke's suggestion.

"With such an arrangement, I would marry your daughter without asking for a dowry," he smiled. "The joint management of our properties would bring me wealth enough."

When he heard those words, the duke had no more doubts. "Let us make arrangements for the marriage to take place as soon as possible," he said.

When the young maiden heard that she was to marry her father's grey-haired old friend, she was heartbroken. She begged the duke not to make her do such a thing.

"If I may not marry my beloved young knight, who lives in his manor house in the forest, at least let me wed a young man, fit to live with a young woman," she pleaded. "Do not tie me to a wrinkled old miser."

The duke brushed her pleas aside.

"I brought you up so that you could make a marriage to improve our family fortunes," he said. "This is the richest offer we shall ever have. Do your duty and behave as a noblewoman should. Do not burden my ears with talk of happiness."

The young maiden returned to her room. She prepared a beautiful dress for her wedding day and she wept.

The duke sent out invitations to his closest friends to be guests at the wedding. He summoned his steward and his master of horse to stand before him. He gave the steward the orders for food and for the preparation of chambers. He turned to the master of his horses.

"My daughter should ride to her wedding on a quiet, well-behaved mount," he said, "one with a fine appearance which will be the envy of those who behold her."

"In that case," replied the master of the horse, "there is only one horse for her to ride and that is the grey palfrey belonging to the young knight who lives in the forest to the west."

"Of course," smiled the duke, "that grey palfrey is the very mount. Send to the young knight and ask him to lend me the horse on the day before the wedding. I will return it to him well-cared for, the day after the ceremony."

The duke did not give a thought for the feelings of the young knight. Great noblemen expected lesser nobles to oblige them with services and goods. That was the way of the world.

The servant of the duke came to the manor house of the young knight as he was returning triumphant from the great tournament. The servant asked if

the duke could borrow the palfrey for three days during the coming week.

"Of course," replied the young knight. "She will be rested by then."

He was glad to do a favour to ingratiate himself with the father of his beloved. From idle curiosity he added, "Why does the duke need my horse next week? Is he going on a journey?"

"No," smiled the servant. "The horse is needed for the wedding of the duke's daughter. She will ride the grey palfrey to the church where she will marry the duke's old friend. Everything is arranged for the two great estates to be joined together."

The young man stood still and his heart turned cold. His beloved was to marry someone else. He would never know another happy hour. For a few moments he considered refusing to lend the grey palfrey. Why should he do anything to help this unwelcome marriage?

Then he thought, "The duke's daughter cannot wish to marry this old man. If I send her my horse, perhaps that will be a little comfort to her. In the midst of her unhappiness, she will have something of mine to remind her that we are at least united in our sorrow."

The next week the knight sent his horse to the home of the duke on the day before the wedding. Then the young man shut himself in his bedchamber and would speak to no one. He sat staring from the window.

Meanwhile, the wedding guests had arrived at the home of the duke. The evening before the ceremony they all dined merrily together. They laughed and toasted the bridegroom and the duke and congratulated them on their splendid alliance. They sat up late, drinking of the free wine, and stumbled to their beds scarcely an hour before they were due to rise.

The fair maiden also spent a sleepless night, but she did not pass her hours in jollity. Like the young knight she sat staring from the window of her bed-chamber. She thought of her grey-haired old bridegroom with his wrinkled skin. Her own young face set into lines of unhappiness.

The next morning, before dawn, the steward went round the house, hammering on the doors, and calling to the guests to awake and mount their horses. "It is a long ride to the church," he called, "we must start betimes."

Groaning and clutching their aching heads the duke and the bridegroom and their friends staggered from their beds. In the half-light they dragged on their rich clothes and groped their way up into their saddles. Two by two they jangled along the narrow forest road, keeping their heads down to avoid the sweeping branches of the overhanging trees. The duke and the bridegroom rode at the head of the procession, and the maiden at the rear, in the care of the steward. The girl wore her lovely dress, but her eyes were blinded with tears. The steward, who had been up all night, dozed in his saddle.

So this bleary-eyed, belching company swayed through the forest in the dim, grey light, which shines before dawn. No one noticed when, from force of habit, the grey palfrey turned down the secret path which was usually taken by the young knight. The maiden sat in the saddle, cold and exhausted, and did not raise her head to look about her. Suddenly she wondered why the rest of the company had fallen so silent, then she saw that she was alone in the

12

wilds of the forest on a narrow path leading she knew not whither. Terror seized her and she opened her mouth to call to the steward.

Then she closed her mouth and thought, "I would rather be killed by the wild beasts than go to the church to marry that old man. Let the grey palfrey carry me where it will."

Back on the main track through the forest, the steward opened his eyes to see that the maiden no longer rode at his side. He thought she had gone ahead to be with her father and with a grunt, he went back to his snoozing.

The sun came up above the horizon. It cleared the tops of the trees and shone down through the leaves. The grey palfrey tossed its head and hurried along the paths it had trod so many times with the young knight. Scenting home, the palfrey cantered across the last few yards of cleared land and snorted before the door of the knight's manor house. The watchman pushed open a grill high in the wall and looked out. "Who is there?" he called.

The maiden was fearful that she had come to a den of bandits, however, she had little choice but to reply.

"I am lost in the forest. Please let me rest for a while and then show me the way to my home," she called.

By this time the watchman had recognized the grey palfrey. He ran to the room of his master and hammered on the door.

"Your grey palfrey is at the gate with a maiden as beautiful as the sun riding on its back," he shouted.

The young knight ran to the door and flung it open. Sitting on his grey palfrey he saw the maiden he loved. She stared at him in astonishment. He led her in through the gates which were slammed shut after her.

The maiden slid from the horse into the arms of the brave young knight.

"How did you get here?" he asked.

"I don't know. I don't know," she sobbed and laughed together. "My eyes were blinded by tears. Somehow the grey palfrey turned away from the track and from the wedding guests and brought me here."

"Then here you shall stay," said the brave young knight. "Our love was meant to be."

He woke his chaplain and called his household together. In front of them all the young knight and the maiden were married.

When the duke and the bridegroom arrived at the church, they turned to wait for the maiden, while the whole company of groaning, sleepy guests dismounted from their horses. The steward arrived, but there was no bride.

What uproar and recriminations there were! What shouting and mounting and dismounting of horses! The duke and his guests and servants searched back through the forest and through the duke's large home. By the time they came to the manor house of the young knight the wedding was over. The couple were man and wife and what was done could not be undone.

The duke stamped with rage. Then seeing there was no remedy, he gave the couple his blessing and left. The young knight and the fair maiden lived the rest of their lives in happiness.

Beowulf

This story, set in Denmark, belongs to the traditions of the Anglo-Saxon tribes which spread across northern Europe after the collapse of the Roman Empire. The story of Beowulf was first found in poetic form as part of the ANGLO-SAXON CHRONICLES. These chronicles were written in England during the ninth to the twelfth centuries.

In the dark days of constant warfare, which followed the withdrawal of the Roman armies from northern Europe, there were many small kingdoms all fighting to save themselves from falling into the hands of a larger foe.

In those days strong, brave, well-trained fighting men were a tribe's only salvation. Such men were admired as heroes. This is a story of Beowulf, a hero of his time.

In the troubled Dark Ages, there lived in Denmark a king named Hrothgar. He gathered a fine band of fighting men around him and for a while brought peace to his kingdom. No one dared attack a land defended by Hrothgar and his warriors. To reward his men, Hrothgar built a great hall, where they could meet together and feast, during the dark days of winter. A hall where they could talk of battles past, and plan what they should do if danger threatened again.

Some years went by and Hrothgar passed his fighting prime, but still young men came to train with him and the kingdom remained safe. Then a danger came which none had foreseen, and Hrothgar and his men stood helpless.

Hrothgar's great hall was called Heorot and it was set in a land of fens and moors. One year a terrible fiend, named Grendel, came to live on the fens with his mother. Their home was in a dank cave below a dark mere and so frightful were these terrible creatures that not even wild animals dared approach them.

One night, on his wanderings across the fens in search of an unwary animal or a lonely traveller, Grendel heard the sound of laughter and music coming from Heorot. Creeping close, he saw the warriors and King Hrothgar laughing together and he was jealous of their happiness. He waited until the small hours of the morning, when the men were asleep across their seats and King Hrothgar sat high above them dozing on his throne. Grendel crept into the great hall of Heorot and slew thirty of the warriors and dragged them away to his lair.

In the morning, when those who were left awoke, they stared at the bloodstains on the floor and the empty places of their comrades and they wept. They knew this was the work of Grendel. The next night the same thing happened. Grendel crept unseen and unheard into Heorot and killed thirty warriors and took them away.

15

The bravest of Hrothgar's men tried to defend the hall against this wicked fiend, but Grendel was not easily seen and even less easily caught. Swords and knives were useless against him as they glanced away from the mist which surrounded him. Soon no warriors would come to feast in Hrothgar's hall and the old king sat alone.

News of the dreaded Grendel reached Beowulf, the son of the king's sister, where he lived in Geatland. Beowulf was brave and strong and well-trained in fighting, but he was young and needed experience in confronting many different foes. As was the custom amongst young nobles, Beowulf called together his friends and set out to fight this new terror, so that they might gain in glory and, if they survived, learn new tricks with which to defend their own people.

Beowulf and his friends sailed across the seas to the shores of Denmark. They strode to the forlorn grandeur of Heorot and stood before King Hrothgar.

"Hail to thee, Hrothgar," called Beowulf, bowing low. "I have come to rid your hall of this fiend, Grendel, who comes in stealth by night. I have slain giants and I have slain sea-monsters. A creature of the mere holds no terror for me."

Hrothgar welcomed his brave, young guest, but shook his head sadly.

"I trust you will succeed where others have failed," he said, "but do not be too confident. Grendel creeps in unseen. Weapons are no use against him. Take care for your life, young man."

But Beowulf felt no fear. That night he and his men feasted with Hrothgar in Heorot, but when the meal was over, Hrothgar went away. Even he dared no longer pass the night in that hall. Beowulf laid aside his sword and took off his coat of mail.

"If Grendel likes to fight without a weapon, then I will oblige him," smiled Beowulf to his men. They settled down to rest, each wondering in his heart if he would ever see his homeland again.

In the darkness before dawn, Grendel came stalking across the fens and the moors. He stood before the door of Heorot and although it was locked with iron bars, Grendel entered. He strode between the tables, his eyes glowing red at the sight of so many warriors to slay. Seizing one young man, he stole his life away, then he reached for Beowulf. His arm was grasped in the strongest grip the fiend had ever felt.

Grendel knew at once that he had met his match and tried to flee, but Beowulf jumped to his feet and seized Grendel's arm in an even tighter hold. Grendel cried out in pain and fought and tugged and wrenched at his arm in his efforts to flee to the safety of his home in the mere. The hall shook and shuddered with the thrashing and struggling of the brave warrior and the fearsome fiend. At last with a scream, which no one who heard ever forgot, Grendel wrenched his body away from his arm and, with blood pouring from his gaping shoulder, ran back towards the cavern in the mere and left Beowulf, clutching the frightful, severed arm, in the hall of Heorot.

In the morning, when the sky was light, Beowulf followed the trail of blood across the moors and found the body of Grendel. Leaving the fiend where he lay, Beowulf returned to spread the good news amongst the Danes.

Great was the rejoicing. King Hrothgar gave Beowulf and his men many fine presents. Hrothgar's warriors returned to sleep in their hall. Beowulf and his men lodged in a nearby house, ready to leave for home the next day.

But Grendel's mother had found his body. Furious with grief and lusting for vengeance, she strode to Heorot that night. Entering the hall while the warriors slept, she seized the young man dearest to Hrothgar and slew him, screaming that she would have vengeance for her son.

In the din and confusion made by the waking, shouting men, she slipped away to the cavern under the mere.

In the morning, Beowulf was brought the dreadful news that now another fiend was killing the men of Hrothgar. Again he showed no fear, but stood before the king and offered to go to the frightful cavern and kill Grendel's mother, as he had killed the fiend himself.

Hrothgar ordered horses to be saddled and, with Beowulf and a band of men, rode out over the moors and fens until they reached the dark mere, under which lay the cavern that had been Grendel's home. Frightful sea-monsters swam about in its murky depths, but when one of Hrothgar's men blew a blast on his hunting horn, they fled. Beowulf stared down into the water and swore that it should not stop him from reaching Grendel's mother and slaying her. He put on his coat of mail. He put on his helmet and took up his sword, then stepped into the cold waters. For a day he groped through the mere. Suddenly he felt himself seized in a powerful grip – Grendel's mother had found him!

With amazing strength, the creature dragged Beowulf into a damp cavern. Looking round he saw that it was lit by a beam of white fire. Now Beowulf could see his enemy and wrenching himself free, he struck at her with his sword. But like Grendel, his mother could not be harmed by a sword made by mortal hands. Flinging Beowulf to the ground, Grendel's mother pulled a dagger and was about to stab him, when the young man saw a beautiful old sword hanging on the wall. He recognized it as the work of the giants of old and with one last effort, he reached up, snatched the sword from its place and used it to cut off the head of the fearful creature.

Out of danger at last, Beowulf looked round the cavern and saw the body of Grendel lying on a couch. He used the sword to cut the head from the body, but then a strange thing happened. The poisoned blood of Grendel melted all but the jewelled hilt of the sword, which remained in Beowulf's hand.

Carrying the heads of the two fiends, and the jewelled hilt of the ancient sword, Beowulf left the cavern and rose to the surface of the mere. How joy-fully he was welcomed by the anxious group of men waiting on the shore. The heads of Grendel and his mother were taken back to Heorot for all to see. Beowulf presented King Hrothgar with the hilt of the sword which had slain his enemies and Hrothgar, in gratitude, gave Beowulf and his men more fine presents.

The Apples of Iduna

The Apples of Iduna is a myth of the Norsemen, or Vikings. They were the Danes, Norwegians and Swedes who raided most of north and west Europe from the sea, during the eighth to the eleventh century. They often settled in the lands they had conquered.

As the great glaciers withdrew at the close of the last mighty ice age, northern Europe was a fearsome, awesome place. Only the gods were young and beautiful and the hope for the world.

The jealous, evil frost giants lived in Jotunheim, ever ready to attack the gods at the slightest sign of weakness.

Beneath the earth laboured the ugly dwarfs and trolls and gnomes, collecting gold and silver and jewels. They were clever smiths and forged beautiful metal work and fine swords, but they crawled like maggots beneath the surface of the world and forever envied the loveliness of the Aesir, as the gods were called.

The Aesir looked at the chaos around them and created Midgard, a garden in the middle of the earth. One day Odin, the son of Thor, with Hoenir, the bright one, and Loki, the fascinating, unreliable, good friend and deceiver, were strolling through Midgard, when they saw two trees, the ash and the elm. From each tree was carved a log in human form. Odin gave the logs souls, Hoenir gave them the power of movement and the gifts of hearing, seeing and feeling, while Loki gave them blood and the bloom of life. So man and woman were created and populated the earth.

Then the Aesir sought to make a home for themselves. They crossed the wide River Ifing, whose waters never froze, and ventured to the broad plain Idawold, set high above Midgard. In the centre of this lovely and sacred place, they built Asgard, the home of the gods. In this beautiful city there was to be neither quarrelling nor bloodshed, but harmony for as long as the gods should rule.

Iduna lived in Asgard. She was the wife of Bragi, the god of poetry, and she was the keeper of the apples of youth. The gods of Asgard did not stay young naturally, they could age, as mortals did. However, if now and then at their feasting, they ate an apple from Iduna's magic casket, they stayed vigorous and young through the ages.

The frost giants and the dwarfs longed to eat the apples of youth, but Iduna never left Asgard and the apples stayed safe in their magic casket. As Iduna took an apple from the casket and gave it to a god, another apple would appear magically to take its place. The beautiful Aesir seemed secure in their eternal youth.

One day Odin, Hoenir and the tricky, unreliable Loki, set out on a journey through Midgard, as they often did. They walked for many hours, surveying the progress of the men and women they had created. As evening approached, the weary, hungry gods slew an ox and building a fire, set the ox to roast. After a rest, Odin reached for the meat, expecting it to be cooked and sizzling with running fat. To his disgust it was still raw. Stirring and feeding the fire, the three gods waited again. Sure that this time the meat would be ready to eat, they once more leaned forward over the blazing fire and attempted to slice some tasty roast ox to put into their empty stomachs. The meat was still as raw as if it had never seen a flame.

It was now clear to all three of them that magic was at work. Looking around, they saw an eagle perched in the tree above them. At once the eagle spoke and admitted that he was the cause of the trouble.

"But if you will agree to share your meal with me, I will cease my mischief and the ox will soon be roasted," he screeched.

As the ox was a large one, Odin, Hoenir and Loki agreed to the eagle's terms, thinking there was plenty for all to eat. Then the flames of the fire leapt high and in a few seconds the meat was roasted. Odin cut the carcass into succulent pieces and the gods were about to eat when, to their indignation, the eagle swooped from the tree, snatched up nearly all the meat and left but a few miserable scraps for the three ravenous travellers.

Flying into a rage, Loki snatched up a stick and tried to beat the eagle away from the food, but the eagle was the mountain giant, Thiassi, endowed with magic powers. The stick stuck fast to the back of the eagle and to the hands of Loki. The eagle soared away into the air and the helpless god was dragged through the sky with his feet crashing against the tops of the trees and his arms felt as if they were being dragged from their sockets.

"Release me!" begged Loki.

"Not until you promise to do me a favour," screeched Thiassi, swooping through the air and blundering through the trees, to increase the suffering of the unfortunate Loki. Then Thiassi went on, "When I release you, say nothing of what has happened to the other gods, but when you return to Asgard, lure Iduna out to walk in Midgard that I may obtain possession of her and the casket of the apples of youth."

Loki was horrified, but in such pain, that he swore a solemn oath to do as Thiassi demanded. Then he was released and walked back through the forest to rejoin Odin and Hoenir, but, he told them nothing of his promise, and they were amazed that he had escaped from the eagle so easily. After a few days the three gods completed their journey and returned to Asgard.

It so happened that at that time Iduna's husband, Bragi, was away from Asgard on a minstrel journey, playing and singing his poetry to all who would listen, leaving Iduna alone.

The cunning and frightened Loki went to see her and asked if she would give him one of her apples. Smiling, Iduna opened the magic casket and taking an apple handed it to Loki. At once another apple appeared in the casket. The stock seemed as secure as ever. Then Iduna became puzzled. Instead of eating the apple, Loki looked at it and turned it over and held it up to the light.

"Is something wrong?" asked Iduna.

"No," replied cunning Loki, "but I am amazed. I thought there were no other apples like these, yet only this morning I saw some growing away from Asgard, down in the land of men."

At first Iduna laughed and would not believe him, but Loki was so insistent that the apples he had seen were exactly the same as Iduna's, that she agreed to go with him to look. Taking her casket of apples with her, so that she might compare them with the ones of which Loki spoke, Iduna went with Loki from the protection of Asgard.

Further and further he led her from the abode of the Aesir, then suddenly he hid and Iduna was alone. At last she realized that she had been tricked and turned to run back to Asgard, but she was too late. The giant Thiassi, still wearing his eagle wings, swept down from the sky and seizing her in his talons, carried Iduna and the casket of apples to his home in the mountains.

Loki slunk back to Asgard and said nothing of what had happened.

At first Iduna was not missed. It was thought that she was with her husband, Bragi, singing in a far grove, where they would trouble no one. Gradually the effect of the apples began to wear off. Lines and white hair appeared to mar the beauty of the Aesir. They fell sick and ached with the pains of age. They searched for Iduna throughout Asgard, but they could not find her. They questioned each other and found that Iduna had last been seen in the company of Loki.

Odin sent for Loki, who stood in fear before him and confessed how he had betrayed Iduna to Thiassi. The whole of the Aesir fell into a fury and threatened Loki with instant death if he did not rescue Iduna and regain the apples of youth.

By this time, with the grey hand of old age upon him, Loki knew he must overcome his fear and turn against Thiassi. He begged the goddess, Freya, to lend him her falcon disguise.

"Dressed as a falcon, I shall not be recognized by Thiassi and I shall the more easily rescue Iduna," pleaded Loki.

So Freya lent Loki her falcon feathers and he flew to the mountain home of the giants. Fortunately, Thiassi was away fishing in the north and Iduna was sitting alone with the casket of apples at her side.

Loki circled around the lonely, sad goddess and transformed her and the casket into a small nut. Seizing this in his claws, he turned and raced for the walls of Asgard and safety. He was not to succeed so easily. Thiassi returned in time to see the falcon fleeing towards the horizon. Recognizing the falcon's feathers as a disguise of the gods, he swiftly pulled on his own eagle's wings and flew in pursuit.

The mighty eagle easily gained on the smaller falcon and Loki, weakened by old age, had to strain every muscle and summon up all his resolution to keep ahead. At last he flapped exhausted over the walls of Asgard and fell to the ground.

Meanwhile, the anxious gods had lined the walls of their lovely city, staring intently into the sky for Loki's return. Seeing the eagle pursuing him, they piled wood shavings onto the ramparts. As soon as Loki had swept over into safety, the Aesir set fire to the wood and Thiassi was caught in the flames and the smoke. Choking and blinded he fell to the ground inside Asgard and was swiftly killed by the vengeful gods.

Loki and Iduna recovered their true shape and once more the gods were able to eat the apples of youth. How sweet they tasted and how happy the gods were to see their wrinkles and grey hair disappear and their youth and loveliness return.

"It is no wonder that the giants try such tricks to obtain the apples for themselves," said Odin.

He ordered that the eyes of the slain Thiassi should be taken up to heaven and turned into shimmering stars. In that way the giant continued to live, and the honour done to his eyes, softened the anger of his brothers at his death.

Aesop's Fables

Traditionally Aesop is thought to have been a Phrygian slave, living in the sixth century B.C., and he is credited with hundreds of sharply observed, short fables.

Mercury and the Woodman

One day, a woodman was felling trees by a river. Suddenly his axe hit a knot in a tree trunk and flew from his hands into the water. The woodman was standing on the bank of the river, lamenting his loss, when the god Mercury appeared before him.

"Why do you wring your hands in grief?" asked the god.

When the woodman explained that he had lost the axe with which he gained his living, Mercury took pity on him and dived into the flowing stream. Presently, he came to the surface with a gold axe in his hand.

"Is this yours?" he asked the woodman.

"No," the man replied.

Again Mercury dived to the bottom of the river and this time he came up with a silver axe in his hand.

"Is this silver axe yours?" he asked.

"No, that is not mine either," replied the woodman.

For a third time Mercury dived beneath the water and this time he came up with the woodman's plain axe.

"That is mine. Oh thank you," smiled the woodman, eagerly reaching out his hands.

Mercury was so impressed with the man's honesty, that he gave him not only his own axe, but the gold axe and the silver axe as well. The woodman hastened to tell his friends of his good fortune, for the gold axe and the silver axe were worth a great deal of money.

The woodman's friends congratulated him on his luck. However, one of the men was envious and determined to see if he also could become rich. He hurried to the river bank and after a little banging and cutting, dropped his axe into the river. Then he stood at the water's edge and wailed and wept. At once the god Mercury stood before him and asked him what was amiss.

When the man said that he had lost his axe in the water, Mercury dived down and came up waving a gold axe in his hand.

"Is this yours?" he asked.

"Yes. Yes. That is mine. Give it to me," said the man, reaching forward and trying to snatch the axe from Mercury's hand.

Mercury was so disgusted by the man's dishonesty, that he not only did not give him the gold axe, he did not retrieve the man's own axe either.

Honesty is the best policy.

The Wolf and the Lamb

Once, a hungry wolf came upon a lamb, which had strayed from the flock. He wished to eat the little creature, but knowing it to be a blameless innocent, sought an excuse for such a cruel deed.

"Are you not that lamb which insulted me last year?" he asked.

"No indeed," bleated the lamb. "Last year I was not born."

"Then you have wronged me by eating in my pastures," growled the wolf.

"That is not possible," baaa-ed the lamb. "I have not yet started to eat grass."

"Well, I am sure you have done me an ill-deed somehow," snapped the wolf. "I know. You have fouled my drinking water, by drinking from my stream."

"I have not touched your drinking water," wailed the lamb. "I have drunk nothing but my mother's milk."

At that the wolf lost patience and killed the lamb and ate it.

"I'm hungry. That is a good enough excuse," he said.

Belling the Cat

Once upon a time, all the mice living in a great house met to discuss how they could protect themselves against the attacks of a big, clever cat, which had come to live in the same house.

Many ideas were put forward. At last one mouse said, "I think I have the perfect solution. We must obtain possession of a bell, which I know how to do, and then we must hang the bell round the neck of the cat. Whenever the cat moves, the bell will ring. Thus we shall always be warned when she is creeping close to attack us."

"Wonderful! Marvellous!" cheered the other mice. "That is the solution. A bell must be hung round the neck of the cat. Why did no one think of that before? Our troubles are over."

Everyone thanked the mouse who had made the brilliant suggestion and a gift of grain was granted to him.

Amongst all the cheers and murmurs of approval, a little voice belonging to a small, unimportant mouse, was heard asking, "But, *who* will hang the bell round the neck of the cat?"

There was a silence, which grew longer, and longer. Then there was a shuffling of feet as all the mice remembered important engagements to which they had to hurry away. No one ever mentioned the idea of belling the cat again.

The Fox and the Grapes

One fine day, a hungry fox was hurrying through a garden, when he saw a bunch of ripe grapes hanging from a trellis against a sunny wall. Wishing to eat the grapes, the fox jumped into the air and pawed at the vine, but all in vain. Try as he might, he could not reach the grapes.

At last the fox walked out of the garden with an angry toss of his head.

"I thought those grapes were ripe," he snarled, "but now I see they are sour."

The Goose that Laid the Golden Eggs

Long ago, there lived a man and his wife, who were lucky enough to own a goose which laid a golden egg every day. However, the man and wife fell to thinking that they were not growing rich quickly enough.

"If we cut the goose open, we can obtain all the eggs at once," they thought. "Why should we wait for merely one a day?"

They killed the goose and slit it open, only to find that inside, it was as other geese. There was no store of golden eggs. So the man and wife did not become rich quickly and, as their goose was dead, they had also lost their one, daily, golden egg. Through their greed, they had lost everything.

The Oak and the Reeds

Once a tall oak tree grew on the bank of a river. It held its head proudly up to the sky and looked down with scorn upon the reeds so thin and small below. One day a mighty wind blew and uprooted the tall oak tree and cast it down into the mud.

The oak tree lay bewildered and humbled and puzzled. It said to the reeds, "How is it that you, who are so thin and puny stand undamaged, whilst I have been destroyed in the glory of my strength?"

"Aaaaaagh," murmured the reeds, swaying in the breeze. "You stood tall and strong and stubborn and fought against something more powerful than yourself. We little beings bow and yield before every wind that blows and the wrath of the storm passes harmlessly over our heads."

The Pedlar of Swaffham

Legend has it that hundreds of years ago, in the village of Swaffham, in the county of Norfolk in England, there lived a pedlar who was plagued by a certain dream.

The dream was always the same. In his sleep a voice came to him and said that if he stood on London Bridge, he would hear joyful news.

At first the pedlar took no notice. For him to go to London would not be easy. He would have to walk there, and sleep in barns or under hedges, along the way.

The dreams persisted. The voice was so insistent that the pedlar became upset and worried. He dreaded going upstairs to bed. At last he said to his wife, "It is no use. I shall have to go to London and stand on London Bridge or I shall know no peace for the rest of my life."

He packed a few belongings, some food, a little money and walked the long road to London.

In those days London Bridge was a bustling place with houses and shops on either side. For several days the pedlar stood on the bridge, first in one spot and then another, but no one spoke to him and no one gave him joyful news.

"I was a fool to come," he told himself, but still he waited.

Finally, when he had nothing but a crust of bread in his pocket and knew that he must depart for Norfolk within the hour, a shopkeeper stepped from his shop and came and spoke to him.

"Satisfy my curiosity," said the shopkeeper. "I have seen you here for several days past. You do not beg, you do not pick pockets, you are not selling anything. Why are you standing here?"

The pedlar replied honestly that he had dreamed that if he stood on London Bridge he would hear joyful news.

At that the shopkeeper burst out laughing.

"You do not want to take notice of foolish dreams," he said. "Why, I keep having this dream that if I go to Swaffham, in Norfolk – a place I know nothing of – and ask for the pedlar's house and go into the orchard at the back and dig under a great oak tree, then I shall find a hoard of treasure. What nonsense! Why, I am sure that if I took any notice of that dream, I should make a long journey to Swaffham and when I got there, find nothing. You be off home, my friend, and take no notice of dreams."

At once the pedlar hurried home to Swaffham. He went into the orchard at the back of his house and dug under the great oak tree. He found a chest of treasure and was wealthy for the rest of his life.

Being a God-fearing man, the pedlar gave some of the money for the repair of the local church and inside it he had a statue raised of himself with his pack on his back and his dog at his heels, walking towards London Bridge, where he had indeed heard such joyful news.

How Arthur Pulled the Sword from the Stone

Stories of the exploits of Arthur and his valiant companions go back to the Dark Ages. They were first gathered together in a best selling book, LE MORTE D'ARTHUR, by Sir Thomas Malory in 1470. Nowadays, Arthur and his knights of the Round Table are popularly shown as dressed in full armour and living in stone castles, as kings and knights did in the days of Malory. Present historical opinion places Arthur, not as a king, but as a successful war chief, living and fighting at the time of the Anglo-Saxon invasions of Britain.

Many hundreds of years ago, Uther Pendragon was king of England. Those were troubled and warlike days. The king was constantly fighting and roving from one end of the land to the other. Thus it happened that when a baby son was born to King Uther and his wife, Igraine, the child was given to Merlin the magician to bring up in safety.

Merlin took the boy, named Arthur, and put him in the care of a knight called Sir Ector. Sir Ector was not an important nobleman, but he was honest and kind. He already had a son, called Kay, and Arthur was brought up as Kay's younger brother.

In the usual way of things in those days, Arthur would have lived with Sir Ector until he was ten or twelve years old, and then returned to the court of his father to be trained as a fighting prince.

Barely two years after Arthur had been given to Merlin, King Uther died. The kingdom fell into chaos, with one great duke fighting another, and with everyone fighting the foreign invaders, who constantly harried the shore.

Those who were aware that the little Prince Arthur existed, knew nothing of his whereabouts. Sir Ector knew that the boy in his care was the son of an important nobleman, but he did not know Arthur was the son of King Uther.

So the years went by, with Arthur living happily on Sir Ector's small estate far in the country, and England was in turmoil because there was no strong king to keep order.

At last, Merlin the magician visited the Archbishop of Canterbury and counselled him to send for all the lords of the realm and all the gentlemen of arms, to meet in London at Christmas.

"As our Lord Jesus was born by a miracle on that night, perhaps out of His mercy, he will show us, by a miracle, who should be king of this troubled realm," said Merlin.

The Archbishop of Canterbury agreed and all the nobles, great and small, were called to meet in London by Christmas day, or risk being put under the curse of the church.

30

Several days before Christmas the nobles assembled at the great church of St Paul, to ask God to listen to their prayers and to help them to choose a worthy king.

When they came out of the church they saw an amazing sight. A huge stone stood four square in the churchyard, where no stone had stood before. Embedded in the stone was an anvil of steel a foot high. Pushed into the anvil was a fair sword and written round the sword in gold were the words:

Whosoever pulleth out this sword of this stone and anvil,
is rightwise king born of all England.

Everyone was amazed. Some of the nobles ran to fetch the Archbishop.

"God has given us a sign," he said. "We must pray once more and then those who think themselves fit to be king may try to pull the sword from the anvil and the stone."

Many great nobles tried to pull the sword from the stone, but none succeeded.

"The man who can claim the sword is not yet here," said the Archbishop. "God will send him. Meanwhile, let ten knights of good repute take turns to guard the sword."

So it was agreed.

Then Merlin the magician again spoke secretly to the Archbishop.

"A tournament should be arranged for New Year's Day," he said, "otherwise those who have not succeeded in pulling the sword from the stone will become bored and go home. All the nobles must be here to acclaim the rightful king, when at last he is found. Moreover, a tournament will attract many people. Surely the boy born to be king will be amongst them."

The Archbishop of Canterbury agreed to this and so it was arranged.

Talk of the great meeting in London and the tournament on New Year's Day had reached the ears of quiet-living Sir Ector. He rode to London with his son, Sir Kay, who had been made a knight the Hallowmass before. Young Arthur, who was not yet old enough to be a knight, rode as a squire to his brother, Sir Kay.

London was of course very crowded and Sir Ector had to take lodgings far out of the city. On the day of the great tournament, Sir Ector, Sir Kay and Arthur rode into town.

Suddenly Sir Kay gasped, "Arthur! I have forgotten my sword. I cannot fight without it. Please go back to our lodgings and fetch it for me. If I ride back, I shall be tired before the tournament starts."

"Very well," agreed Arthur, who was a good-natured lad. In any case, it was his duty as a squire to serve his brother.

Arthur rode back along the road, as quickly as he could. When he reached the lodging house, he found to his dismay that it was locked and shuttered.

"The lady of the house has gone to watch the tournament," called a child, playing in a nearby field. "There is no way of getting into that house until she returns tonight."

Upset, Arthur rode back towards the jousting field. Without a sword Kay would not be able to take part in the tournament. It was all very upsetting.

As he rode past St Paul's churchyard, Arthur saw a magnificent sword sticking in an anvil high on a huge stone.

"Well, whoever owns that sword cannot want it very much to leave it lying about like that," thought Arthur. "I will pull it out and take it to my brother, Kay, and he will have a fair sword with which to fight in the tournament."

Tying up his horse, Arthur climbed on to the stone, seized hold of the sword with both his hands and heaved it from the anvil. Then remounting his horse, he hurried to catch up with Sir Ector and Sir Kay. The sword Arthur held in his hands was, of course, the magic sword, which he had found unguarded because all the knights were at the jousting.

"Kay! Kay!" called Arthur, spurring up beside his brother. "The lodging house was locked and I could not fetch your own sword, but I found this fair sword left pushed in an anvil. Will it do for you?"

By this time, Sir Kay had been talking with other knights and nobles and he had heard all about the sword in the stone.

"Did you get this sword from St Paul's churchyard?" he asked Arthur.

"I'm not sure," replied Arthur. "You know I have never been to London before, but it was a fine, big church. Besides, if people leave good swords lying about pushed into stones, they deserve to lose them. That is your sword now, Kay. You use it and win."

Kay was a good young man, but for once temptation was too great for him. He went to his father, Sir Ector, and showed him the sword.

"Father," he said. "I have the sword from the stone, therefore I must be king of England."

Sir Ector looked at the sword and looked at his son. He knew his son had no right to be king. He took the sword and Sir Kay into St Paul's church. Arthur went along with them, hoping he would not be rebuked for touching the sword.

Sir Ector put a Bible into Sir Kay's hand and said, "Now tell me how you came by the sword."

"Sir," said Sir Kay, "my brother, Arthur, gave it to me."

Then Sir Ector turned to Arthur, "How did you get the sword?" he asked.

"I rode back to the lodging house, which was locked, hence I could not bring Kay his sword. As I came back here, I saw this sword in the anvil in the stone and I thought that my brother Kay should not be swordless. As this fine sword was lying unwanted in a churchyard, I pulled it from the stone and gave it to Kay. If I have done wrong, then I am sorry."

Sir Ector looked long at the boy he had brought up as his own.

"You have pulled the sword from the stone," he said, "and now you must be king of England."

Arthur stared in amazement at the man he knew as his father.

"Me?" he said. "Why should I be king of England?"

"Because God wills it," replied Sir Kay, "and because you pulled the sword from the stone."

"It was easy, anyone could do it," said Arthur.

"Really?" said Sir Ector. "Then push it back in and let me try."

Arthur climbed onto the huge stone and rammed the sword into the anvil. Sir Ector climbed up beside him and pulled and pulled at the handle of the sword, but he could not move it.

"You try, Kay," said Sir Ector. Kay scrambled up onto the stone and with both his hands and all his strength, tried to pull the sword free. He did not succeed.

"Now you try Arthur," said Sir Ector, his face and his voice as serious as Arthur had ever seen.

Arthur put his hands upon the sword and easily pulled it free.

Then Sir Ector and Sir Kay knelt before the young man.

Arthur was distressed.

"My father and my dear brother! Why do you kneel before me?" he asked.

"Arthur," replied Sir Ector. "I am not your father and Kay is not your brother. We are not of the same blood, but to tell the truth, I never dreamed that you were as high born as it seems you are."

Sir Ector told how Arthur had been brought to him by Merlin and Arthur wept, for he loved Sir Ector and Sir Kay dearly.

"Even if I am to be king, you will not leave me, will you?" he asked, and Sir Ector and Sir Kay promised to stay with Arthur as long as he needed them.

The three of them went to the Archbishop of Canterbury and showed him the sword and told him how it had been gained.

On the twelfth day, the Archbishop called all the nobles together. Arthur put the sword back into the stone and anyone who wished, tried to pull it out. No one succeeded. Only Arthur could pull it free.

Many of the great lords were angry and said it would shame them to be ruled by a boy. They refused to agree that Arthur should be king.

From Candlemas to the next Christmas to the next Easter, the quarrels raged, but Arthur gathered clever faithful men around him. He learned to lead men and to win battles, and eventually he became King of England. Sir Ector and Sir Kay stayed with Arthur all their lives and Arthur ruled his realm from Camelot. He was a great and good king. Some people say that he never died, but is sleeping in a cave in the Welsh mountains, waiting to lead his country once again.

A traditional English story

The Lambton Worm

The worm, or wurm, is often referred to in old English stories. It was a monstrous, fearsome creature of the serpent species, and the tellers of these old stories obviously assumed that wurms were well-known to their listeners. Whatever these terrible beasts were which crept over England some seven hundred years ago, they are not to be seen nowadays. The River Wear and the town of Chester-le-Street, referred to in this story, still exist, in the north of England.

Long ago, in England, at about the time of the Crusades, the son and heir of Lambton Castle cared for neither God nor man. He did not learn his duties on his family estates, he did not attend church and if anything displeased him he called out curses in a loud voice, to the scandal and dismay of all who heard him.

One Sunday, having spent the day before drinking, the young man was fishing in the River Wear. Many times he cast his line over the water, but he did not catch anything. The servants and country folk, passing by on their way to the chapel at Brugeford, heard the heir of Lambton cursing and profaning, and were deeply shocked.

Within a few minutes the disreputable young fellow felt a tug on the fishing line. Thinking that at last he had caught a fine fish, he hauled in his catch, only to find that it was a loathsome serpent or worm. Cursing his luck yet again, the heir snatched the worm from his line and threw it into a nearby well, which folks say is still known as Worm Well.

Not many weeks after this incident, the heir of Lambton took himself off on the Crusades. Some say because he had repented of his wicked ways, others say because his family wished to have a rest from him and hoped that the dangers and novelties of a long voyage abroad would teach the young man some sense.

Meanwhile the worm lay unheeded in the well, growing longer and larger with every passing hour. Soon it outgrew the well and crawling down to the river, spent its days curled round a rock and its nights lying at the foot of a nearby hill. In a month or two, it was long enough to entwine itself round the hill three times. The local people called it Worm Hill from that time on.

At first the horrible worm had been content to hunt wild creatures, but as it grew larger, it began to prey on domestic animals. It drank milk from the cows, ate chickens and lambs, and chased the dogs and the horses. As the years went by, it needed more and more food and soon the land north of the river was laid waste. The farms were deserted as no one dared to live there.

The worm then turned its eyes to the southern side of the river, where Lambton Castle stood. The land was fair and the animals fat. The worm slithered across the river bed and wriggled a loathsome trail towards the castle.

35

The Lord of Lambton was old now and past his fighting days. No one knew what to do. Panic and dread filled the castle, and everyone shrieked and wailed and wished that the heir of Lambton had not been such a ne'er-do-well. He should have been with them to defend the castle as was his duty.

At last a steward spoke up and suggested that as they were not fortunate enough to have a young fighting lord they should try to please the worm and perhaps, in that way, they might be spared.

"I have heard," said the steward, "that the worm likes milk. Let us therefore fill the trough in the courtyard with milk and with luck the worm will be satisfied."

The terrible worm slid into the courtyard, drank the milk and retired across the Wear. It entwined itself around its hill and went to sleep without doing further harm.

The next day the worm was again seen approaching Lambton Castle. Again the trough was filled. It took milk from nine cows to fill the trough and so the household had to do without. This caused discontent and it was suggested that the trough need be only half-filled, so that there could be rice pudding for supper in the servants' hall. Why should the servants do without their favourite food just because Lord Lambton was old, and his heir did not know his duty?

The next day, when the worm again slithered towards Lambton Hall, the milk from five cows was put into the trough, and the milk from the other four cows was given to the servants.

The worm flew into a rage and lashed furiously with its tail, uprooting valuable trees from the castle park.

"This is too bad," old Lord Lambton roused himself to say. "My great-grandfather planted those trees. I can't have them uprooted by a worm. The servants will have to do without the milk and that is that."

The worm was the terror of the neighbourhood. Many knights and brave men came to slay the fearsome creature, but they did not succeed. Even though these gallant men fought bravely, the worm had the power to join itself back together wherever it had been cut asunder.

The worm prevailed against all who came to slay it and stayed in possession of Worm Hill.

After seven long years, the heir of Lambton returned from the Crusades, toughened, experienced and reformed, looking forward to taking his place as manager of the fair lands of Lambton. However, as so often is the case, he found that things had changed while he had been away. His rich inheritance was a wasteland, the servants were a terrified rabble, and his dear father was sinking white-haired into his grave.

"Really, this is too bad!" sighed the heir. "Cannot a fellow sow a few wild oats and turn his back for a year or two without the place going to pieces entirely! I knew I should have to fight the heathen and put everyone right abroad, but I did expect things to be in order in England."

Feeling rather irritated, the heir of Lambton crossed the river and surveyed the worm as it lay curled and asleep round the foot of Worm Hill, huge and loathsome and fearsome. No one lost any time in telling the heir that the worm had killed every man who had gone against it, whether noble or common, large or small, brave or desperate.

"Thank you for that information," said the heir of Lambton. Having learned many useful things during the Crusades, one of which was to think before acting, he went to consult the Wise Woman of Chester-le-Street.

He was not received cordially.

"All this trouble and destruction is your fault," she screeched at the heir. "If you had not pulled the worm from the river and thrown it into the well and cursed and blasphemed on the sabbath day, none of this would have happened. I don't know how you have the courage to show your face amongst respectable folk!"

"Yes, yes, well I'm frightfully sorry, but we're all young once," said the heir, "and now I am here to put things right. As you are so wise and clever and the years have imparted wisdom as well as loveliness upon your person, can you find it in your heart to give me good advice?"

Seeing that the heir was now a reformed man, the Wise Woman of Chester-le-Street said this to him, "Take your best suit of mail and have it studded with spearheads. When you come to fight the worm, take your stand on a rock in the middle of the River Wear, hold your best sword in your hands and confront the worm face to face and put your trust in God. If you are fortunate enough to overcome the worm, you must slay the first living creature you meet on your way home otherwise, for nine generations, no lord of Lambton will die in his bed."

The heir thanked the Wise Woman and returned to Lambton Castle. He sent his strongest suit of mail to be studded with spearheads. He went to pray in Brugeford chapel and swore to fight the worm with all his might and, if he overcame it, he would slay the first living creature he met on his way home.

When his armour was ready, the heir of Lambton took his finest sword in his hand and, at the hour when the worm usually awoke, he took his stand on a rock in the middle of the River Wear. Soon the horrible monster uncoiled its slimy length from around Worm Hill and slithered towards the river. Southwards it swam, on its way to despoil the lands of Lambton, but as it passed the heir, he struck it a terrible blow on its head.

Amazed and full of rage, the monster turned and coiled its tail round the heir, thinking to crush him to death as it had crushed so many others. However the Wise Woman of Chester-le-Street had given good advice. The tighter the worm pulled its coils, the more it wounded itself on the spearheads studding the heir's armour. It cried with pain as gaping holes were torn in its flesh, and the river ran with blood.

Pulling his arms free from the seething coils, the heir hacked at the worm with his sword and again the cleverness of the Wise Woman was revealed. As the heir of Lambton slashed pieces from the enormous coils of the worm, they were carried away down the river and were unable to reunite, as they would have done, if the heir and the worm had been fighting on land.

The struggle was fierce and desperate, but at last the worm was dead and gone.

The heir of Lambton stood exhausted, but alive and victorious.

All this time the fearful household of Lambton had been locked up inside the castle, praying for the safety and victory of their young lord. The heir had told them that if and when the worm was slain, he would blow a blast on his bugle. Then an old hound was to be released to run towards him that he might slay it as the first living thing to meet him after his victory.

The heir, suddenly filled with exaltation at the realization of his success, blew a mighty blast on his horn and turned to walk back to Lambton Castle. He saw the gates open, but his heart turned to ice, as his dear, aged father ran out laughing and calling out his joy at the safety and triumph of his brave son.

In his happiness, the old man had forgotten about his son's promise to kill the first living thing to meet him on his way home.

Filled with horror, the heir blew another blast on his horn and the old hound came bounding from the gates. But it was too late. The father reached his son a stride before the hound came leaping up at him.

The heir stared at his sword, still dripping with the blood of the worm.

"Who but we three knows who reached me first?" he thought as he plunged the blade into the hound.

So peace and prosperity were returned to the lands of Lambton, and those around them, and the heir lived richly and married well.

However, the Fates were not to be defied. The vow had been broken. For nine generations the Lords of Lambton met violent deaths.

The Lost Islands

Parts of the land to the west of Britain are sinking. In several places, at a particularly low tide, stumps of old forests and remains of ancient villages can be seen sticking up out of the sea. People say that if you sit on the seashore and listen, you can hear the old church bells tolling as they rock to and fro with the tide.

Hundreds of years ago, the Little People lived all over Britain. Now, after many invasions and with the noise of modern life, the Little People have retreated to live in the lonely places of Wales and Scotland and far Cornwall. They are secretive and keep themselves to themselves, but some of the old Celtic folk, who have the power of second sight, can see them. The Little People dress in green, except for their hats, which are red. It does not do to offend them for they have magical powers. Most people think it wise to stay right away from the Little People or Faerie Folk, as they are sometimes called. However, one Welshman found great benefit from mixing with the faeries. His name was Griffith and he lived at a port called Milford Haven.

Many years ago, fine markets were held at Milford Haven. The country folk for miles around would bring their goods to sell. The Little People came to the market too. They never spoke, but if they wanted to buy any article, they would put down money at its side then, if the stallholder thought the price was fair, he would pick the money up. The faeries would then take the goods and go. If the price was not enough, the stallholder would leave the money lying until more was added to it, or until the faeries took up the money and left without buying anything.

The faeries who went to Milford Haven were honest, never stole and the local people were glad to trade with them. Very few people could see the faeries, most traders merely saw the money appearing on their stalls and the goods going. However, Griffith a corn merchant, could always see the Little People and so could a butcher who lived in the centre of town. Griffith and the butcher sold much corn and meat to their faerie customers.

"There must be plenty of them to need all those supplies," Griffith would say to the butcher.

"Indeed," would be the reply. "And where do they live, I ask myself. It is not in the valleys near here, I see no sign of them on my walks with my dog. Either they must be very lazy, that they grow no food for themselves, or they must live somewhere where there is no room to farm."

Everyone puzzled about where the Faerie Folk lived, but no one knew. Then one day, Griffith was walking high up by St David's churchyard, when he happened to glance out to sea and saw some islands where he had never seen islands before. Having inherited the second sight from his mother,

Griffith knew that these were the Green Isles of the Ocean, the lost islands of long ago.

"If the islands are in the mood to show themselves, then I will go to look at them," he thought.

He started down towards the seashore, but at once the islands disappeared. He walked back up to St David's churchyard and again he could see the islands. Griffith understood at once what was happening.

"I can see the islands only when I am standing on sacred land," he muttered.

A lesser man would have stayed in the churchyard and admired the islands from there, but Griffith was clever. He cut the piece of turf on which he was standing and carried it down to his boat. Then he stood on the turf in the boat and looked seawards. He saw the islands clear and bright. Standing on the turf all the way, Griffith steered towards the islands and landed on the largest. At once he met some of the Faerie Folk, who bought corn from him. They greeted him in surprise and laughed when they learned how he had found his way to their home, then they showed him the beauties of their little islands.

"Many islands have disappeared beneath the waves," they said, "but some have become invisible by magic and it is on these islands that we live, safe from you big trampling mortals."

Then they sent Griffith home, with his arms full of gifts and they continued to trade with him for many years and made him a rich man. However, the Faeries made Griffith give them the sacred turf which had guided him to the islands and, no matter how often he stood in St David's churchyard staring out to sea, he never saw the islands again.

Lazy Jack

Lazy Jack or Idle Jack is a favourite character in English folk lore. More often than not he is the hero who wins the hand of the fair lady. He still appears regularly on the English stage in the pantomimes which are performed all over the country every Christmas.

Once upon a time, there was a boy called Jack, who lived with his widowed mother on a dreary common, in the rain-swept country-side. The mother earned a poor living by spinning, but Jack was lazy and earned nothing. At last his mother lost all patience with the boy and told him that if he did not find some work, she would turn him out of the house.

"Dear me!" thought Jack. "What a pass I am come to."

He went out and hired himself for the day to a farmer. The farmer gave him a penny and Jack was well pleased. However, he was not used to handling money and on the way home, he lost the penny in a stream.

"You stupid boy," said his mother. "You should have put the penny in your pocket."

"You're right," agreed Jack. "That is what I shall do next time."

The next day Jack went out again and hired himself to a dairyman. At the end of the afternoon, Jack was given a jugful of creamy, warm milk, and putting it into his pocket, the lad walked home.

"I did as you said, Mother," called Jack, stepping indoors, but when he lifted the jug from his pocket, he found he had spilled all the milk on the journey home.

"Where have you spent all your life?" groaned his mother. "Don't you know you should have carried it on your head?"

"You're right," agreed Jack. "That is what I shall do next time."

A day or so later, Jack found the strength to work for another farmer. In payment the farmer gave him a cream cheese. Jack put the cheese on his head and walked home. For once, the rain had stopped and the sun was shining. The cheese melted and ran through Jack's hair and over his shirt.

"You stupid boy," shrieked his mother, who liked cream cheese. "You should have carried it carefully in your hands."

"You're right," agreed Jack, who was nothing if not good-natured. "That is what I shall do next time."

On the morrow, Jack worked all day for a baker whose cat had recently given birth to kittens.

"Take a kitten for your payment, Jack," smiled the baker.

Jack took the kitten and carried it carefully in his hands, but the kitten did not wish to leave its mother and scratched Jack so much he had to let it go. Again Jack arrived home with nothing.

"You stupid boy," said his mother, when Jack told her what had happened. "You should have tied it with a piece of string and dragged it behind you."

"You're right," agreed Jack. "That is what I shall do next time."

The following day Jack hired himself to a butcher who gave him a shoulder of mutton as payment. Jack took the mutton, tied it with string and dragged it along behind him all the way home. By the time he reached there, the meat was not fit to eat.

"You ninny," sighed his mother. "You certainly take after your father's side of the family not mine. You should have carried it on your shoulder."

"Thank you for all your helpful advice, Mother," smiled Jack. "That is what I shall do next time."

On the following Monday, Jack hired himself to a cattle-keeper, who gave him a donkey in payment for his work. Now the donkey was heavy, but Jack was strong and with much heaving and grunting, on his part and also that of the donkey, Jack pulled the donkey on to his shoulder and set off for home. On the way he passed the home of a rich merchant, who had a rather strange daughter.

The girl had never laughed in her life and the doctors had said she would never be cheerful until she saw something she thought was funny.

"To think I have to pay good money for advice like that," moaned the merchant. He was fond of his daughter and wishing to see her happy, he promised her hand in marriage, and a fine dowry, to any young man who could make her laugh.

As luck would have it, the merchant's daughter was looking from her window as lazy Jack stumbled past carrying the braying donkey on his back. The girl had never seen anything so ridiculous and burst out laughing. The merchant was delighted and inviting Jack indoors, asked him if he would like to marry the girl and accept a fine gift of money.

Jack agreed and he and the merchant's daughter lived happily together for the rest of their lives. And as Jack was a kind-hearted lad, he saw that his old mother had everything she needed.

"My boy Jack, may be lazy and stupid," smiled his mother, "but he managed to do the right thing when it mattered."

The Smith and the Little People

The Celts were the people who lived in the British Isles before and during the Roman occupation. When the Roman administration finally withdrew in about 400 A.D., there were fresh invasions by Anglo-Saxons, who overran roughly the area now known as England. The Celts were driven back to Wales, Scotland and Ireland and the small islands round the west coast. Celts were well-known for their storytelling gifts and love of talking.

Not so long ago, on one of the islands washed by the cold, green Atlantic Ocean, there lived a blacksmith. He had but one son, who was a good, strong, healthy boy and the joy of his father's heart.

When the lad was fourteen years old he fell ill and took to his bed, listless and depressed. No one could find what was wrong with him. Nothing could cure him. He lay still, thin, pale and old-looking. People whispered that for sure he would soon be dead.

Strange to say the boy did not die. Month in, month out, he lay on the bed, but the thing which amazed his father was that the boy developed an enormous appetite. He ate everything which was set before him and then called for more. His distressed father was worn out and became poor by feeding his lazy, wizened son.

Fortunately, one day, a wise man happened to visit the forge and asked the smith why he looked so sad. When he heard the story, he said, "I am sure it is no longer your son who lies on that bed. He is a changeling. Your son has been stolen by the Little People."

The smith was more distressed than ever.

"I thought so! I thought so!" he groaned. "My poor, dear son! What can I do to rescue him?"

"You must find the courage to stand against the Little People," said the Wise Man. "Can you do that?"

"To save my son, I can," replied the smith.

"Then first we must make sure that I am right, and then we must get rid of the changeling," said the Wise Man.

He told the smith to collect as many empty egg shells as he could from his friends. Then to take them into the son's bedroom together with a bucket of water. Next he was to fill the egg shells with water and carry them, two at a time, across the room as if they were very heavy, and then set them down with great effort at the side of the bed, in sight of his son.

The smith did as he was told, and as he set the egg shells down, a voice called from his son's throat, "Ah ha! What foolishness! I have lived for five hundred years and I have never before seen anyone so silly as to try to carry water in egg shells."

The smith was now convinced that his son was gone and that a changeling lay in his bed. He again consulted with the Wise Man.

"It is serious news I must give you," sighed the Wise Man. "If your changeling is one of the ancient Little People, then your son is imprisoned with them under the Green Knole." He pointed to a huge green mound which had stood outside the village since before time began.

The poor smith went pale.

"How shall we ever get my son free from that place?" he asked.

"Have courage and do exactly as I say," replied the Wise Man.

This time he told the smith to light a huge fire at the side of the changeling's bed and, when the creature asked what the fire was for, to say that he would see presently. Then, when the fire was roaring and red, the smith was to seize the changeling and fling him into the hottest part.

"If we have been mistaken and the invalid is still your son, he will beg you to save him and you must pull him back," said the Wise Man, "but if he is the changeling, then he will say nothing, but fly away through the roof."

Shaking and fearful, but determined to save his son, the smith returned home and built a huge fire at the side of his son's bed.

The thin, dull creature on the bed stared at the flames with fear growing in his eyes.

"Why do you build that fire?" he asked.

"I will show you presently," replied the smith and, when the fire was blazing red, he picked up the lad and tried to toss him on the flames.

A weird cry rang through the house. A terrible flapping noise filled the room, then there was a crash as a hole appeared in the roof, and the boy was gone.

"That is good news indeed. Everything is going well," smiled the Wise Man, when the poor exhausted smith told him what had happened. "Now, you will truly need all your courage to snatch your son back from within the Green Knole."

He told the smith that once a month, at the full moon, a door opened in the side of the Green Knole.

"You must take a Bible to defend yourself against the anger of the Little People, a sword with which to block open the door, and a crowing cock hidden under your coat. You must go through that door and enter the Green Knole," said the Wise Man. "You will find yourself in a fine, large room full of Little People. Working at a forge at the far end you will see your son. You must take him by the arm and pull him out of the Green Knole with you. The Little People will try to stop you, but if you are firm, you will succeed."

At the next full moon, the poor smith stood before the Green Knole. His heart thundering in his breast, he almost fainted with fear as he saw a door swing open in the grassy side of the hillock. Jamming the door open with his sword, the smith walked forward and found himself in dazzling light filled with laughter and chatter and surrounded by Little People. However, he had eyes only for the figure of his son, stooped and tired from working as a slave all those long months.

The smith pushed his way through the laughing, dancing Little People, who turned and frowned at him.

"What do you want here?" shouted one.

"I have come for my son. He must stay here no longer," replied the smith.

At that the Little People shouted with rage and snatched at the smith's arms. He clasped the Bible firmly and no harm came to him. More Little People crowded round, jostling the smith and trying to push him from the knole. This time the cock struggled out from under the smith's coat and crowed and scratched and flapped round the room.

The Little People were frightened and startled, wondering if dawn had come and daylight was about to burst upon them. In the confusion the smith caught the arm of his son and dragged him to the doorway. The two found themselves rolling out into the fresh air. The sword was thrown after them and the door in the Green Knole slammed shut.

The smith took his dear son home. It was indeed his own son, with all his sweet loving ways, but yet he was not as he used to be.

He sat quietly in a corner of the room and would say not a word to anyone.

"The Little Folk might just as well have kept him," sighed his heart-broken father.

A year and a day after the escape from the Green Knole, the smith was making a sword for an important gentleman, who had ordered the finest workmanship. Try as he might, the smith could not get the sword as he wished it.

Suddenly, to his surprise, his son was at his side.

"Give the sword to me," he said and taking the metal, he wrought it in the most delicate way, until he had made the finest weapon the smith had ever seen.

After that the enchantment seemed to drop away from the boy. He became a normal cheerful lad and grew into a fine young man. He was never bothered again by Little People from the Green Knole. He had, however, learned something in his months of imprisonment, for he became the finest sword maker in all the islands and he and his father became rich men.

How Finn found Bran

Ireland was never conquered by the Roman legions, but remained a Celtic stronghold, retaining its tribal traditions and, most of all, the gift of storytelling.

Long, long ago, in the days when MacArt was king of Ireland, there existed a band of soldiers known as the Feni of Erin. They were tall and bold and fearless and no enemy could stand against them; even their friends were afraid of them.

The captain of these fearsome men was Finn, son of Cumhal, whose castle was on the Hill of Allen, not a very long walk from Kildare. Finn was the bravest of the brave and a terrifying sight as he strode through the middle of a fight, waving his magic sword, with his long hair streaming down his back.

Even more feared than Finn was his faithful hound, Bran. Not only was this creature huge and tireless with long, snapping teeth, but it had one claw much sharper than the rest. This claw was not only sharp but venomous. A scratch from it would never heal, but would fester until the unfortunate victim died. Most of the time, Finn kept a golden shoe tied over this vicious claw, but when danger pressed him too close, he would call Bran to him and take off the shoe. Bran would fly at his master's enemies and there were very few with the courage to stand and face him.

Some folk wondered how such a dog as Bran came to be, but the old people knew that Finn had fetched him from Faerie Land. This is the story of how it happened.

Times had been peaceful, which was unusual, and one day Finn decided to go walking, alone and unattended. After a while he met a man whose face was unfamiliar. This in itself was strange, for Finn knew all the men who lived on his land.

"Who are you to be walking here?" asked Finn.

"I am a clever man in search of work," replied the stranger.

"In what way are you clever?" asked Finn.

"I never sleep," replied the man. "A master must have a use for a man who is always awake."

"That is true indeed," smiled Finn. "Follow me. I will employ you."

Hardly had Finn taken another step, when he was confronted by a second stranger.

"Who are you who walks so boldly over my land?" asked Finn.

"I am a clever man in search of work," replied the stranger.

"In what way are you clever?" asked Finn.

"I can hear the slightest sound," replied the man. "I can even hear the grass growing from the ground."

50

"Can you indeed!" smiled Finn. "Then you had better follow me and I will employ you." He did not immediately see the use of such a talent for hearing, but thought it better for the man to be in his employ than working for an enemy.

Scarcely a hundred paces further along the road, Finn met a third stranger. Again he asked the man what he was doing and again received the same reply – that he was a clever man looking for work. This stranger claimed that he was so strong that once he gripped something no one could make him let go.

"In that case, join these other men and work for me," said Finn.

Finn met four more men who, like the others, were given work. One was an expert thief, one was a skilled climber, the third claimed he could throw a stone, which would turn into a wall upon landing, and the fourth said he was such a fine marksman that he never missed a shot.

Now Finn was no fool and with such unusual things happening to him, one after the other, he rightly concluded that the faeries were at work and perhaps to his advantage. So he strode onwards to see what the rest of the day would bring.

Looking around it seemed to Finn that the landscape suddenly changed. He found himself close by a palace quite unknown to him. As night was falling, Finn knocked at the palace gate and asked for shelter for himself and his men. He was allowed into the palace and there he found the king and queen in deepest sorrow.

"Our first two sons were stolen by faeries or demons or some such creatures," wept the king. "Now another lovely baby has been born to us and we are afraid that this child will be stolen too."

Then it seemed to Finn that he understood why he had met the seven strangers, and why their footsteps had been led to this palace.

"My men and I will guard your new baby," he smiled. "Have no more fear."

Finn sent the man who never slept to sit watching the baby in its chamber. He told the man who could hear the grass growing, to sit in the ante-chamber and listen for anyone approaching. Finally, he instructed the man with the strong grip to sit by the baby's cradle.

"Whatever approaches," said Finn, "be it demon, monster or faerie, seize it and never let it go."

The king's household settled down for the night and at first all was peaceful. Then, as midnight struck, the man sitting in the ante-chamber said, "I feel so drowsy."

"So do we," yawned the many courtiers who also sat in the ante-chamber, inquisitive to see what the night would bring.

The man who could hear the grass growing, cocked his head and said, "Far in the distance I hear the approach of sweet music. Do you know what it can be?"

At his words terror filled the faces of the courtiers.

"It is the Musical Harper," they cried. "His playing lulls everyone to sleep long before he arrives. How can we watch over the baby if we are asleep?"

At that the man sitting in the baby's chamber laughed and said, "Nothing ever puts me to sleep. I will keep you all awake."

Getting to his feet, the man walked continually round the palace, shaking the guards and the courtiers so that no one slept.

This left the man with the strong grip sitting at the side of the cradle. Suddenly he saw a long, skinny arm come right through the wall and reach over where the baby lay.

"Steal the child, would you!" roared the man. "Well you will be unlucky this time." Leaping to his feet, he seized the mysterious hand, and a terrible struggle followed in which the man was thrown all over the room. He did not relax his grip and finally, with one mighty heave, he pulled the hand and arm from the unseen body.

All the courtiers rushed forward to look at the weird trophy, and in the excitement and jostling, no one noticed a second hand push through the wall and snatch the baby. As the infant cried in alarm, the courtiers turned their heads in time to see it disappearing through the wall, and the wall closing behind it. Everyone rushed outside and searched through the darkness, but in vain. The king and queen were heartbroken.

No one was more distressed than Finn, who had failed to guard the baby as he had promised. He swore to the king that he would never rest until he had found the child again. Calling his seven men, he strode out of the palace and back home.

Near Finn's home, lying on the shore, was a boat which had been seven years and seven days a-building. Taking his seven new servants with him, Finn set sail until they reached a rocky shore. Pulling the boat well up the beach, Finn and his men walked inland until they came to a lonely house. Its walls were high and covered with slippery eel skins.

Finn called the man who was an expert climber.

"Climb to the top of that house. Put your eye to the chimney and tell me what you see," he ordered.

The man had not boasted in vain. He climbed easily over the slippery eel skins, peered down the chimney and returning reported to Finn that sitting inside the house was a one-eyed giant, whose arm had been torn from his body. In his remaining hand the giant held a baby and playing on the floor were two handsome boys.

Finn knew he had found the stolen children. Turning to the man who had boasted of being an expert thief, Finn told him to go into the house and steal all three children.

Silently the thief lifted the latch of the door and crept into the house. Without a sound he picked up the two boys. Then gently, so that the giant did not realize what was happening, he took the baby from the enormous hand. He turned to go, but on the way back to the door he saw three chubby puppies playing amongst the rushes on the floor. Being a thief, he could not resist taking the little dogs, and laden, he ran out to rejoin Finn and the others.

With the children in their arms the group of men turned and ran for the

shore, but they had not gone far before they heard a mighty baying and glancing back saw a great, tawny hound, with eyes that glowed like lamps, bounding after them. It was the mother of the puppies.

"Now it is your turn to work," said Finn, turning to the man who had boasted he could throw a stone which would turn into a wall as it hit the ground.

As the men ran hard for the shore, the stone-thrower picked up stone after stone and threw them behind him. As each stone struck the ground, a fine wall rose up, but this did not stop the mother dog. On she bounded after her puppies.

"Throw down a puppy for her," shouted Finn. For a moment the dog paused to sniff happily at the little creature, then on she bounded.

"Throw down another," panted Finn and this time the mother seemed satisfied, as she stayed behind with her two puppies. Finn and his men reached their boat and dragged it thankfully into the sea.

They rowed for many hours and at last, within sight of the shores of home, they thought themselves safe and rested on their oars. However, looking back the way they had come, they saw a terrifying sight. A ball of light flashed and darted in the water. All about it, the sea foamed and frothed as if someone were beating it into a fury.

One of the servants called, "It is the giant. I can see his great face with his one eye glaring."

Finn turned to the man who was a fine marksman and said, "Now is the time to show us how good you are with a bow."

At once the man pulled a bowstring to his ear and sent an arrow flying straight and true into the giant's terrible eye. The great creature threw his remaining arm high into the air, crashed back into the sea and was never heard of again.

Thankful for their deliverance, Finn and his men hurried to the palace of the king and restored the children to their delighted parents.

"What can I give you as a reward?" the king asked of Finn.

"No reward," smiled Finn, "but I will keep the puppy for I believe it has come from an enchanted land and will be a good friend to me in times of peril."

So Finn set off to walk to his own castle and on the way, strange to say, the seven servants were lost to sight, but the puppy remained.

Who can doubt that what the old people say is true and that the dog, which Finn called Bran, indeed came from Faerie Land.

The Green Children

This story is told by two old English chroniclers, Ralph of Coggeshall and William of Newbridge. The events are supposed to have taken place in the twelfth century, some say in the reign of King Stephen. This would have been some two generations after the Norman conquest, when people were speaking a mixture of Anglo-Saxon and Norman-French.

One bright sunny day, some good people from the village of St Mary's in Suffolk, found two children wandering and crying near a wolf pit. The children, a girl and a younger boy, were like normal humans in shape, but their skin and hair were green. The children seemed to be dazzled by the sunlight and confused. They spoke in a strange language and did not appear to understand what the villagers said to them.

Not knowing what else to do, the people of St Mary's took the children to the house of Sir Richard de Caine. His was the biggest household in the district and he had room in which to shelter the children. Even Sir Richard, who was a man of the world, could not understand what the children were saying. They were treated kindly and meat and bread was set before them. The children appeared to be hungry, but pushed the bread and meat aside and continued to weep. Then, by chance, some green broad beans were brought in from the gardens. Eagerly the children snatched at them, but opened the stalks instead of the pods and when they found no beans inside they once more fell to weeping. A member of the household showed the children how to open the pods and find the fat beans inside. At last the children ate and became more composed in their manner.

The children stayed with Sir Richard de Caine. At first they ate only green food and the boy became depressed and sickly. Sadly he died, but the girl learned to eat the same food as the rest of the household and she lost her green colour and took on the appearance of a normal human being. After a while she came to speak the Anglo-Norman language of her benefactors and at last she was able to tell her story.

The girl said that she had lived in a land where the light was always dim and dappled, where all the animals and the people were green, as she had been. She said that her home was called St Martin's Land and that although the people were Christian, she thought they also worshipped St Martin. The sun never rose in St Martin's Land, but a bright country could be seen far away, across a wide river. One day she and her brother were tending their flocks, when they came to the entrance of a large cavern. They heard the sound of sweet bells and could not resist going into the cavern to see what was making the beautiful music. On and on and up and up they wandered, through twisting passages, until suddenly they came out into brilliant sunlight. They had never seen the sun, nor such bright daylight before. Their eyes hurt and their heads ached. They blundered about in confusion and could not find their way back to the entrance into the cavern. After hours and hours, when they were hungry and exhausted, they were found by the villagers.

Many times after this, Sir Richard ordered a search to be made for the entrance to the cavern, but it was never found. The girl remained in service in Sir Richard's household and when she was grown up she married a man from Lenna.

The Fisherman and the Rich Moor

The great Spanish peninsula reaches to within sight of the northern coast of Africa. Much of Spanish history is concerned with the conflicts between the Moors of Africa and the kings and queens of Spain.

Once long ago, on the shores of the blue Mediterranean Sea, there lived a kindly Spanish fisherman. This man was not poor, he made good catches of fine fish and he took care of his money. He lived in a comfortable house. However, the fisherman knew that not everyone was as fortunate and sensible as he was so, every feast day, he would go into the streets and look for a poor man. Then he would invite the man home to eat a fine meal and to sit for one day in warmth and comfort.

One Christmas, the fisherman went out as usual in search of a poor unfortunate. His eyes fell on a Moorish slave, thin and miserable looking. At first the fisherman hesitated because Moorish pirates were always raiding round the Mediterranean coast and were hated and dreaded by the Spaniards. If a Moor was hungry and unhappy, then it was only what he deserved, in the eyes of the fisherman.

Then the fisherman thought to himself, "It is Christmas. I must be charitable to my enemy. It is easy to be kind to those who deserve kindness. Today I must help this man, even if he deserves to be a slave."

The fisherman invited the Moor home with him, gave him warm clothes, set him in a comfortable seat near the fire and fed him well. The Moor was surprised and grateful. At the end of the day he returned to his master. Shortly afterwards, the fisherman learned that the Moor had been ransomed by his family and had returned home. That seemed to be the end of the matter and the fisherman continued with his good works and his fishing.

A year or so later, while he was far out at sea, the fisherman was captured by Moorish pirates and taken to the slave market in Algiers. He stood in chains, thinking of the miserable life which lay ahead of him and scarcely bothering to look at the rich Moors who came to inspect him. One master would no doubt be as harsh as another. One Moor stopped and looked closely at the fisherman. He bought him at once and took him home.

Then he said, "Are you not a fisherman and do you not take poor unfortunates into your home on feast days?"

"Yes, master," replied the fisherman in surprise.

Then looking more closely at the Moor, he recognized him as the man he had entertained at his fireside one Christmas.

"I will repay one good deed with another," smiled the Moor and he freed the fisherman and arranged for him to be shipped home. "But take my advice," called the Moor, as the fisherman was leaving, "you are growing old. Do not go to sea again. Stay by your fireside, where pirates cannot capture you."

The fisherman took that good advice and lived the rest of his life in happiness in his own home, thanks to the gratitude of the Moor.

A tale from Italy

St Mark and the Saving of Venice

Venice is an ancient Italian, merchant city. Built out from the shore and scarcely above sea level, it is in constant danger from storms blowing in from the Adriatic Sea.

Once long ago, an old fisherman lived in the city of Venice. He was a poor man without a home of his own. However, he had his fishing nets and his own boat, and each night he tied up in the shelter of a marble bridge near the palace of the Doges and he was happy enough. One February, a terrible storm arose. The wind howled and the sea raged higher and higher. The fisherman's boat was torn from its moorings and washed out towards the open sea. After great struggles the frightened man managed to land near the Riva San Marco. Wet and shivering he prayed for the storm to abate and waited for dawn to break, but the storm grew worse and the night became blacker and the fisherman feared that the end of the world had come. Suddenly a stranger walked down the steps from San Marco.

"Will you row me across to San Giorgio?" he asked, pointing across a narrow stretch of water to a small island.

"Are you mad?" gasped the fisherman. "No ship could cross that raging sea, least of all my little boat."

"We shall come to no harm," replied the man, "and moreover I will pay you well for I must reach San Giorgio tonight."

The fisherman shrugged. He liked the idea of earning good pay and the island was not far off, perhaps he could reach it in safety. He set off with the stranger and to his amazement the waves became smooth in his path and he easily reached San Giorgio.

"Wait for me," instructed the stranger, stepping ashore. In a few minutes he returned with a young knight of great beauty, dressed in full armour. They stepped into the boat and asked the fisherman to row them to San Niccolo di Lido.

"That is a long way away!" gasped the poor fisherman. "If we try to go there, we shall all be drowned for sure."

"I will pay you well," said the stranger, "and we shall be safe."

Something in the man's manner reassured the fisherman and again he launched forward into the huge waves and lashing wind. Again the sea turned calm in his path and they reached their destination safely. At San Niccolo di Lido the two passengers went ashore and came back with an old man dressed as a bishop.

"Have no fear," he said, smiling at the fisherman. "Take the three of us between the two castles which guard the gateway to the open sea."

The fisherman was horrified, for this was the place where the sea raced and roared worst of all, but he felt that he could not refuse after going so far.

He rowed his little craft between the two guardian castles and then truly almost died of fright. Advancing between the castles, with all sails set, was a huge black ship filled with screaming demons.

"Venice!" they shrieked. "Venice! We will have Venice tonight!"

Onward surged the black ship with the horrible demons leaning forward over the rails, reaching out grasping, scaly hands towards the beautiful palaces of Venice. Laughing to each other and shrieking in tune with the howling wind.

"Row us in the path of that ship!" ordered the young knight.

The fisherman obeyed. Then he saw the stranger from San Marco, and the young knight from San Giorgio, and the bishop from San Niccolo di Lido, stand up boldly and, with no hint of fear, make the sign of the cross at the ship of howling demons. At once it disappeared and the sea became calm.

The trembling fisherman rowed each man back to whence he had come, but at San Marco, he thought to ask for the good pay which had been promised to him.

The first stranger took a ring of gold from his finger. "I am Saint Mark," he said. "Tonight you took me and Saint George and the bishop, Saint Nicholas, to save Venice from demons. This is Saint Mark's ring from the city treasury. Show it to the Doge and tell him your story and he will reward you."

Next day the fisherman did as he was told. The Doge looked into the treasury, but Saint Mark's ring was missing. Then the Doge believed the fisherman's story. He rewarded him and ordered a great procession of thanks to go from San Marco to the island of San Giorgio and out to San Niccolo di Lido.

Beneath the bridge, where the fisherman used to shelter, was carved a picture of the Madonna with a fishing boat, in memory of the brave old man.

60

The Best Teacher

Rumania is a small European country of mountains and forests. In the old days it was full of gipsies and dashing nobles riding their fine horses in battle against each other or the invading foe. It also must have been inhabited by people with a great sense of humour, as so many of their folk tales are full of laughter and fun.

Once long ago, there lived a man who was blessed with a fine house, healthy animals and fertile land. This man was also fortunate enough to have a handsome, loving son, but the boy had never known anything but good times and had never had to deal with adversity.

"The lad must have experience of dealing with ill-luck," said the father.

From then on he gave his son all the awkward jobs. However, luck was with the young man until the day his father sent him into the forest to bring back timber. Only a rickety old cart was free for the work and the father watched his son harness two oxen to the cart.

"If that cart breaks up today, then it will be good experience for the boy," he thought.

The father smiled at his son. "If that cart breaks up when you are alone in the forest, necessity will teach you what to do," he said.

"Right, Father," replied the lad, who was good and loyal, but not the cleverest young man in the world. He thought that Necessity must be some handyman who lived in the forest and helped travellers in trouble.

The son drove the oxen far into the forest where there were good trees suitable for felling. He worked hard, cutting down the trees, sawing them up and loading them on to the cart. When the cart was full, he collected the oxen from where they had been munching at the patches of forest grass, reharnessed them and set off for home. However, as he drove over a patch of rough ground, the cart lurched and one of the axles broke.

"I hope that Necessity fellow is nearby," thought the son. He stood up and shouted, "Necessity! NECESSITY! NE – CESS – ITY!"

No one answered.

Then the young man ran up first one path, then another, always shouting at the top of his voice, "NECESSITY! NE – CESS – ITY!"

Still there was no reply.

The son became worn out.

"I will not bother searching for Father's clever friend any more," he said. "I will do the job myself. Father gave me useless advice."

The young man went back to the cart, took off his coat, unharnessed the oxen, took some wood from the cart, mended the axle, reharnessed the oxen and drove home, having made a fine job of both the repair and collecting good timber. His father was pleased with him, but the boy was not pleased with his father.

"I could not find that fellow, Necessity, anywhere," said the son, "He did not teach me anything. All I learned was that if a job needs doing, it is best to do it myself, then it is done quickly and well. If I go looking for help from other people, I can look for ever."

"There you are," smiled the father. "Necessity did teach you a good lesson. I told you he would."

A legend of the River Rhine

The Lorelei

The River Rhine is one of the great waterways of Europe. It flows through Switzerland, Germany and across the lowlands of Holland into the North Sea. Mountains, forests and castles line its route and dark, melancholy legends are told about those who lived on its banks.

A little way above the city of Koblenz, a huge rock stands high out of the River Rhine. This is the Lorelei Rock. Trippers and merchants may look up at the great rock with wonder nowadays, but in olden times, folk looked up with fear and kept off the river as daylight faded.

Many, many years ago, a beautiful and heartless water nymph lived at the top of the Lorelei. Her hair was golden, her skin was white, her lips were curved and pink. She sang with a voice that charmed away the wits of men. Every evening, the water nymph became visible to human eyes and no man could resist her beauty nor the loveliness of her song. Sailors foolish enough to be near the Lorelei at sunset would steer their boats straight for the huge rock. As they stared up at the lovely nymph, their craft would be dashed to pieces and the unfortunate men would drown in the cold river waters.

One year Ronald, the son of the Count Palatine, swore that he would outwit the nymph of the Lorelei.

"I will not be drowned," he boasted. "I will climb the rock and seize the Lorelei maiden and make her my wife."

He bribed a fisherman to row him towards the huge rock at close of day. Through the twilight they saw the white form of the nymph as she shook out her golden hair. Ronald heard her teasing voice singing and laughing.

63

"You are not rowing fast enough," he shouted at the fisherman. "She will vanish before I can climb the rock."

But the fisherman was rowing slowly and cautiously. He did not intend his boat to be dashed to pieces, as had so many others.

"Faster!" shrieked Ronald and when the fisherman would not obey him, the young man threw himself into the water, swam towards the rock and was swept away and drowned, like all the other young men who had tried to capture the Lorelei. The heartless nymph laughed until dawn hid her from human sight.

The Count of Palatine was heartbroken. He ordered that the nymph must be killed, so that she could tempt no more men to their deaths. The next day four tough old soldiers made their way towards the high rock, they were skilled in mountain climbing and were hard of heart. They scaled the rock and as evening fell and the Lorelei nymph came into sight, it was clear that soon she would be within reach of the soldiers.

"We will fling you from the top of the rock into the river below," they shouted. "You will be dashed to pieces and that will be the end of your evil ways."

For a moment the nymph faltered and seemed afraid, then she gave a shaky laugh, "The Rhine is my father," she said. "He will not let you harm me. He will save me from you."

She took the pearls which entwined her hair and the necklaces from around her throat. Then she tore the strings of jewels apart and, leaning far out over the river, she threw the precious stones one at a time into the rushing torrent.

"Father! Father!" she called. "Save me! Waters of the Rhine, carry these stones to my father, tell him I am in peril. Ask him to send his foaming steeds to save me from my enemies."

Then the waters of the Rhine seethed and roared and rose up like two white horses and washed over the top of the rock, carrying the Lorelei maiden away and out of sight.

Never again did she sing from the heights above the river.

The soldiers hurried home and told Count Palatine that the nymph was gone. Everyone rejoiced that no more men would be lured to their deaths, but for all his life the count mourned the death of his dear son.

The Story of Perseus

Greece is a small country of mountains and islands lying at the south east of Europe. Many people believe that the culture of its early city states formed the foundation for European civilisation. According to legend, the gods of ancient Greece lived on Mount Olympus. They married and quarrelled and felt jealousy, as humans do. They also frequently interfered in the affairs of men, helping their favourites and harming those who had offended them. This is the story of Perseus, who enjoyed the favour of the gods.

Long ago, Acrisius was the king of the small Greek kingdom of Argos. Fear filled his heart, for he had stood before an ancient oracle and given gifts to the priestess, hoping to hear prophecies of riches and prosperity. Instead he was told that his death would be caused by his own grandson.

Hastening home, Acrisius built a brass tower and in it he imprisoned his only child, his daughter Danae.

"There she shall stay for the whole of her life. She will not marry and I will have no grandson to kill me," said Acrisius.

However, the cruel father had reckoned without the power of the gods. Zeus looked down from Mount Olympus and saw the beautiful Danae pining with loneliness in the tower of brass. He flew down and, taking the form of a shower of gold, entered the tower and took Danae as his human wife. In the course of time a little son, named Perseus, was born. Four years went by with Acrisius knowing nothing of the happiness which now filled the lonely tower. Then one day, as the king was walking past, he heard the sound of a child's voice coming down from the high windows. Filled with suspicion, he rushed into the tower and up the steps to the chamber, where his daughter lived. Before his horrified gaze a lovely, little boy sat playing with golden toys.

"Who is this?" screamed Acrisius, turning to Danae.

The frightened girl snatched little Perseus into her arms.

"It is my son," she replied and, as Acrisius stretched out his hands to seize the boy, she went on, "he is the child of Zeus and you harm him at your peril."

White with fury and trembling with fear, Acrisius stood staring at his daughter and the grandson who was destined to kill him. How he longed to seize the child and dash his brains out on the stones of the floor however, fear of Zeus stayed his hand.

Dragging Danae and the boy with him, he called to his servants and strode to the seashore. There he put Danae and little Perseus into a wooden chest and ordered them to be pushed out to sea, where the swift currents carried them far from land.

"I have not harmed a hair of their heads," he growled. "I have cast them out into the hands of fate. If Zeus cares for them so much, let him save them, now they are his affair, not mine. I hope they die, but if they do not, may it be many years before they find the path to bring them back to Argos."

Acrisius turned his back on the shore and returned to his palace. For years he heard no word of his daughter and he thought he was rid of her and her child, but the prophecy of the oracle was not forgotten.

The great god Zeus was fickle in his loves. Already his eyes were turning to admire the beauty of other maidens, however he heard the cries of Danae as she drifted, hungry and thirsty, across the sea. Zeus ordered Poseidon, the god of the oceans, to calm the heaving waves and to carry the wooden chest containing Danae and Perseus to the island of Seriphus. Here lived Polydectes the king and his brother, Dictys.

It was Dictys who was fishing from the rocks when the wooden chest came swaying ashore. Dictys found the exhausted mother and child and took them to the royal palace, but it was Polydectes, who fell in love with Danae and married her. Thus Perseus became the stepson of a king and was brought up and trained in the accomplishments suitable to a prince.

Seeing Danae and Perseus so well settled in the world, Zeus turned his attention elsewhere. And so the years went by.

With such parents as the beautiful Danae and the mighty god, Zeus, Perseus grew up to be a beautiful and charming young man. The goddess Athene noticed him and smiled upon him and she persuaded another god, Mercury, to help her guide Perseus's footsteps along the path of good fortune.

One day Polydectes said to Perseus, "You are a young man of ability and yet you have no achievements to boast about and with which to impress the rulers of this world. If you are to achieve greatness, you must perform some mighty deed."

All this was plainly true, as Danae, Perseus and the whole court agreed. After much discussion it was decided that Perseus should set out to slay Medusa, the Gorgon. If he could accomplish this feat, then indeed his fame would echo round the world.

The Medusa was a truly frightful creature. Once a beautiful, golden-haired maiden, she had offended the goddess Athene. In revenge Athene had transformed each lock of the girl's golden hair into a snake. Medusa's lovely eyes had become bloodshot yellow. The skin of her face had turned to livid green. Scales grew over her body. Her hands became hardened brass and her teeth were like those of a wild boar. She was sent to live with two other creatures as repulsive as herself, and their task was to guard those wrongdoers who, after their deaths, had been sent to eternal torture in the underworld.

These three monsters were called Gorgons. They were all winged and ferocious. Medusa herself was the most vicious of all, as her nature had become embittered by her ugliness. Indeed, so filled was she with hatred, that one glance from her eyes could turn an attacker to stone.

Perseus knew that slaying Medusa the Gorgon would give him the renown for which he longed. He also knew that it would be no easy task. The young man turned to the goddess Athene, and to Mercury, and asked for help.

"In order to slay the Gorgon," said Athene, "you must take with you a pair of winged sandals, a magic wallet and the helmet of darkness. These three things are in the possession of nymphs whose whereabouts is known only to the three Grey Sisters who live far away on the shores of the great sea."

At once Perseus set out to visit the Grey Sisters and, with Athene and Mercury to guide him, he soon reached his destination. He found the sisters sitting together and handing one to the other, the single eye through which they could see and the one tooth with which they could eat.

"Grey Sisters, pray tell me where to find the nymphs who keep the winged sandals and the magic wallet and the helmet of darkness," called Perseus.

The three Grey Sisters cackled with laughter. "Why should we help you?" they screeched. "Do not bother us, young man."

Silently Perseus crept closer to the Grey Sisters. While one of them was wearing their single eye, he stood still. When they passed the eye from hand to hand, and for that minute could not see, he crept forward once more. At last he made a sudden dash and snatched up both the eye and the one tooth. Now the Sisters could neither see nor eat.

"Tell me where to find the nymphs who keep the winged sandals and the magic wallet and the helmet of darkness," called Perseus, "or you will starve in blindness for the rest of your short days."

Frantically the Grey Sisters groped about them.

"Have you the eye? Have you the tooth?" they screeched one to the other.

"Scramble about as you like," shouted Perseus. "You will not find what you are seeking. I have your eye and I have your tooth and I will never return them until you tell me what I wish to know."

Then, grumbling and whining, the Grey Sisters told Perseus how to reach the nymphs. With a smile of triumph, he threw the eye and the tooth between the sisters' six searching hands and rose into the air. He was far, far away before any one of the weird creatures could fit the eye into her forehead and look round to find him.

The nymphs knew that Perseus enjoyed the favour of Athene. They gave him the winged sandals, the magic wallet and the helmet of darkness. Mercury handed to Perseus a sickle-shaped sword, with which to cut off the head of Medusa. Athene gave him a burnished shield.

"Listen to me carefully, handsome, young Perseus," said Athene. "You must not look upon the face of Medusa, or surely you will be turned to stone. When you reach the lair of the Gorgons, you must hold my burnished shield high in your hand. Look at the reflection in the shield to find your way. When you see the Medusa, strike her head from her shoulders with the sword of Mercury, put the head into the magic wallet and flee before the other Gorgons can kill you."

Perseus thanked Athene for her gifts and her help. He strapped the winged sandals to his feet and carefully holding the helmet, wallet, shield and sickle-shaped sword, he flew swiftly to the abode of the Gorgons. All around stood brave men and wild creatures, turned to stone by the fearful Medusa.

68

Perseus put the helmet of darkness upon his head and he became invisible. The winged sandals carried him into the air to hover over where the Gorgons lay. He grasped the sickle-shaped sword in his right hand. With his left hand he raised the burnished shield of Athene high above his head and tilted it to look towards the ground. In its glittering reflection Perseus saw the three frightful Gorgons lying hideously asleep.

The green of Medusa's face glowed livid. Even though she slept, the snakes which were her hair, slithered and heaved their coils round her shoulders. Fearful that she might awake and look at him with her bloodshot, yellow eyes and petrify him even through the reflection in the burnished shield, Perseus struck. He severed Medusa's head with one clean slash of Mercury's sword. Still groping behind him, not daring to look directly at the Gorgon with his own eyes, Perseus put the severed head into the wallet and pulled the thongs closed. He sighed with relief and for a moment relaxed. That terrible head was hidden from sight, an unwary glance in the wrong direction could no longer turn him to stone.

Suddenly there was a mighty rustling of wings. Perseus, still trembling from the shock of combat, saw a huge winged horse, ridden by a fearsome warrior, spring from the neck of the slaughtered Gorgon. The horse flapped and pounded its hooves amongst the stone statues of the Gorgon's victims. The warrior called to the remaining monsters, "Your sister is slain. Awake and take vengeance! I, Chrysaor, and Pegasus, the horse, appeal to you."

The two living Gorgons opened their eyes, looked at their sister and screamed with rage. They flapped their wings and rattled their scales and pushed claws forth from their brazen hands, then rose into the air, slashing and striking everywhere around them.

"Who has done this? Fight us too," they screeched in their harsh voices.

Perseus pulled the helmet of darkness firmly on his head. Clutching the wallet containing the Gorgon's head, he let the winged sandals carry him far from that dreadful place. The Gorgons screamed and raged and searched, but the powers of the gods were with Perseus. The helmet of darkness made him invisible and he escaped. Nevertheless, such was the horror of what had happened that the young man did not pause, he flew for hour after hour over the desert as long as his strength lasted. As he went, drops of the Gorgon's blood fell from the wallet on to the hot sand and became the poisonous snakes, which swarm over Africa to this day.

At last when he was weak with tiredness, Perseus came to the kingdom of the giant Atlas. Clutching his precious possessions, the young man asked for shelter.

Atlas was suspicious. He had an orchard filled with apples of pure gold and many sought to gain his confidence, only to try to rob him. He looked at the dishevelled, blood-streaked, exhausted Perseus, and at the glittering helmet, the burnished shield and the winged sandals on which the young man had descended from the skies. Most of all he looked at the blood-stained sword and the leather wallet from which dripped blood, which turned into wriggling snakes.

"And who might you be?" asked Atlas.

"I am Perseus, the son of Zeus," replied Perseus, longing for rest and food and feeling no desire to be questioned at length. "I have slain the Gorgon, whose head I carry in this wallet."

Then, as Atlas showed no sign of offering hospitality, Perseus added in a threatening voice, "I have only to lift the Gorgon's head from the wallet and show it to my enemies for them to be turned to stone. It is better for those I meet to be my friends."

Atlas thought of his golden apples and of how easy it would be for this young man to steal them.

"I will send him on his way before he finds out the apples are here," thought Atlas.

"I have no rooms, nor food fit to set before the son of a god," said Atlas. "You had better fly on further and look for shelter elsewhere."

Perseus was furious.

"Miserable old man!" he shouted. "All I asked was for simple food and rest. If you will not give me that, then you will never give anyone anything."

Turning aside his own gaze, he snatched the fearsome, bloody head of the Medusa from the wallet and held it up before the face of Atlas. The old man could not resist staring at the monster about which he had heard so much. He gazed and gazed and never stopped gazing for he had turned to stone. His beard and hair became forests, his arms and legs, great rocks. He became the Atlas Mountains which stand in North Africa to this day.

Perseus put the head back into the wallet. He ate and drank and rested in the home of Atlas. The next day, recovered from the strains of his adventure, he went on his way. Athene watched over him and Mercury flew at his side to help him. After a long journey across the desert, he came to Aethiopia, the kingdom of King Cepheus.

This was a land in a sorry plight, the king's wife, Cassiopea, had boasted that her daughter, Andromeda, was more beautiful than the sea nymphs, the Nereides. Furious with wounded pride, for Andromeda was indeed beautiful and there was truth in Cassiopea's boast, the Nereides asked their protector Poseiden, the god of the oceans to punish the whole kingdom. Floods and storms were sent to devastate the land and a huge monster rose up from the sea and devoured all those not swift enough to run from its path.

"These terrible happenings can only be the work of the gods," said the king, Cepheus. "I will consult with the oracle of Jupiter-Ammon in the Libyan desert to learn how we have offended the mighty ones and find out what we must do to placate them."

He returned to his kingdom white faced and distraught.

"You have offended Poseiden with your boasting," he said to his wife. "The Nereides are jealous of the beauty of Andromeda. The sea monster will never cease to plunder our shore, until Andromeda is given to it to be eaten."

So it was that as Perseus circled over the shore of Aethiopia, he saw beautiful Andromeda chained to a rock, with the waves washing round her feet. He turned to look at the clifftops where the king and his court stood,

70

making no move to help the unfortunate maiden.

Perseus landed to ask what place this was, where no one came forward to help a young woman chained down before the rising waves.

"Alas!" groaned King Cepheus. "There is nothing I wish more than to save my only, beloved child, but a terrible monster will cease raiding my land, only if he is given my daughter as his prey."

Already Perseus was in love with Andromeda.

"I have slain the Gorgon," he said. "Why should I tremble before a mere monster of the sea? If I slay this creature and save your child, will you give me her hand in marriage and let me take her to my home in Greece?"

"Yes! Anything! Save her! Save her!" gasped the desperate king.

Putting on his helmet of darkness and taking the sword of Mercury in his hand, Perseus rose into the air and flew towards the approaching beast. It heaved its terrible head from the parting waves and opening its jaws, was about to tear Andromeda to pieces, when the invisible Perseus killed it with a single blow. Then releasing Andromeda from the rock, Perseus carried her to the shore.

The wedding was arranged, the great hall of the palace of King Cepheus was filled with feasting guests. Suddenly the door flew open and the warrior, Phineas, and his armed followers strode into the room and confronted Perseus.

"This marriage cannot take place," said Phineas. "Andromeda was betrothed to me. The contract was signed. She must be my bride and the wife of no other."

Perseus stood up.

"And where were you when Andromeda was chained to the rock and the waves were parting to send forth the sea monster?" he asked. "I saw you not then, nor heard your voice prating of marriage contracts. Andromeda is mine."

King Cepheus interrupted.

"Let us talk this over," he said. "Perhaps it would be better if Andromeda did not marry Perseus. After all, none of us knows anything about him and Greece is a long way away. The marriage arrangements with Phineas were beneficial to the kingdom. Let Andromeda marry Phineas and Perseus can take some other reward. I am sure we can easily find something. A chest of gold perhaps? Or we have some very nice jewelry that Perseus might like to take to his mother."

Perseus's heart was filled with rage at such perfidy.

"Do you seek to buy off the son of Zeus with necklaces and bracelets?" he shouted. "I killed the monster in order to win Andromeda in marriage and Andromeda I shall have."

He drew his sword and rushed at Phineas.

Phineas drew his sword and fought back, so did his followers, so did the soldiers of King Cepheus. Even a hero such as Perseus could not fight against such odds. Stepping back he picked up the blood-stained wallet.

"All who are my friends, turn aside their eyes," he shouted.

Then dragging the head of the Medusa from the bag, he brandished it high in the air. His enemies were turned to stone, but Andromeda, who loved him and had turned away her gaze, was saved.

The next day Perseus and his lovely bride journeyed to Seriphus in Greece where they were eagerly greeted by Danae, the mother of Perseus. There they lived happily, until Perseus said to his mother, "Now I have proved my worth by the slaying of the Gorgon, I wish to return to our native land to claim my rightful inheritance from your father, King Acrisius."

Danae nodded, for it was right that Perseus should inherit the throne of his ancestors, but she counselled her dear son to be careful.

"It was foretold that King Acrisius, my father, would be killed by his grandson," she said. "Acrisius will fear you and might even do you harm."

"This is nonsense," laughed Perseus. "I do not wish to kill the old man. The priestess must have misunderstood the oracle and given the wrong prophecy."

Longing for the sight of his homeland, Perseus returned to Argos and sought to kneel before his grandfather, King Acrisius.

The old king fled in fear and took shelter with King Teutemias of Larissa. Still Perseus followed his grandfather, wishing to make peace with him.

"Arrange some games," he said to King Teutemias. "Let my grandfather watch me secretly and see that I am no monster, but a worthy grandson."

On the day of the games, Perseus entered the contest for throwing the discus. Acrisius watched from amongst the crowd of royal courtiers. He saw his grandson step forward and swing his arm. Then Perseus seemed to trip. He threw awkwardly. The discus flew over the crowd and struck a blow to the head of Acrisius. He fell dead. Thus the prophecy was fulfilled. Through no wish of his own, Perseus had killed his grandfather.

The sorrowing young man buried Aristius with fitting ceremony and returned to Argos. However, he could not be happy in a kingdom which he had inherited in such a tragic way. He exchanged kingdoms with King Megapenthes of Tiryns and there he lived happily with Andromeda and later founded the towns of Mycenae and Midea.

The head of the Gorgon did not stay in the possession of Perseus. He thought it wise to present it to the goddess Athene to thank her for her favour. She fixed the head in the centre of her burnished shield and brandished it high in the face of her enemies.

Middle East

MIDDLE EAST

The Epic of Gilgamesh   78

Aladdin or the Wonderful Lamp   88

David and Goliath   102

Joseph and His Coat of Many Colours   108

The Epic of Gilgamesh

Assyria and Babylonia, or Syria and Iraq. The names of the states change in the Middle East, but the country remains the same where the Tigris and Euphrates rivers drain down to the Shatt al Arab and the Arabian Gulf. Under the huge mounds of shifting sand are buried the secrets of Nineveh and Babylon and Gilgamesh of Erech. It is thought that the Epic of Gilgamesh was first written down in 2100 B.C., although it was without doubt, an oral tradition long before. King Assur-bani-pal was a patron of literature, who created a library in ancient Nineveh. Historians believe that it was in this library that the story of the hero, Gilgamesh, was first scratched on to clay. Not long after the twelve tablets of the Epic of Gilgamesh were written, Nineveh fell to invaders. In the tradition of conquering hordes, they burned the library and trampled the words of wisdom into the dust under their horses' hooves. Buried beneath the debris of centuries, the broken tablets of the Epic of Gilgamesh lay untouched until they were discovered and pieced together by European excavators in the nineteenth century. Missing fragments of the story, cultural differences and translation difficulties all make the understanding of Gilgamesh a difficult task. Here follows an attempt to tell his story, so very long after he saw his last sunset.

Gilgamesh was a hero, brave and clever, but also harsh and unrelenting. He rescued the city of Erech from seige by an invading foe, then the city was his. Everyone obeyed the word of Gilgamesh or woe and grief was their portion. To the strong went the spoils and Gilgamesh was strong. This was the way the people liked things to be and while Gilgamesh ruled, no other power needed to be feared.

Gilgamesh was the son of the daughter of the old King Sokkaros, who was the first king in Babylonia after the great flood. No one could say who was the father of Gilgamesh. Was it the god of the Sun? Was it the eagle which saved the baby's life when he was flung from the top of a high tower? So often the gods stayed their wrath in the face of Gilgamesh. Strange warriors whose fiery glances shrivelled other men, stood aside to let Gilgamesh pass. Surely the father of Gilgamesh came from the sun and Gilgamesh was kin to shining ones of the heavens, for why else would his enemies quail before him?

Like all mortal men, Sokkaros died and his grandson, Gilgamesh, drove out the enemies who had been harrying the fading power of the old man.

The glittering glory of Gilgamesh dazzled the people. He wore precious jewels and gold necklaces, his clothes were the finest. He was a man of the city.

However, there were those in Erech who forgot how recently the enemy had been at the gate. They begged the goddess Aruru to make another hero, a man quite different from Gilgamesh, a man who could defy Gilgamesh, the harsh ruler, and frighten him into softening his government.

At last, weary of constant whining and pleading, Aruru fell into deep thought. Inside her mind she created a picture of a man totally unlike Gilgamesh. She washed her hands, then she took some clay and fashioned it in the likeness of the man in her mind. She threw the clay to the ground in the far mountain country, and so was created Eabani, the wild man.

Eabani lived like the animals, hunting his prey in the scrubland, eating plants with the flocks of gazelles and lapping at the waterholes with the beasts of the desert. His body was hairy and the flowing locks which grew from his head reached to his waist like the tresses of a woman. Nevertheless, he wore the clothes of a god, for the goddess Aruru had created him.

Eabani lived in the wilderness, away from the protected life of the city. He grew strong and fearsome. Tales of the wild man who ran faster than the animals and swam more sleekly than the silver fish, reached Gilgamesh. Perhaps his father, the god of the sun, Shamash, whispered into his ear that Eabani had been sent to humble him. Gilgamesh became suspicious. He sent a skilled tracker, named Tsaidu, and a beautiful girl, named Ukhut, from the temple of the goddess Ishtar to find Eabani.

"Tempt him with stories of life in the city," said Gilgamesh. "Get him into your power, then bring him to Erech that I may look at this rival."

Tsaidu and the beautiful Ukhut travelled into the wilderness. They waited at the watering hole where Eabani customarily drank, and saw him lean down and lap like the beasts. They walked before him in their graceful silks and lovely jewelry. The soft hair of Ukhut was shining and smooth, not stiff and rough like the hair of the creatures of the wilderness. Her skin, sheltered by the walls of the temple of Ishtar, was delicate, not coarse from the sun.

Eabani fell in love with Ukhut. For six days and seven nights he stayed with her at the waterhole, listening to stories of life in the city. He longed to visit this abode of men.

"Come with us to stay in the city and visit the great Gilgamesh," urged Ukhut and Tsaidu.

Suddenly Eabani remembered his friends the gazelles, the water creatures and the herds of animals. He ran to speak to them, but some had moved on, while most of the rest had forgotten him in the short time he had spent with Ukhut. Those who did remember him would no longer obey him.

"Where were you for six days and seven nights?" they asked. "One who comes and goes is no use to us."

Ukhut and Tsaidu again said, "Come with us. You are handsome. Why waste your good looks on the beasts? Come to the great palace and meet Gilgamesh, that dazzling ruler of men."

So, disillusioned with life in the wilderness, Eabani agreed to go to the town. On the way the gods whispered in his ear.

"You were created to humble Gilgamesh," they said. "Be prepared to fight him."

Eabani had a mind of his own. Life in the city sounded alluring and he wanted Gilgamesh to be his friend. Eabani thought of the customs of the animals, the only customs he knew. When two strong animals met, they always fought before they could be friends. A combat was needed to settle which of them was to be the leader.

"Perhaps I should challenge Gilgamesh to a duel so that from the start we will know which of us is greater," thought Eabani.

He asked the opinion of Ukhut, who was wise in the ways of the city. "Fight Gilgamesh, if you must," she said, "but remember he is strong and aggressive. He has an army of bodyguards lining the walls of his palace. He is not a man to take orders from others and most important of all, he is a favourite of Shamash."

Eabani spoke no more of a combat. He was a wise young man.

Meanwhile Gilgamesh eagerly awaited the arrival of the hairy man of the wilderness, whom the goddess Aruru had created especially to humble him. Should he kill him, or imprison him or surround him with so much luxury that he becomes a weakling? It was not an easy decision. Care had to be taken not to offend Aruru.

The two young men met. And so it was proven that the plans of even a powerful goddess may go awry. Gilgamesh and Eabani liked one another. Gilgamesh gave up his plans to harm Eabani and Eabani gave no thought to humbling Gilgamesh. Perhaps Gilgamesh was bored with the conversation of lesser men, maybe the monotony of natural life had palled with Eabani, or it could have been that confronting an equal came as a release to both of them. For whatever reason, from the first meeting Gilgamesh and Eabani were as brothers.

Once, as was natural, Eabani became homesick for the colours and sounds of the open country. When he spoke of leaving the city, the god of the sun, Shamash himself, intervened. He came as a vision to the two young men.

"Eabani shall stay in comfort in the palace," he said. "Gilgamesh shall give Eabani a seat next to the throne and the kings who come to pay tribute to Gilgamesh shall kiss the feet of Eabani."

So it was done and Eabani stayed in the city of Erech.

Then a dream came to trouble Eabani. In it he saw a frightful monster threatening and pawing at the foot of a sacred cedar tree which guarded the forest home of the goddess Ishtar. At the same time Shamash whispered into the ear of Gilgamesh, "Do not rest here. Go to the forest. Slay the monster Khumbaba."

Both young men knew that a task had been set which they must perform. The ways of the gods are full of guile and Gilgamesh went to consult his mother, the priestess Rimat-belit. They asked her advice on how to reach the Forest of Cedars and which path to take to the sacred tree and the home of Ishtar.

Rimat-belit, who had walked with the gods in her youth, told her dear son all that she knew. She watched him leave, and her heart was with him. She turned and called out to Shamash.

"Why did you choose my son for this terrible task?" she asked. "Could not another have risked his life? You have sent my dearest boy to fight that terrible creature which spreads evil throughout the land. Now you must watch over him every moment he is away. Do not turn to other things. Care for my son with all thy splendour until he returns to his home."

So Gilgamesh and Eabani found their way to the Forest of Cedars. It was a still and silent place, for the evil of the monster Khumbaba spread through the trees like an ill wind. Long before the monster was seen, its invisible power had struck, making everyone who entered the woodland weak and sick. After walking in the forest for only a short while, Eabani lingered at the wayside.

"I am ill," he said. "My arms are weak. My hands will not do what I tell them."

No harm came to the great hero Gilgamesh because the god Shamash had heard the cries of Rimat-belit and he was watching over him. Gilgamesh strode through the forest, his glory undimmed, found the frightful monster and slew it. Eabani struggled forward to be with his friend, but he was weak and helpless.

In triumph Gilgamesh returned to the city of Erech. He walked every step wearing the blood-stained, torn clothes in which he had fought the monster Khumbaba, and his friend trailed like a shadow behind him.

Gilgamesh walked through the streets of Erech showing off his gory apparel and boasting of his valiant deed, then he took off the torn clothes and washed away the blood. He put on his golden, kingly robes and wore the flowers of victory round his brow. He had never looked more noble nor more handsome and in that moment were sewn the seeds of his future sorrows.

The goddess Ishtar looked down to see the hero who had slain the monster at her door. When she beheld how handsome Gilgamesh appeared in his victor's crown, she fell in love with him. She came to the palace and asked Gilgamesh to be her husband.

"I am a goddess," she said. "Marry me and your flocks will increase, your enemies will flee and all nations will pay tribute to you."

Gilgamesh laughed.

"All this may be," he said, "but for how long? You have had many husbands, oh lovely goddess, and you have tired of all of them. You have cast them aside and taken their riches. Why should my fate be different? I will not marry you."

Ishtar returned to heaven in a rage at being scorned. She whispered spiteful words into the ears of the other gods and turned many of them against Gilgamesh.

"Gilgamesh must be punished for his impudence," said the gods Anu and Anatu.

They created a mighty bull, whose breath would spoil the crops of the earth for seven years, and they sent the bull to fight Gilgamesh.

"Kill the bull," they called to Gilgamesh. "If you do not, he will kill you and rampage through your lands which will lie withered for seven years."

Gilgamesh was a hero. He felt not one moment of doubt and taking up his weapons he walked forward to face the bull.

The fight was long and exhausting and Gilgamesh was hurt and tired. The dirt kicked up by the bull choked in his throat, sweat ran down his forehead and blurred his eyes, while the blood from his wounds slid out with alarming swiftness – but Gilgamesh killed that huge bull before the bull could kill him.

The sickly Eabani could only stand and watch.

Then the scorned goddess Ishtar burned with fury. She stood on the walls of Erech and screeched at Gilgamesh, "Curse you! Curse you, who have scorned me! How dare you be strong enough to defeat a bull sent by the gods! You will be punished!"

At that Eabani found the strength to stand before Ishtar.

"Gilgamesh defeated the bull in fair fight," he said. "That should be the end of the matter. You are wrong to carry on with the feud. Leave Gilgamesh in peace."

Ishtar turned flaming red with fury and her hair rose like a mane about her head.

"Cursed be you too!" she hissed at Eabani.

From that moment, there was no more hope for his life.

The beautiful girl Ukhut, who had waited by the waterhole for Eabani so long before, was already dead. She came to Eabani one night in a dream.

"Eabani," she said, "it is time for you to come with me down to the land of the shadows. Come with me down the path of no return, to the house where no one who enters ever leaves. Now you must live in the land without light, where dust is our food and the feathers of the birds are our clothes."

Eabani rose no more from his bed. Twelve days later, he was dead.

Gilgamesh was filled with grief. No more would he walk in the sunlight with his dear friend. No one was left with whom he shared the same memories, because part of his own life was lying in the grave with Eabani.

Suddenly Gilgamash was seized with a great fear of death. He decided to seek out his ancestor, Ut-Napishtim, the only man ever to be made immortal by the gods.

"Ut-Napishtim must tell me the secret of everlasting life," thought Gilgamesh. "Death must not take me to the land of shadows."

Finding the home of an immortal is not easy. Immortals do not live as other men. They do not eat or drink as other men. They guard their secrets carefully.

Gilgamesh walked towards the lonely, forbidden place. The land rose from the plain into high mountains and the rocky slopes of the valleys pressed menacingly on either side. Wild beasts grunted and stalked what looked like an easy meal. This was the country Eabani had loved. The hairy man of the wilderness would have known every trick used by the wild animals, but Eabani was no longer with Gilgamesh.

Sin, the moon-god, slipped down from the sky and taking Gilgamesh by the hand, led him through that place of peril. When they came to Mashu, the Mountain of the Sunset, even the moon-god would not stay.

"Go no further, Gilgamesh," he said. "This is a place of danger."

Gilgamesh would not turn back. He looked towards the sky which was spread with the colours of sunset. By day and by night the pink coloured clouds hung above the Mountain of Mashu. No one could explain why, but they were always there. This was the entrance to the far world where life was different, where men were not as other men and where the immortals lived.

Gilgamesh stepped forward and his path was barred by the Scorpion men. These terrifying creatures had human shape, but were covered with shimmering, shining skin, like that of a scorpion. They shrivelled men with their gaze and to behold them was death. They guarded the portals of Mount Mashu from sunrise to sunset as they were the servants of the sun. Their numbers were so great, they covered the mountains from peak to valley.

Gilgamesh looked at them and was afraid. They dazzled him and he became confused, but he did not die under their glance because he was partly a god.

Seeing that this was no ordinary man, the Scorpion men came forward and spoke to Gilgamesh. He told them that he was seeking his ancestor, Ut-Napishtim, in order to learn the secrets of immortality.

"Go back," counselled the Scorpion men. "Ut-Napishtim does live beyond the portals of Mashu, through the land of the sunset, but you will never survive the journey. After the sunset you will come to a region of thick darkness. For twenty-four hours you will travel through the night – a terrible choking night and more barriers lie beyond that. If we let you through, we shall be sending you to your death."

Gilgamesh stumbled to his feet.

"I am going forward," he said.

His manner was rough and his eyes were threatening. Even in grief and confusion, Gilgamesh was still the man who had ruled Erech with a hand of iron.

The Scorpion men stood aside and let him walk through.

Gilgamesh walked under the flaming sunset and into the thick, choking darkness of twenty-four hours of night. Steadfast he strode forward, like the true hero that he was. At last the blackness lightened. A faint gleam, then a strong light filled the sky and Gilgamesh found himself in a beautiful garden. It was lovely, but it was strange. Nothing was real. The fruit was made of jewels and the tops of the trees were lapis lazuli, while the leaves were green but dry.

"These are the gardens of the gods," thought Gilgamesh.

Gilgamesh was tired and dirty, his clothes were torn, and his legs bleeding, from his many falls in the darkness. He still grieved for his dead friend, Eabani, and he was anxious to find the right road to the home of his ancestor, Ut-Napishtim.

From her palace on the sea shore, the goddess of the sea, Sabitu, looked out and saw this doom-laden figure. She saw a desperate man, torn by deep emotions, yet still ferocious and menacing.

Sabitu locked her doors and pulled the shutters down over the palace windows.

84

"Trouble, I can do without," she thought.

Gilgamesh looked at the shore spread out before him. His father, Shamash, whispered in his ear, "You must cross the sea to reach Ut-Napishtim. To do that you need the advice of Sabitu, the goddess of the sea."

Gilgamesh walked to the sea-bleached doors of the palace. He knocked. He called. He hammered and shouted. Still Sabitu would not let him in.

"A man who can get this far into our different world is a man to be feared," she thought.

She was right. The fury that had made Gilgamesh the conquerer of Erech, consumed him. He raised his axe and brought it down with a crash and splintered the wood of the palace doors.

"Let me in or I will destroy your precious home," he shouted.

At once Sabitu ordered the doors to be opened and food was set before Gilgamesh. Trying to hide her nervous shivering, she asked him what he wanted.

"Tell me how to cross the water to reach my ancestor, the immortal Ut-Napishtim," he replied.

"Do not go," said Sabitu. "It is too dangerous. Already you have come too far into this strange land. You do not know the peril you are in, return to your home while you still have the strength."

Gilgamesh would not listen.

"Very well then," said Sabitu, "Adad-Ea is the ferryman of your ancestor, Ut-Napishtim. He is the only one who can take you across these treacherous waters. Ask him to ferry you to the far strand."

Adad-Ea was as reluctant as Sabitu to help this desperate man who had come out of the great darkness.

"Go home and do not bother me," he said.

Gilgamesh raised his axe and smashed the rudder from Adad-Ea's boat.

He turned and looked at the ferryman.

"Take me across to Ut-Napishtim or I will smash the rest of your boat and you will never take anyone anywhere again," he said.

Adad-Ea hastily consented. Gilgamesh cut a new rudder from the forest and they journeyed across the water.

Ut-Napishtim was surprised to see the boat approaching as it was not time for Adad-Ea to visit. He was more amazed when he saw Gilgamesh in the boat.

Eagerly Gilgamesh rose to his feet, planning to wade ashore to talk to this man who knew the secret of immortality, but he was too weak to scramble over the side of the boat. He felt sick.

"Seasickness! Seasickness!" he groaned. "I must be seasick. How strange! I have never been seasick before."

Adad-Ea looked at his unwanted passenger.

"It is not seasickness that ails you," he said. "Look at your skin."

Gilgamesh looked down and found that he was breaking out into sores.

"You should never have come here," said Adad-Ea. "Everyone told you that, from the Scorpion men onwards, but you knew better."

Gilgamesh gripped the side of the boat and pulled himself up so that he could talk to his ancestor.

"I have come so far and suffered so much, and I will find out the secret I came to learn," he thought.

"Greetings, noble ancestor," he called, "I am Gilgamesh, a mighty warrior and worthy descendant of your honoured self. The gods granted immortality to you. Tell me why, that I too may earn this precious gift."

Ut-Napishtim shifted from foot to foot.

"You look unwell," he said. "This is not the time to talk. Sleep for a while. We will discuss your question later."

Gilgamesh would not be deterred.

"Tell me the secret of immortality!" he shouted.

"Be reasonable!" begged Ut-Napishtim. "How can I do such a thing? The gods would be furious. Death is the destiny of all mankind, it is not given to man to avoid death, or know the hour at which it will strike. Annunaki the greatest god and Mammerum, the maker of destiny, decide these things. It is not for you or me to interfere. Be content, immortality is not so desirable a thing."

Gilgamesh broke into a cold sweat and the sickness made his head ache. The sores on his body stung, but still he clung to the side of the boat and shouted across the shallow water, "Undesirable or not, I notice you did not refuse immortality when it was offered to you. Why is it good for you, but not for me?"

"I was very special," protested Ut-Napishtim. "I was favoured by the god Ea. He ordered me to build a big ship and take people and animals into it. I did as I was told and when a great flood deluged the earth, everyone on my boat lived. If it had not been for me, animals and mankind would have perished. In gratitude the gods made me and my wife immortal. I cannot ask them to do the same for you. You may be a great warrior, but so are other men."

Gilgamesh was filled with disappointment, for once even his ferocious spirit flagged and his head drooped. Ut-Napishtim felt sorry for him.

"Come ashore and I will try to heal you," he said.

Gilgamesh was carried to a bed. Ut-Napishtim ordered sleep to breath upon him. For six days and nights Gilgamesh slept and all the while the wife of Ut-Napishtim treated his sores with ointment.

When Gilgamesh awoke, he was taken to a special spring where he bathed, his sores were finally healed and his strength restored.

Once more he asked for the secret of immortality.

"The gods will not grant it to you," replied Ut-Napishtim. "It is useless to ask."

Ut-Napishtim's wife smiled at Gilgamesh's handsome face.

"There is a plant growing at the bottom of the sea," she whispered, "Adad-Ea, the ferryman knows where to find it. Eat this plant and you will never grow old."

With this Gilgamesh had to be satisfied. Adad-Ea showed him how to

86

collect the sea-plant. They made a great bundle of it and then Adad-Ea guided Gilgamesh back through the darkness and under the sunset, past the Scorpion men, through the valleys of the wild beasts and back to the land of men.

As he drew within sight of Erech, Gilgamesh came upon a spring of sweet water. He knelt down and gave thanks to the gods for bringing him safely home from such a perilous journey. As Gilgamesh prayed, a serpent scented the sea-plant and slipping forward, carried it away in its mouth. Gilgamesh never saw the magical herb again.

He wept bitterly for it was clear that the gods did not intend him to be immortal.

Gilgamesh strode into Erech. Everywhere he looked he was reminded of Eabani and his grief returned. He went from temple to temple begging the gods to let Eabani come back to the upper world. At last the god Ea agreed. A hole opened up in a hillside, a cold wind blew and suddenly Eabani was standing in the sunlight – a pale grey shadow of the Eabani who had lived on earth.

"Do not waste your time in grief," he said to Gilgamesh. "I am a fortunate spirit. You gave me proper burial and put furnishings and clothes and food in my tomb. In my existence in the land of shadows I dwell in luxury with delicate meals to eat and fine clothes to adorn me. You saved me from the shame of those whose bodies are left to rot in the fields. They are beggars in the other world and know no comfort."

Eabani smiled, turned his head and he was gone.

So ends all we know of Gilgamesh. It is to be hoped that he found happiness during the rest of his life. Or did he spend his time gazing at the eternal sunset over the Mountain of Mashu, longing for immortality?

Aladdin or the Wonderful Lamp

The Arabian Nights stories were not known in Europe before the year 1704, when a French professor named Antoine Galland published a French translation of a book of Arabic tales. This was a great success, but contained only a small selection of the original stories. In the nineteenth century, Sir Richard Burton made a translation of Arabian stories running to ten volumes. Most of the stories are supposed to have been told by Scheherazade in serial form. This was to hold the interest of her husband, the sultan, so that he would not have her executed, as had been the fate of his previous wives. Since the original translations, the stories have been retold and broken up into separate tales to suit the purposes of the tellers. This story about Aladdin is one of the Arabian Nights stories which was set in China.

Long ago, in China, there lived a poor tailor, named Mustapha. He worked hard and made a modest living for his wife and only child. However, his days were filled with distress because of the idleness and disobedience of his son, Aladdin.

Aladdin was a wild and wayward boy, who preferred to spend his days playing in the streets and chatting in the public squares, rather than working in his father's tailors shop. At last, worn out with work and sorrow, Mustapha died. Now there was nothing to restrain Aladdin's behaviour, for he had no fear of his gentle mother.

The boy made no attempt to work or learn a trade, but ran wild in the streets with a gang of like-minded idlers. His sad mother earned what money she could, but their home became poor and threadbare and often there was no food in the cupboard.

This continued until Aladdin reached the age of fifteen years. Then a stranger came to town, a sorcerer from Africa. This stranger walked the streets looking at the boys who ran without restraint. He saw something in Aladdin's face which suited his purpose. He spoke with the merchants in the market place and learned much of Aladdin's family history.

Then, wearing his finest clothes and his richest jewels, the sorcerer approached Aladdin and asked, "My dear boy, is your name Aladdin and are you the son of Mustapha, the tailor?"

Impressed by the apparent wealth of the stranger, Aladdin replied meekly that this was so, but that his father was now dead.

At once the sorcerer threw his arms round the boy's neck and with tears in his eyes cried, "Then you are my nephew and I am your uncle. Your father, Mustapha, was my dear brother. Oh, how like him you are! Oh, how grieved I am that he is dead and that I shall never see him again!"

The sorcerer asked Aladdin where he lived, gave him some money to take home to his mother and said that he would have supper with them the next evening. Aladdin ran home and eagerly told his mother about the rich and generous uncle who was coming to visit them.

His mother was puzzled and suspicious. "Your father had no brother, nor did I," She said. "You have no uncles. This man has made a mistake." However, she could not resist taking the money and with it bought food and prepared a good supper for the next evening.

At suppertime the sorcerer arrived with gifts of fruit and wine and more gold coins, which he gave to Aladdin. He embraced the boy and again he wept and said how much Aladdin reminded him of his dear, dead brother, Mustapha. He turned to Aladdin's mother, greeted her respectfully and begged to be shown where Mustapha had sat to eat his meals and to work. When this was done, he again made a great display of weeping and grieving and said he wished he had not spent so long away from China, and that he was heartbroken he had not seen his beloved brother before he left the world of the living.

The sorcerer gave presents of jewels to Aladdin's mother and assured her that he really was Mustapha's brother, and that he had been out of the country for forty years travelling in Africa and India.

"However, now I am back," he smiled, "and I should like to make up for my neglect of my family by helping you and my dear nephew, Aladdin."

The poor mother could think of no reason why the rich stranger should help them, unless his story were true, and graciously took the gifts and hoped that their days of poverty were over. The three of them ate supper together and then the sorcerer took his leave, promising to visit again the next day.

So things continued for several days, until Aladdin and his mother trusted the so-called uncle completely. Then the cunning sorcerer started to do what he had been planning from the beginning.

"Aladdin," he called one bright morning. "This humble home in which you and your mother live, is not good enough. Come with me outside the city walls and we will choose a fine mansion, with lovely gardens, where the three of us may live together, with servants to wait on us. You are all the family I have left and I want to take care of you."

This sounded very agreeable to Aladdin and, putting on some of the fine clothes bought for him by the sorcerer, he said farewell to his mother and walked out through the city gates. On and on they walked and although Aladdin saw many houses, which to him seemed beautiful and pleasing, his 'uncle' found fault with all of them and led the boy further and further from the city. At last they reached the foothills of the mountains and, as the sorcerer had intended from the beginning, they stopped in a narrow valley between two low hills. This was the place the sorcerer had seen in his magical dreams and it was to find this place that he had journeyed all the way from Africa.

Turning to Aladdin, he said, "Gather up dry sticks and make a bright fire. I am about to show you many wonderful and frightening things, but you will thank me in the end."

Aladdin was puzzled, but did as his 'uncle' said and soon a great fire was blazing in the narrow valley. The sorcerer threw some incense on the flames and chanted magic words. At once the earth before him rolled back to reveal a stone with a ring fixed in it. Terrified, Aladdin turned to run, but his 'uncle' caught him by the arm and gave him a blow round the ears and told him to stay close. This seemed strange behaviour for the man who, until then, had been so kind.

"Remember, I am your uncle and you should obey me as if I were your father," snarled the sorcerer. He continued on in a more wheedling tone, "Aladdin, under this stone is a great treasure and only you may enter to get it. Do not be afraid. If you do exactly as I say, no harm will come to you, only great riches."

The talk of treasure calmed Aladdin's fears and he agreed to do as his 'uncle' instructed.

The sorcerer pointed at the stone.

"Take hold of the ring and lift the stone," he said.

Aladdin could not restrain his laughter.

"Uncle!" he gasped. "How can I, a boy, lift such a heavy weight? You must help me."

"No!" snapped the sorcerer, again letting his mask of kindness slip. "You must do it alone. If I help you, all will be ruined. Pull on the ring and the stone will rise. Try it and see."

Lured on by the thought of riches, Aladdin pulled on the ring and to his amazement, the stone swung back easily to reveal a short staircase leading down to a door.

"Go down the stairs and open the door," said the sorcerer. "Go through and you will find yourself in a palace with three great halls. On either side of you there will be gold and silver, but you must not touch it. Walk carefully through the halls. Take nothing, and do not let your clothes brush against anything. You will then enter a garden. In the garden will be many lovely fruit trees, but you are to walk to the far side where you will find a lamp burning in a niche. Put out the lamp. Throw away the wick and the oil. Place the lamp in your waistband and hurry back to me."

Then, as Aladdin started to descend the steps, the sorcerer called him back and, pulling a ring from his own finger, placed it on one of Aladdin's.

"This ring is a talisman against evil," he said. "It will keep you safe from any dangers lurking beyond my sight. Now hurry through the palace and bring back the lamp and we shall both become rich."

Aladdin decended the steps and pushed open the door. He found himself in a great palace, exactly as his 'uncle' had described. On either side of him were vessels containing silver and gold, but Aladdin touched none of them. Gathering his clothes closely about him, so that they brushed nothing as he passed, Aladdin hastened through the three halls and out into the beautiful garden. Still obeying his 'uncle', the boy walked across the garden to where a lamp burned in a niche. He took the lamp, put out the light, threw away the wick and the oil, then tucked the lamp into his waistband.

92

The boy turned to retrace his steps. However, he could not help staring at the beauty of the fruits hanging from the trees – some were milky white, some hung in green clusters, some glittered like crystal and some were as red as strawberries.

"My uncle did not forbid me to touch the fruit in the garden," thought Aladdin. "I will take some home to my mother."

He wandered amongst the trees, picking handfuls of the pretty fruit. He was disappointed to find that it was hard and not like the soft, luscious fruit of the upper world, but he took it anyway. Aladdin, having been poor all his life, did not know that the milky white fruits were pearls, the green fruits were emeralds, the crystal fruits were diamonds and the red berries were rubies. Filling his waistband and the front of his jacket with as many of the pretty baubles as he could fit in, Aladdin hurried back to where the sorcerer waited.

At the foot of the short, steep flight of steps, Aladdin paused for breath.

"Lend me your hand and help me up into the air, Uncle," he panted.

"Give me the lamp first," snapped the sorcerer, whose temper was frayed from waiting.

Aladdin glanced down to where the lamp was buried under the fruits he had picked in the garden.

"Oh, I cannot get it out now," he called. "I will give it to you as soon as I am out of this hole."

At this the sorcerer lost his temper completely and, convinced that Aladdin was trying to cheat him of the lamp, he threw more incense on the fire and chanted some magic words. At once the stone closed back over the staircase and the earth rolled back over the stone as if it had never been disturbed.

Aladdin was trapped.

Still consumed with rage, the sorcerer hurried back to Africa, carefully avoiding Aladdin's home town, in case anyone should enquire after the lad. The truth was that the sorcerer had learned of the existence of the lamp from studying his magic books. After many years he had worked out the position of the trapdoor. He had learned that he could only gain ownership of the lamp if it were given to him willing by someone who did not know its value. For that reason he had sought out a fatherless boy, whom he could take away without question, and he had chosen Aladdin because of his bold, fearless manner. Then, just as it seemed he would gain the prize he sought, Aladdin had not willingly given him the lamp and all the sorcerer's hopes were ruined.

"Let the little wretch rot underground," fumed the furious sorcerer, as he hurried on his way.

Meanwhile, Aladdin was trapped in the darkness below the stone.

"Uncle! Uncle!" he called. "I will give you the lamp. Let me out."

However, there was no one to hear his cries and soon the boy realized that he must help himself. Feeling his way downwards, he tried to push open the door leading to the palace.

"At least in the palace it is light," he thought. "And I might find a way out through the garden."

The door to the palace was shut fast and no banging or pushing would open it. Poor Aladdin crouched in the darkness on the steps and clasped his hands together, intending to pray to Allah for help. However, in clasping his hands, he rubbed the ring which the sorcerer had given to him and which he had completely forgotten about until that moment.

Immediately a monstrous and terrifying genie appeared.

"What is your wish oh Master? I serve whoever wears that ring."

Frightening though the genie was, Aladdin was delighted to see anyone or anything which might help him from the underground darkness.

"Whoever you are take me out from this place," he said.

In a moment he found himself standing on the ground where he had lit the fire in the company of the sorcerer. There was no sign of the opening in the ground or his cruel 'uncle'. Thankful for his deliverance, Aladdin hurried home to his mother and at once fell into an exhausted sleep.

The next day when he awoke, he recounted his adventure to his mother and then begged her for something to eat.

"Alas, son," she replied, "there is no food in the house. Now your so-called uncle is gone, there is no one to give us money to buy more."

Aladdin rummaged amongst the things he had brought back from the underground palace and picked up the lamp.

"I will take this to sell in the marketplace," he said. "It will fetch enough to buy food for a meal or two."

His mother picked up a cloth.

"Let me polish it for you," she said. "It will fetch a better price if it looks shiny and new."

She had hardly given the lamp one good rub when a genie, even larger than the genie of the ring, stood before them. Aladdin and his mother gazed at it in terror. The huge creature stared down at them.

"I am the slave of the lamp," it said. "Your wish is my command."

This was too much for Aladdin's mother, who fainted, but Aladdin snatched up the lamp and holding it in his hands, stared boldly back at the genie and said, "I am hungry. Bring me a fine meal."

The genie disappeared and in a few seconds was back holding a silver tray. On the tray were silver dishes containing delicious food, silver flasks holding good wine and beside them were beautiful silver goblets. The genie set down the tray and vanished.

Aladdin and his mother, when she regained her senses, sat down and enjoyed the meal. Then they talked about what they should do.

It was clear that with the help of the slave of the lamp they could become immensely rich. However, they were afraid that neighbours would gossip and that they would be accused of being thieves. They decided to live in modest comfort by selling the silver tray and dishes, brought by the genie. They would rub the lamp and ask for more food and silver only when they needed it.

Several happy years went by and Aladdin grew into a man. From his visits to the shops of the silver merchants he became familiar with fine jewelry and after a while, he realized that the fruits he had picked from the underground garden were, in fact, precious gems. He said nothing, but kept them hidden and went on living his contented life.

This might have continued had it not been for the Princess Buddir, the daughter of the sultan. One day, when Aladdin was strolling through the city, he heard the cracking of whips and saw the servants of the sultan running along the pavements calling to the shopkeepers to close their shops and shutter their windows.

"Everyone must get off the streets," shouted the servants. "The Princess Buddir will pass this way to the baths. No one may look on her face."

With their whips, they drove all the people indoors – all except Aladdin. No sooner had Aladdin heard that he must not look on the face of the princess, than he formed a desire to do so. He ran swiftly ahead of the royal procession and hid behind the door of the bath house. Soldiers approached. Maid servants approached and finally the princess herself shimmered through the doorway in her lovely clothes. Thinking no strangers were present, Princess Buddir removed her veil and Aladdin was able to see her beautiful features.

At once he fell in love and, as soon as he could, the young man hurried home and told his mother that he had decided to marry the daughter of the sultan.

First his mother laughed, then she became worried.

"What foolishness is this, Aladdin?" she asked. "The likes of you can never marry the daughter of the sultan. Why your head might be struck from your shoulders for even thinking of it."

However, Aladdin was not to be dissuaded.

"I have the slaves of the ring and of the lamp to help me," he said. "And, moreover, I have a hoard of jewels more precious than those in the whole of the rest of China."

Then he told his mother that the fruits he had picked so many years ago were really fine jewels. He begged her to put the gems on a dish and take them to the sultan the very next day.

"Give them as a present," said Aladdin. "Then tell the sultan you have a fine son who wishes to marry the Princess Buddir. He must be impressed by a family which can give away such jewels."

Reluctantly Aladdin's mother agreed to do as he asked. The next day she put the jewels on a plate, covered them with a napkin and stood in the palace before the sultan's divan. For a week she waited on the sultan every day, but he did not speak to her. Viziers and great lords were always given attention before an unimportant woman. At last the sultan became curious to know what this persistent woman carried beneath the napkin. He ordered her to speak.

"Mighty lord, forgive my bold request," whispered Aladdin's mother, shivering with fear. "Allow me to make it, then depart, for I know you can never grant what I ask."

The sultan felt sorry for the frightened woman and promised not to punish her. Aladdin's mother said that her son wished to marry the Princess Buddir.

At first the sultan laughed in derision, but when he saw the jewels, he was astounded. They were finer than his own! He spoke to his vizier, who was his chief advisor.

"Should I not agree to the marriage?" he asked.

Now, the vizier wished the princess to marry his own son.

"Take the jewels," he whispered, "and tell this woman to return in three months time to discuss wedding arrangements."

So it was done and Aladdin's mother hurried home to tell her son that the sultan had accepted the jewels. It seemed that the first steps towards the marriage of Aladdin and Princess Buddir had been successfully taken.

However, from that moment, the vizier did not cease to tell the sultan how much more suitable it would be for the princess to marry a man of good family, like his own son. He gave the sultan many fine presents and soon Aladdin's mother was forgotten. Her jewels were put in with the royal collection and a date was arranged for the wedding of Princess Buddir and the vizier's son.

One day when Aladdin's mother was out shopping, she was amazed to see a procession of great lords in their finest clothes and to learn that they were on their way to the wedding of the Princess Buddir. Hurrying home, she told Aladdin that they had been betrayed and that Princess Buddir was at that moment marrying another man. Filled with anger, Aladdin rubbed the lamp and summoned its slave.

"What is your wish, oh Master?" asked the mighty genie. "I serve whoever holds the lamp."

"The sultan has betrayed me," said Aladdin. "He is marrying his daughter to the son of the vizier. Tonight, when they retire to bed, bring them both here to me."

The genie bowed.

"Your wish is my command," he boomed in his deep, echoing voice and then he disappeared.

Back at the palace, the wedding feast drew to its close. The bride and bridegroom were taken to their bedchamber, but no sooner was the door shut, than the astonished couple found themselves transported to the home of Aladdin.

"Take the bridegroom away and keep him prisoner until the dawn," ordered Aladdin and the genie obeyed.

Aladdin turned to the terrified princess. He told her of her father's deceit. He explained to her that she was his own promised bride and that he could not allow her to be married to another man. He drew a scimitar and placed it at the princess's side.

"No harm will come to you," he said. "Tomorrow you will be taken back to the sultan's palace."

At the first light of dawn the genie brought the shivering bridegroom before Aladdin. The unfortunate young man had spent the night outside Aladdin's chamber, enchanted into stillness and wearing only a night shift. He was frozen through with cold.

"Transport the two of them back to the palace," ordered Aladdin.

As suddenly as they had been taken away, the princess and her bridegroom found themselves back in their bridal chamber. The princess told her mother what had happened. The bridegroom told his father, the vizier. The sultan was informed. He ordered the whole affair to be kept secret and for three more days the wedding parties continued. Each night the bride and groom were taken to their room, and each night Aladdin sent the genie to bring them to his house where the bridegroom shivered with cold outside the door, while the princess lay terrified at the side of a drawn scimitar.

The sultan consulted with the vizier. It was clear to them both that there was a curse on the marriage and it was declared cancelled.

Meanwhile three months had passed since Aladdin's mother last visited the sultan to discuss the marriage of her son and the Princess Buddir. Again she went to the palace and bowed before the sultan and asked if he had given consideration to plans for the wedding. The sultan was filled with impatience. He had been glad enough to take the jewels as a present, but he wished to see no more of this low-born woman. He consulted with his vizier.

"Make conditions for the marriage that this woman cannot possibly fulfill," advised the vizier. "Then you will have kept your promise, but the affair will be over."

The sultan turned and smiled at Aladdin's mother and said, "I must have proof that your son can support my daughter in royal state. Tell him to send me forty trays made of solid gold. Each tray must be loaded with jewels and carried by a beautiful slave, magnificently dressed. If your son can send me these things, then he may marry my daughter."

Aladdin's mother bowed and left, and the sultan smiled, thinking never to see her again. However, after he had spoken to his mother, Aladdin withdrew to his chamber and took up the magic lamp. He rubbed it and in a moment the mighty genie of the lamp was standing before him.

"What is your wish, oh Master?" he asked. "I obey whoever holds the lamp."

Aladdin told the genie what the sultan had said and that same day a procession of forty magnificently dressed slaves, carrying forty solid gold trays, laden with precious jewels, walked to the palace of the sultan. Crowds rushed to see them pass and the sultan was astounded. He sent for Aladdin to be brought before him. Wearing the most magnificent clothes the genie of the lamp could supply, Aladdin walked into the sultan's palace.

By this time, the sultan was eager to welcome such a rich son-in-law into the family. The marriage contract was drawn up and arrangements made for the wedding to take place that very day.

Aladdin looked from a window of the palace and said to the sultan, "Grant me the use of that land which lies before us, oh mighty one, and on it I will build a palace the like of which has never been seen before, and in that palace I will live with your daugher."

Greedy to see even more riches appear before him, the sultan nodded. With the help of the genie, in one night, Aladdin caused to be built a palace of marble and jasper and agate. The walls were set with bricks of gold and silver alternately. The windows and doors were ornamented with diamonds and rubies and emeralds.

The sultan was delighted. The wedding took place and for several years, Aladdin lived happily with his princess in the lovely palace.

Far away in Africa, the sorcerer had regretted his hastiness in giving up the magic lamp so easily. He determined to make another attempt to find it and once more journeyed to China. Entering the city where Aladdin lived, the sorcerer soon heard tales of the rich Prince Aladdin, who was married to the Princess Buddir, and who lived in a palace the like of which had never before been seen by mortal man.

The sorcerer hurried to the palace and, after one look, knew that this must be the work of the genie of the lamp. Returning to his inn, the sorcerer shut himself quietly in his room and, casting his spells, he learned that the magic lamp was kept on a shelf in Aladdin's bedroom in the palace. Smiling happily to himself, the sorcerer visited a coppersmith and bought a dozen new copper lamps.

He dressed as a poor streetseller and waited by the gates of Aladdin's magnificent home. Soon after dawn, Aladdin rode out with his men for a days' hunting.

When he was safely out of sight, the sorcerer strolled under the windows of the palace calling, "New lamps for old. I give new lamps for old. Who would like a new lamp in exchange for an old one?"

The street urchins laughed at hearing such a strange cry. Several of them hastened home and came back with chipped old lamps, and in return the sorcerer gave them shiny, new copper ones.

A maidservant, looking from a window of the palace, saw what was happening and ran to speak to Princess Buddir.

"An old man is out in the street offering to give new lamps for old," she laughed. "Did anyone ever see such a foolish thing before?"

"It cannot be true," laughed the princess.

She remembered the old lamp which Aladdin kept in his bedroom.

"Fetch that old lamp from your master's room and offer that to the old man," she said. "See if he will exchange a nice new lamp for that old thing?"

The maidservant took the magic lamp from the shelf and carried it into the street.

"Will you give me a new lamp for this?" she asked.

The sorcerer's heart leaped for joy.

"Willingly, my dear," he replied and giving the girl a new lamp, he thankfully clasped the magic lamp to his chest and hurried back to his room at the inn. As soon as he was alone, he rubbed the lamp and at once the fearsome genie appeared.

"What is your wish, oh Master?" he asked. "I serve whoever holds the lamp."

"Take me, and Aladdin's palace and everything in it, back to my home in Africa," said the sorcerer. "And do it now."

"To hear is to obey, oh Master," said the genie.

At once Aladdin's palace, with the princess and servants in it, disappeared from its place by the palace of sultan and was transported to Africa. The sultan, happening to glance from his window to admire the riches of his daughter's home, rubbed his eyes in astonishment. He sent for the vizier and the grounds of the palace were searched, but no trace of the palace could be found.

The vizier was no friend to Aladdin, having always suspected that he had obtained the princess's hand by unfair magic means.

"Send soldiers to arrest that villain," he suggested.

And it was done.

In his fury, the sultan ordered Aladdin to be put to death. However, the common people, who loved Aladdin for his generosity towards them, stirred in rebellion and the sultan was forced to think again. Aladdin was dragged before him.

"Bring my daughter back safely within forty days," said the sultan, "or I shall have you hunted down and killed indeed."

Aladdin was thrown out into the streets of the city, with neither servants nor riches to help him. For several days he wandered aimlessly, asking passers-by if they had seen his palace or his princess or an old lamp. No one had. At last, weak and hungry, Aladdin stumbled down a rough slope and as he fell, he rubbed his hand along the ground. In so doing, he rubbed the ring, which the sorcerer had given him at the entrance to the underground cavern. At once the genie of the ring stood before him.

"I serve whoever wears the ring," said the genie. "What is your wish, oh Master?"

Almost weeping for joy, Aladdin asked the genie to bring back his palace and the princess to their rightful home.

The genie shook his head. "I am the genie of the ring, not the genie of the lamp," he said. "My powers are not so great. I cannot bring your palace here, but I can take you to it, if that is your desire."

"Indeed it is," Aladdin said, and on the instant he found himself standing outside his palace, which was now situated on a plain in Africa, not far from a big city.

Glancing up at the palace, Aladdin saw that he was standing beneath the windows of the rooms of the Princess Buddir, his wife. By chance a servant girl looked from one of the windows and was overjoyed to see Aladdin standing below. She let him in by a small side door, and soon Aladdin and the princess were in each others' arms.

After many tears and much talk, the princess learned that she had been the cause of her own grief in giving the old lamp to the streetseller. Aladdin guessed that the streetseller was the sorcerer he had met so many years before and learned, in his turn, that the sorcerer kept the magic lamp tucked in his jacket, where no one but he could touch it.

"Still do not give up hope," said Aladdin to his princess. "We shall outwit this wicked man yet."

He slipped from the palace by the side door. So that his strange Chinese attire might not attract attention, he persuaded a poor passer-by to exchange clothes with him. Unnoticed, Aladdin walked into the nearby town and sought out the shop of a man selling potions. He asked for a small bottle of a certain mixture.

"Be off with you," laughed the shopkeeper. "That potion costs a piece of gold. A poor fellow like you can never afford it."

However, Aladdin pulled a well-filled purse from his pocket and the bottle was soon in his hands. He hurried back to the palace and crept silently to the princess's rooms.

"At supper tonight, be friendly with the sorcerer," he said. "Smile and sing and make him think you are reconciled to your new life. Then ask him to drink your health in a cup of wine you will give him. He will do it to please you. In the wine must be this potion. As soon as it has passed his lips, he will fall into an endless sleep. When this happens, send one of your women to fetch me."

The brave princess did as Aladdin instructed. Although she hated the evil sorcerer, she ordered her servants to sing for him and smiled and laughed at his words. When she asked him to toast her health in a glass of wine, the sorcerer drained it to the last drop. Then he fell back and never woke again.

"Quick. Fetch my husband," ordered the princess, and her most trusted servant hastened to Aladdin.

Aladdin ran quickly to the room. He ordered the princess and her maids and slaves to wait quietly. When he was alone with the sorcerer, he bent over him and pulled the magic lamp from his jacket. He rubbed the lamp and was overjoyed to see the genie appear.

"Your wish is my command, oh Master," said the genie. "I serve whoever holds the lamp."

"Leave this sorcerer to sleep in the desert," said Aladdin, "but transport the palace and the rest of those within it back to our home in China."

There was a gentle bump as the palace left the ground, and another as it landed, and that was all anyone felt of the long journey home.

The sultan, still laden with grief, was looking from a window, when to his amazement, he saw a palace appear before him. It was the palace of Aladdin and his daughter. He ran towards the jewelled entrance doors and embraced his dear child and begged Aladdin to forgive him for the harsh way he had treated him.

"Indeed there is nothing to forgive," replied Aladdin, "for you simply did what was your duty."

After that Aladdin took good care that the magic lamp never left his sight. They were troubled by the sorcerer no more. When the sultan died Aladdin and the princess ruled the land together and lived long and happy lives.

David and Goliath

Long, long ago, Samuel was a prophet to the Jewish people and Saul was their king. However, Saul sinned and lost favour with God. God spoke to Samuel and told him to go to Beth-lehemite to anoint a new king, whom he would find amongst the sons of a man named Jesse.

Samuel went to Beth-lehemite and seeking out Jesse, asked him to bring his sons to join him in making a sacrifice to the Lord. Out of respect for the prophet, Jesse did as he was asked. One by one, Samuel looked at the sons of Jesse, but as each one passed before him, Samuel heard the Lord whispering in his ear, "Do not be beguiled by this man's goodly countenance, nor his fine build. You see his handsome appearance, but God looks into mens' hearts."

Seven sons of Jesse walked before Samuel, but none was pleasing in the sight of the Lord.

"Have you no other sons?" Samuel asked of Jesse.

"I do have one other," replied Jesse, "but he is merely a lad and he is out keeping the sheep."

"Then bring him to me," said Samuel. "I must see all your sons, even the youngest."

He waited wearily until the boy came and stood before him. The young man's face was bright with good health. His glossy hair hung on either side of his beautiful countenance.

"Anoint this boy," said the Lord. "He is the one."

Meanwhile, King Saul, unaware of the prophet's task, was becoming more and more troubled. His mind was disturbed as he became subject to fits of rage. He terrified everyone around him.

"Music will help me," said Saul. "If only someone would find a man who could play sweet music. I am surrounded by fools and knaves and when they drive me to madness I need music, soft, lovely music, to calm my shattered nerves."

One of his servants found the courage to speak.

"It is said that David, the son of Jesse of Beth-lehemite, plays music which charms the ear," he whispered, "and also he is valiant, clever and handsome and is loved by the Lord."

"Yes, yes," snapped Saul, who was accustomed to hearing peoples' virtues exaggerated. "So long as he plays sweet music, send for him."

102

Messengers left the court of the king and fetched the boy David from where he was still tending his father's sheep. He stood before King Saul and found favour in his sight.

"You will be my armour-bearer," said King Saul, "and you will stay near my side. You will keep this harp close to your hand and when the fits of madness come upon me, you will play. Sooth the demons in my head with sweet music and make me well again."

So David stayed in the court of King Saul.

In those far off days, war frequently troubled the land. Before David had been long at court, the Philistines gathered a great army together and marched upon the land of the Jews. King Saul summoned his soldiers and went to face his enemies. Each army stood in formation on a mountain slope, with a valley between them. Both sides hesitated, for battle is a terrible thing.

Then a champion strode out from the camp of the Philistines. He was a giant of a man called Goliath of Gath. He was a magnificent and terrifying sight. On his head was a helmet of brass. He lightly wore a coat of mail, which would have weighed any other man to the ground. Brass armour protected his shins and his breast and he brandished a spear like a battering ram. His shield-bearer walked before him, with confident insolence.

Goliath ran his eyes over King Saul's army. To and fro he looked, taking his own time.

At last he called in his booming voice, "Why are you bothering to stand in battle array, you midgets of King Saul? There is no need for you to *try* and fight. Here am I, a champion of the Philistines, ready and willing. Send out one champion of your own against me. Then none of the rest of you mice need raise a sword. If your champion kills me, then we will be your servants. If I kill your champion, you will be our servants. Thus the blood of only one man need be shed. I lay this challenge before the army of Saul. Send one champion against me and let us settle the quarrel."

His voice died away into a long, long silence. Neither King Saul nor any of his men stepped forward. With good reason, they were all afraid of Goliath of Gath.

Now David, the son of Jesse of Beth-lehemite, was still a boy and not old enough to go with the army. Finding himself left behind and not needed by King Saul, he took the opportunity to visit his father. He was very welcome, for his three older brothers had gone to fight the Philistines.

"We are short of hands to help with the sheep," said Jesse. "Go out and tend them, David."

Forty days went by, with neither the return of the three older boys, nor any word of their fate. The truth was that the armies were facing stalemate. Each stood on its mountain-side and each day Goliath of Gath paraded up and down the valley calling for a champion to come down and fight. No one dared to accept his invitation.

In those days, when men turned out to defend their country, they took their own food along with them. Whatever the outcome, good or ill, campaigns were at least short. After forty days, Jesse became concerned that his three

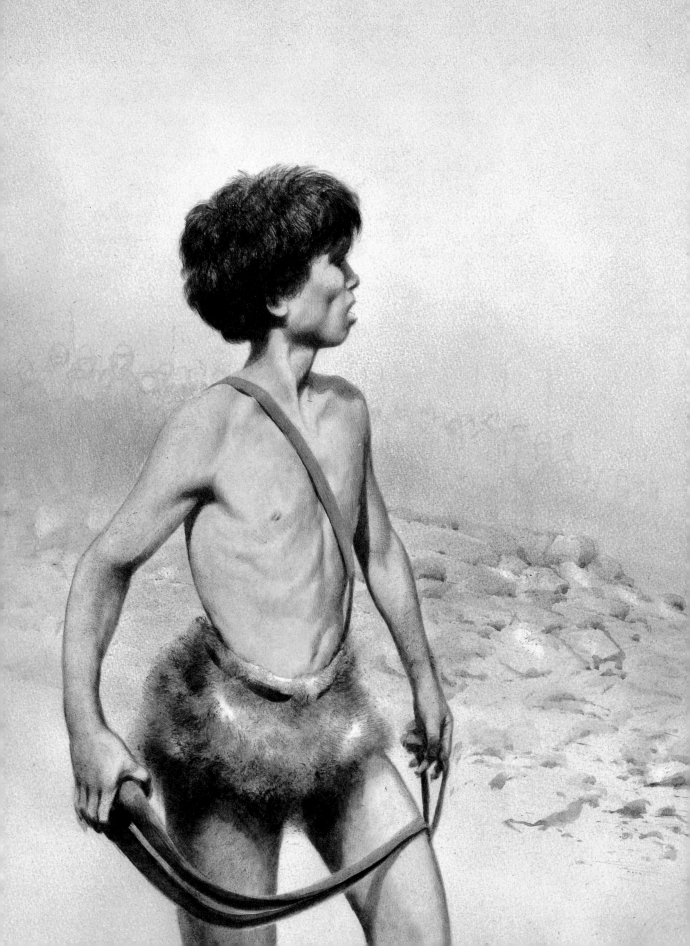

sons were running out of food. He gave the boy David a supply of loaves and cheeses and told him to find the army and give the food to his brothers.

On the day that David found the army, the men were preparing to do battle. It was clear that no one was willing to fight Goliath alone and the only alternative was a full pitched battle. David hurried from group to group, asking the whereabouts of his brothers. He heard the chatter about Goliath and how no one dared fight him, not even King Saul himself. Now the whole army was going to have to fight. He looked down into the valley and saw a mighty man swaggering up and down with his shield-bearer grinning before him.

"Is that Goliath?" asked David, thinking that he looked more like a blowhard than a hero.

David hurried along the hillside, searching for his brothers. Still he kept glancing down at Goliath.

"Do you mean to say everyone in the army in frightened of that man?" he asked. Hearing the descriptions of Goliath, he had expected to see a monster breathing fire, rather than a flesh and blood man.

Goliath's thundering voice jeered and laughed at the army of King Saul, and David burned with fury.

"What will be given to the man who goes down and silences the laughter of that mocker of my brethren?" he asked.

A group of soldiers laughed at David.

"Whoever slays Goliath will be loaded with riches and given a daughter of King Saul in marriage," they said, "but you look a little young for the job."

At last David found his eldest brother, Eliab. Eliab was astounded to see the boy in such a dangerous place.

"What are you doing here?" he gasped. "You should be back with the sheep. Oh, I know. You have slipped away to watch the fun, as you think. Well fighting is a man's work. Go home and keep out of this."

David was annoyed at such a reception.

"Fine words to greet me, when I have come all this way to bring you food," he said. "And as for this being no place for me, well I think that it is. If no one here is willing to fight Goliath, then it is indeed fortunate that I have arrived."

He went and stood before King Saul.

"There is no need for anyone to feel fear because of Goliath," he said. "I, your majesty's servant, will go to fight with that braggart Philistine."

King Saul shook his head.

"You are only a boy," he said. "You cannot fight a trained soldier."

David stood his ground.

"A shepherd boy I may be," he said, "but shepherd boys know how to fight. Lions and bears come to take my father's sheep, but I kill them first. If I can kill a lion and a bear, why should I not kill this impudent Philistine who dares to challenge the chosen of the Lord?"

King Saul sat in silence.

"Go out to fight," he said at last, "and may God be with you."

106

The king gave David his own helmet and coat of mail, thinking to help the young boy. David put them on, but took no more than two steps.

"These are not for me," he said. "They weigh me down and make me feel awkward."

He took off the armour and stood in his shepherd clothes. He swung his sling in one hand and a stick in the other. He put five smooth stones in a pouch at his side. He smiled at King Saul and the host of soldiers.

"I will go like this," he said. "It is better."

The slim boy walked down the hill into the valley to confront Goliath, the mighty warrior of Gath.

Goliath was surprised to see a lad walking towards him and did not at first realize that this was a champion from Saul's army.

"Go home, boy," he laughed.

When he understood that David did indeed intend to challenge him, he was furious.

"Am I dog," he roared, "that a shepherd with a stick is sent to drive me off? Come here boy and let me tear you apart and throw your limbs to the birds of the air and the beasts of the fields."

David felt no fear.

"You come armed with sword and spear and have a shield to protect you," he called in his clear, young voice, "but I come against you with the Lord of Hosts at my side. God will deliver you into my hands."

Then Goliath said no more, but set his mouth in a straight line. The time for talking was over. Boy or not, this challenger, who talked so big, must be cut to pieces. Goliath walked forward, a trained soldier, eager to do his work.

David walked towards Goliath. He was not trained. He did not know the rules. He did not take up battle stance. He looked at Goliath with the eyes of a shepherd boy looking at a lion. He did not know the correct way to parry a sword, or how to deflect a spear, but he did see that Goliath's forehead was unprotected by armour. Taking a stone from his pouch, David slung it at Goliath and knocked him unconscious. The mighty man pitched to the ground and fell on his face. David ran to him and snatching up his sword, hacked Goliath's head from his shoulders. The fight was over almost before the watchers knew that it had started.

The army of the Philistines turned and fled in fear and the land of King Saul was saved from invasion. David was made a mighty captain in the army of Saul. A glittering future lay ahead of him. However, King Saul was jealous, for David had been victorious, while Saul had been shamed. The path of David was not to run smoothly.

Joseph and his Coat of Many Colours

The dramatic and emotional story of Joseph is well-known to readers of the Bible. It takes its place in the history, traditions and stories of the Middle East, where the sons of Jacob lived, thousands of years ago.

Long ago, in the land of Canaan, there lived a shepherd named Jacob. He had many flocks and many wives and many children. However, his favourite son was Joseph. Jacob loved Joseph so much, he could not help but show him favour over his other children. Joseph's brothers, the sons of Jacob's other wives, became jealous of this young boy who, it seemed, could do no wrong.

When Joseph was seventeen, his father gave him a coat of many colours. This was a luxury for a shepherd boy. The other sons looked at Joseph, handsome in his elegant coat, and were more envious than ever.

Joseph himself did not help the situation. He dreamed unfortunate dreams. The dreams he had were so vivid that when he woke he could not shake them from his mind.

"Brothers, listen to me," he said. "Last night I dreamed that we were binding sheaves in the field. My sheaf stood tall and straight, but the sheaves made by the rest of you drooped over and bowed before mine."

His brother were not pleased.

"So, being favoured above us in life is not enough," they scowled. "In your dreams also, we must bow down before you."

Unfortunately Joseph continued to dream these powerful dreams and with the tactlessness of youth, continued to talk about them.

"Father," he said, standing before Jacob, "last night I dreamed that the sun and the moon and eleven stars knelt before me."

Much as Jacob loved Joseph, he felt it was unseemly talk from a young boy. "If you are trying to say that, because of this dream, your mother and I and your eleven brothers should kneel before you, then that is not right," said Jacob. "Do not talk in such a way, Joseph."

Although Jacob rebuked Joseph, still he took note of the strange dreams and wondered if his favourite son was destined for greatness.

Time went by and one year Jacob's flocks were feeding in the land of Shechem. Jacob became anxious for their welfare and sent Joseph to find them.

"Speak to your brothers, who are tending my animals," instructed Jacob. "See if all is well with them and with the flocks. Then come home to me."

Joseph did as his father told him and after days of searching, he found the flocks in the land of Dothan. His brothers looked up and saw Joseph, in his coat of many colours, approaching from a long way off.

"Here he comes," they said, "doubtless with more dreams to tell us how high and mighty he is!"

The brothers looked around and saw that they were far from home and in a lonely place. "This is a good spot in which to rid ourselves of our 'beloved' little brother," they said. "Let us kill Joseph and tell father that the wild animals took him. How will anyone at home ever know that we are not telling the truth?"

Fortunately for Joseph one of the brothers, Reuben, was more compassionate than the others.

"He is only a boy!" said Reuben. "We cannot kill him. Remember he is the son of our father. His blood must not be on our hands."

Still the other brothers wanted to kill Joseph. Reuben became desperate, unlike the others, he did not hate his young brother.

"Leave him in a pit," he begged. "He will die, but at least you will not have shed his blood."

The other brothers agreed to this and Reuben was content for he intended to creep back later and rescue Joseph from the pit.

A little while later Joseph arrived at his brothers' camp, with the messages from home on his lips; hoping for a friendly greeting and food and drink. Instead his coat of many colours was dragged from his back and he was flung into a deep pit. Satisfied with the terrible revenge they were taking on the young dreamer, the brothers sat down to eat, while Reuben took his turn at tending the flocks. Not long afterwards some Ishmeelite traders came riding by. This gave one of the brothers an idea.

"Why not make some profit from this affair?" he said. "Let us sell Joseph to the Ishmeelites. Thus we are getting rid of him, without killing him and making some money as well."

It seemed the perfect plan.

Joseph was sold to the Ishmeelites for twenty pieces of silver and taken to the land of Egypt. By the time Reuben returned from his duties with the flocks, the merchants had gone. There was little hope of finding them. Reuben looked into the empty pit and was beside himself with grief.

He wept and tore his clothes and shouted to his brothers, "The boy is gone. What have you done with him?"

The brothers laughed and said, "He is gone and that is all there is to it."

They killed a baby goat and spilled its blood all over Joseph's coat of many colours. When the grazing was finished and it was time to drive their flocks home, they took the coat and showed it to Jacob.

"We found this near our flocks," they said. "Surely it is the coat which you gave to our brother, Joseph?"

Jacob looked at the blood-stained coat in horror. "I did send Joseph to find you," he said. "This is his coat. A wild beast has killed my dearest boy."

Then Jacob rent his clothes and put on sackcloth. He would be comforted by no one, for his heart was broken.

Far away in Egypt, Joseph had been sold to Potiphar, an important man, who was captain of the guard to Pharaoh. Now Joseph was an intelligent boy, who grew to be a charming young man. Potiphar found that all tasks given to Joseph were well done. All arrangements were made correctly. All transactions were done honestly. As the years went by, Joseph became manager of the entire household. Potiphar had to concern himself with nothing but raising food to his lips. Joseph himself was rewarded well and lived a rich life, dressed in fine clothes.

"I am a slave, but God has smiled on me," Joseph thought.

However, Potiphar's wife was discontented. The household was managed by Joseph. Potiphar was often away on army service. Potiphar's wife felt bored and neglected. She looked at Joseph's handsome face and fell in love. Joseph knew only too well that such a love could bring only disaster to him. He avoided his master's wife and she took offence. Her love turned to fury and when Potiphar returned home, she told him a story full of lies.

"Joseph is in love with me," she said. "He keeps pestering me. I am not safe in the house while you are away. He has betrayed the great trust you place in him."

Joseph was thrown into prison. His days of fine clothes and good food were over. He was thirty years old and it was thirteen years since his brothers had sold him into slavery. However, Joseph was a man who always made the best of things. His faith in God was strong and he set himself to help those about him. Soon Joseph was managing affairs in prison, as he had managed the household of Potiphar. The prison governor trusted Joseph and all the arrangements inside the prison walls were left to him. Yet, despite the governor's trust, Joseph was still a prisoner.

Time went by and one day the butler and the baker of the Pharaoh were sent to prison and put into Joseph's charge. The two men were terrified at having offended the Pharaoh and they dreamed strange dreams.

"What can these dreams mean?" they said one to another. "If only we were free and could speak to an interpreter of dreams, we might learn what our fates will be."

Joseph said to them, "God is the giver of all dreams. Tell your dreams to me and God will tell me their meanings."

Eagerly the two men babbled out their stories. "In my dream," said the butler, "I was standing in front of a vine. The vine had three shoots. They budded and came into blossom and bore fruit quickly, while I watched. Then I picked the fruit and put it into Pharaoh's cup, which suddenly appeared in my hand. Then Pharaoh was before me and I leaned forward and gave him the cup of fruit."

The butler looked anxiously at Joseph.

"What does all that mean?" he asked.

Joseph said, "The three shoots were three days. In three days Pharaoh will free you and take you back to the palace and you will serve him his food, as you used to do."

The butler sighed with relief.

"Oh, I am so thankful," he said.

"Then," said Joseph, "when you are free, remember me still in prison, try to obtain my release."

Next the baker spoke up, hoping for a favourable interpretation of his dream.

"I dreamed that I had three white baskets on my head," he said. "The top basket was full of pieces of food for the Pharaoh to eat, but before I could give them to him, birds from the air swooped down and ate them."

Joseph looked at him sadly.

"The three baskets are three days," he said, "but the meaning of your dream is that in three days, Pharaoh will lift your head from your shoulders and hang up your body, and the birds of the air will come and devour you."

The baker sat sunk in gloom.

On the third day, as Joseph had forseen, the baker was beheaded and the fortunate butler was restored to his position in the palace of Pharaoh. However, the butler immediately forgot his companions in the prison and did nothing to help Joseph.

For two more weary years Joseph stayed in prison. Then Pharaoh himself had a puzzling and disturbing dream. He dreamed that he was standing at the side of the river. Seven fat cows came up out of the water and munched the grass in a meadow. Then seven more cows came up from the river. They were lean and diseased. The lean cows ate up the fat cows. Then Pharaoh awoke.

The next night Pharaoh had another vivid dream. In this dream seven ears of corn grew on one stalk. They were fat and good. Then at their side, seven thin shrivelled ears of corn sprang from the ground. The east wind began to blow. The seven thin ears of corn devoured the seven fat ears. Then Pharaoh awoke.

The dreams had been so real and so alarming that Pharaoh called together all the magicians of Egypt and asked them what the dreams could mean. No one could tell him. Pharaoh became more and more agitated and everyone in the palace was afraid of his ill-humour. Suddenly the butler remembered Joseph. Hoping to gain favour with Pharaoh, the butler told him that there was a young Hebrew man in prison who had correctly interpreted dreams for him and the baker.

At once Pharaoh ordered Joseph to be brought before him. The surprise in the prison was great. Quickly Joseph shaved and the prison governor gave him new clothes, that he might look presentable to appear before the ruler of all Egypt.

"I have had two dreams," Pharaoh said to Joseph and told him about the cows and the corn, "I have told all this to my magicians, but none can explain the meaning. Do you know what my dreams mean?"

Joseph said to the great Pharoah, "Both dreams are one. They have the same meaning. God is telling Pharaoh what is about to befall. The seven fat cows and the seven fat ears of corn are seven good years. The seven lean cows and the seven withered ears of corn are seven years of famine. This is the message

112

which God is sending to mighty Pharaoh. For seven years there will be plenty in Egypt. The crops will be rich and food will be abundant. Then will come seven years of bad harvests and famine. All the good years will be forgotten and hunger and death will stalk the land. God sent the dream twice to assure Pharaoh that these things will truly come to pass."

Joseph paused to collect his thoughts. He continued, "As God has seen fit to send this warning, then let Pharaoh choose a man of wisdom and skill and set him to manage all the affairs of Egypt. Give him officials to help him and during the seven good years, let this man take a fifth of the food and store it against the seven lean years. Let food be stored in the cities for all the people who live there and in the countryside for when the crops fail."

It seemed to Pharaoh and all his court that they were listening to words of wisdom and Pharaoh said, "Joseph, since God has revealed all these things to you, then you are the man who must prepare us against the seven years of famine."

He ordered that Joseph should be put in charge of the royal household and that everyone, save only Pharaoh himself, should obey him. He gave Joseph command over the land of Egypt. He gave him a ring from his finger and fine clothes and a gold chain to hang round his neck. Pharaoh gave Joseph one of his best chariots in which to drive. He gave him an Egyptian name and an Egyptian wife and Joseph ruled in Egypt.

Everything came to pass as the dreams had foretold. For seven years the harvests were good. Food was plentiful as never before. Joseph gathered stores of corn like the sands of the sea. In the eighth year the crops failed. The seven lean years had started. People living in Egypt were fortunate. When the shops in the towns were empty of corn, and when the farmers could no longer reap crops from their fields, the people went to Joseph's stores. There they were able to buy corn and survive and pray for the passing of the seven years of hardship.

Outside Egypt people were starving. After two of the seven lean years had gone by, Jacob and his family were short of food and desperate. Hearing that there was corn in Egypt, Jacob sent his eleven sons with pack animals to buy corn and bring it home, but Jacob would not send his youngest son, Benjamin. Benjamin was Joseph's full brother. He was the only other son of Joseph's mother. After Joseph's disappearance, so many years before, newly born Benjamin had become Jacob's favourite, as Joseph had been.

"I will not send Benjamin on such a long journey," said Jacob. "Some harm might befall him. My heart must not be broken a second time."

The hungry brothers made the weary journey and asked their way to the food stores, where Joseph was supervising the selling of corn to foreigners. During his many years in Egypt, Joseph had not only grown into a man, he had become like an Egyptian in looks and speech. His Egyptian wife had borne him two sons whom he loved. His family now filled his life. His old father and jealous brothers, were a distant dream.

One day as he was going about his work, Joseph turned his head and saw his brothers standing before him. Suddenly he remembered his old life as though he had stepped away from it only yesterday. He was overcome with homesickness and longing for his own people. However, he could not forgive those men who had sold him into slavery. The more longing he felt for his old home, the more Joseph resented his brothers for what they had done to him. He stood unrecognized before them, in his aristocratic clothes and his rich jewelry. Hatred for his brothers overwhelmed Joseph and he determined to make them suffer.

"You are not genuine buyers," he said to them harshly. "You are thieves. You have come to spy on our stores and riches, then you will rob us."

The brothers were terrified by the rage of this great man of Egypt. They protested their innocence and hastened to explain that they were twelve sons of Jacob, an honest herdsman.

Joseph seized on their words. "Twelve sons?" he said. "There are eleven of you only. Your story does not hang together. You are spies!"

The brothers all spoke at once. They were confused by the official's behaviour towards them. They told him about their brother Benjamin, the only full brother of a Joseph who had died as a boy, and how Benjamin was the favourite of their father and that was why he had not made the journey. Joseph learned for the first time that he had a full brother. A brother who had taken no part in selling him into slavery. He longed to see him.

"I will release you to take corn back to your family only if you promise to return with your brother Benjamin," he said. "I will keep one of you here in Egypt. He will be released when you return with Benjamin."

This did not please the brothers. They did not wish to leave one of their number behind as they knew that their father would never consent to let Benjamin go. Not expecting Joseph to understand their own tribal language, they spoke to each other in front of him.

"Which of us shall be left here?" they asked. "When will he ever be released? What a terrible situation and why is this Egyptian being so difficult with us? He is not troubling any of the other foreigners buying corn."

Then Reuben spoke.

"It is a judgement on us," he said. "All those years ago, I tried to stop you from harming Joseph. This is God's vengeance for our wickedness to our brother, the son of our own father."

Hearing the brothers talking in the language of his childhood upset Joseph. Suddenly his Egyptian friends and even his Egyptian family seemed like strangers. Why had he been sent away from where he belonged? He turned aside and wept. Then, with his heart still hard against his brothers, he took one of them named Simeon and imprisoned him. He ordered the sacks of the remaining brothers to be filled with corn as they wished. He also commanded that the money the brothers had paid for the corn be secretly put into their sacks and that they should be given provisions for their journey home.

The brothers hastened on their way, reluctantly leaving Simeon behind. On the road home, they discovered that their money had been given back to them and they were afraid. Why had they been treated in such a strange way? They had been spoken to harshly, and yet they had been given the corn free. The whole thing must be a trick to get them into more trouble.

Jacob listened to his sons' story and shook his head.

"I will not send Benjamin to a man who behaves in such a strange way," he said. "For sure, I should never see the boy again and my grey hairs would go down in sorrow to the grave."

So the brothers stayed at home. Simeon remained in Egypt and time went by.

Still the crops failed and still the famine raged. The time came when all the corn the brothers had brought from Egypt was eaten.

"Go to Egypt for more corn," said Jacob.

The brothers would not go. They remembered the strange behaviour of the rich official who had command of all the food and was the favourite of the Pharaoh.

"We must take Benjamin with us or we dare not go," they said.

Jacob became impatient.

"Why did you have to tell the man you had another brother?" he asked. "If you had not told him about Benjamin, we should not be in this trouble."

"But he questioned us," replied the brothers. "He asked us about our father and if we had any other brothers. We had to tell him the truth. How were we to know he would ask to see Benjamin? Why should anyone in Egypt care about Benjamin? How could we have expected such a thing?"

At last starvation forced Jacob to let Benjamin go to Egypt. He insisted that his sons took not only money for the second purchase of corn, but also the money that had been returned to them the first time.

"Whether it was a mistake, or whether it was a trick, it is best to take the money we owe," he said.

The brothers also took a present for Joseph, hoping in this way to win the favour of this unpredictable man. With apprehension in their hearts, they set out.

Again the brothers stood before Joseph. Again they asked for corn. They asked for the release of Simeon, their brother and pointed to Benjamin standing with them. They held out double money for the corn, explaining that the money for the first supply of corn had been returned to them.

Joseph looked at Benjamin, his own full brother, and his heart was filled with joy. Leaping to his feet, he ordered his servants to take all his brothers to his house. He ordered a great feast to be prepared. The brothers were treated as honoured guests. Their asses were fed. Joseph was friendly and asked them for news of their home and father. Still the brothers were afraid. Why should they be treated in such a special way?

Joseph told his steward to give the brothers all the corn they wanted, and as before, to put the purchase money into the sacks with the corn. He also told him to put a silver cup into Benjamin's sack.

"After these men have left on their homeward journey," ordered Joseph, "ride after them. Search in the sack and find the silver cup and ask them why they have stolen it."

All this was done and again the brothers stood before Joseph, this time accused of theft. At last Joseph said that he would pardon them, but that Benjamin must stay with him as his servant, as it was in Benjamin's sack the cup had been found. In this way Joseph hoped to keep his dear brother with him. However, Judah, one of the brothers stepped forward and, caring not that Joseph was the greatest in the land, save for Pharaoh, explained that he could not possibly return to Jacob without Benjamin.

"After the loss of his son, Joseph, my father loved Benjamin most of all," said Judah. "If we return without Benjamin, my father will go down with grey hairs to his grave. Let me stay, but let the boy go."

Joseph could keep his secret no longer. He ordered his servants to leave the room and he said to his brothers, "I am Joseph."

They were puzzled.

"I am Joseph whom you sold as a slave," said the strange Egyptian official.

The brothers stared at him and in the face of the mature man, they began to recognize the features of their brother. They felt only greater fear.

Seeing this Joseph said, "Do not fear. Now I see that all was the work of God. He caused me to be sent into Egypt, that I might store the corn and save you, my brethren, from destruction. God made me the favourite of Pharaoh and the ruler in Egypt. Now go home to my father and tell him that Joseph lives. Tell him that I am rich and powerful. Tell him to come to me with all his children and his childrens' children and his flocks and herds, and I will care for him. He shall dwell in the land of Goshen."

Now in the eyes of the great Pharaoh, Joseph could do no wrong, for he had saved the land from famine and made Pharaoh very rich from the sale of corn. Pharaoh agreed that Joseph's family could live in the land of Goshen and sent many wagons to make the journey more comfortable for the women and the young children.

When Jacob heard that Joseph lived, his heart was filled with joy. The old man made the journey to Egypt with his family. As they arrived in the land of Goshen, Joseph rode out in his chariot to meet his father. They fell into each other's arms and wept and Jacob said, "Now, when death comes for me, I shall die a happy man, for I have seen that you, my dearest son, are alive and well."

Africa

AFRICA

The Story of Untombinde   120

The Horns of Plenty   126

The Proud Princess   129

The Battles of Horus   134

The Cunning Man   139

The Clever Monkey   142

Tricky Mr Rabbit   144

The Story of Untombinde

This, and the following two stories, were told by the Zulu and Sesuto tribes of southern Africa. Like many of the stories from this area they are serious, reflecting the dignity of successful warrior tribes. These tribal lands were good cattle country, with flowing rivers and green pastures, and stories about rich kings with many wives were often told.

L ong ago, at the boundaries of a far kingdom, there was a haunted pool. A monster lived in the depths of the pool and brave men were afraid to go there.

Untombinde, the daughter of the king, was tall and beautiful and knew no fear. She had heard that the waters of the haunted pool glittered like precious stones and tasted richer than the finest milk. Untombinde wished to go there.

One year when many rains had fallen and all the rivers were full, Untombinde asked if she might visit the pool. Her father and her mother forbade her to go.

For a year Untombinde dreamed of the beautiful waters of the haunted pool and again, after the rains had fallen, she asked if she might go there. Again her parents forbade it.

Another year went by. The rains fell in abundance and for a third time Untombinde asked if she might visit the haunted pool. Her parents saw that they would enjoy no peace until they agreed, so they gave their consent.

Untombinde behaved like a girl setting forth on her wedding journey. She chose two hundred village maidens to walk with her in procession and told them to sing and dance as if they were journeying to meet her bridegroom. The laughing girls formed two lines, one on either side of Untombinde and set out eagerly on their adventure.

A short way along the road, the girls met a party of merchants.

"Are we not beautiful?" asked the dancing girls. "Who is the loveliest amongst us?"

The merchants gazed at the two hundred young maidens, but said none of them was as lovely as their leader, Untombinde, who stood taller than all the rest.

"She is like a graceful tree, swaying in the wind," said the merchants.

Happily Untombinde went on her way, but some of the girls were furious that their beauty had been slighted. They slew the merchants and left them by the roadside.

Before the sun had set, the procession of girls reached the haunted pool. They were hot and tired. Pulling off their brass anklets and bracelets and their beaded skirts, the girls plunged thankfully into the cool waters. They laughed and splashed and swam in liquid more lovely than they had ever seen before. As one by one the girls left the waters of the haunted pool, they found that their clothes and ornaments had vanished. They wailed and cried. Soon all the maidens, except Untombinde herself, were crying at the water's edge.

"It is all the fault of Untombinde!" shrieked one of the maidens. "She brought us to this unfortunate place. Now our clothes and valuables have gone and we are cold and alone and night is falling."

"It must be the monster of the pool who has taken our clothes," sobbed another girl. "No one else is here. We must beg his forgiveness for disturbing the peace of his home. We must tell him it is the fault of Untombinde. We must beseech him to return our clothes."

One by one the girls knelt and shrieked and wailed for forgiveness. One by one the clothes and ornaments of each girl were restored. Only Untombinde stood tall with her proud head held high and refused to beg for forgiveness.

"A beautiful princess, admired by all, as I am, will never beg before a monster," she said.

Her speech so infuriated the monster that he seized Untombinde and dragged her below the surface of the pool and swallowed her. The maidens fled in terror back to their kraal and told the king and his wife what had happened.

"This is terrible," gasped the king. "I knew no good could come of going to such a haunted place. Now I shall never see my lovely daughter again. Oh woe is me!"

Not content with mourning his lost daughter, the king called together his young warriors and told them that he wanted vengeance.

"Sharpen your spears. Put on your war array!" ordered the king. "Go to the haunted pool and slay the monster."

The warriors obeyed the commands of their king.

From far off the monster heard their feet running over the ground. He heard the rattle of their spears on their shields. He heard their battle cries and he rose from the pool to meet them. The mighty monster opened his jaws wide and swallowed every last warrior.

"Who are these people who will never leave me in peace?" groaned the monster. "I will spoil their fields and destroy their kraal and be rid of them."

Bowed down with the weight of all the people he had eaten, the monster waddled towards the kraal, eating everything that lay in his path. At the kraal, the monster was confronted by the king himself.

By now the monster was so bloated with all he had swallowed, that he could scarcely move. The king stepped forward, raised his sword, and with

one slash cut open the monster from throat to stomach. Immediately all the warriors and Untombinde herself fell out into the sweet air. They breathed and laughed and lived again. The monster died in a pool of blood and the whole village rejoiced.

Now it also happened that near the kraal where Untombinde lived were the wide lands of a great king. This king had many wives and many children, however, there was one wife who had no children. In the usual way of things this wife would have been despised and sent to live in disgrace in the poorest hut, but she was the daughter of another powerful king and her husband did not dare treat her with disrespect. This made the other wives very jealous.

"Why should a wife who has born no children live as well as we do?" they asked. They hated the childless wife and treated her unkindly whenever the chance presented itself.

One day, as she so often did, the childless wife was sitting weeping, when two pigeons alighted before her. They offered to give her a child in return for the seeds of the castor plant, which the wife kept in her hut. Joyfully she fetched the seeds and scattered them before the pigeons. The birds ate their fill, then they pecked at the side of the woman until they drew blood.

"Now you will bear a child," they said and flew away.

To the joy of the woman, nine months later she gave birth to a son. He was a handsome boy and as his mother's family was so rich, the boy was made the heir to his father, and his mother was made head wife and queen. At once all the other wives were filled with hatred and their children were consumed with jealousy.

The new queen was afraid that her son might be killed by one of the other wives or children. She wrapped him in the skin of a boa constrictor and kept him hidden away. Even as the years went by, the queen still kept the child hidden. People began to whisper that the little boy had died or that he had turned into a snake. Still the queen would not show her child to the other wives or children. She was too frightened. Soon people began to forget that the queen had ever had a child. The family from which she came became poor and everyone lost their respect for this strange woman. She was put to live in the farthest, poorest hut and despised by all, as if she were indeed childless.

By this time, the boy had grown into a young man. He could not understand why he lived such a strange, secret life. At last he told his mother that he would no longer live with her.

"It is you who are making me an outcast," he said. "It is because of you that my brothers and sisters wish to kill me."

He left home and his mother could not find him, search as she might. She could get no help or sympathy from her husband nor the other wives. They thought the child had perished years before.

Still, ever hopeful that one day the boy would return, the sad mother built a hut for him and every evening, she put meat and drink within it.

Now stories always become more interesting with the telling. Through all the neighbouring villages people said that the lost heir to the king still lived and that he was handsome as the sun. Many princesses offered to be the bride of this mysterious and hidden young man.

The king welcomed all the girls to his village, but told them he did not know the whereabouts of his lost son. Then the princesses were married to the king's other sons, and the mystery remained.

One day, the tall and graceful Princess Untombinde heard the story of the lost prince. At once she decided that this man must be her husband. She went to the village of the great king.

"Your king has an heir as handsome as the sun, an heir whom no one has seen," she said. "I have come to be his bride."

The mother of the lost heir looked at Untombinde and wished that her son would return to marry such a beautiful princess. The king said that his heir could not be found and that Untombinde should marry one of his other sons. To the amazement of everyone, Untombinde refused. She also refused to leave the kraal of the chief.

"I will stay here until the missing heir returns and then I will be his bride," she vowed.

The mother of the heir was so touched by the courage of Untombinde that she built a hut for the girl and told her to wait in it until her son returned. As night fell on the first day of her stay, Untombinde retired to sleep in her new hut. To her surprise the mother brought meat and sour milk and set it beside her.

"This is bridal food," said Untombinde. "Why do you leave it here at night?"

"For years I have set out food for my missing son," replied the mother. "Now I will put bridal food in your hut and hope that he will return."

Untombinde slept through the night and in the morning found the food untouched. The next night the mother again put food into the hut. In the morning Untombinde saw that the hut had been entered and some of the food had been eaten.

"Did you not see who came into the hut?" asked the mother.

"I saw nothing," replied Untombinde.

On the third night, the mother again put food into the hut. In the blackest darkness, Untombinde awoke. Someone was touching her arm. A man's voice asked who she was.

"I am Untombinde and I am waiting to marry the king's heir," she replied.

"The heir was lost many years ago," replied the voice. "Why do you not marry someone else?"

Untombinde replied that only the heir to the king was fit to be her husband. Some of the food was eaten and she was left alone. Yet when Untombinde felt the latch on the door, it had not been unfastened.

By this time the mother of the heir was filled with excitement. She felt sure that it was her son who was visiting Untombinde and eating the food, but still the girl had not seen her visitor and could not say who he was.

The next night food was left and at the darkest hour, Untombinde heard the

124

voice of a man in the hut with her. The voice told her to make a fire and, in the glow from the flickering flames, Untombinde saw that she was talking to a snake.

"I am the king's lost heir," said the creature. "Years ago I went to hide under the ground because I was afraid that my brothers would kill me. Now this is the only form I can take."

Brave Untombinde showed no fear, she begged the snake to wait until dawn and speak to his mother, who still mourned his loss. The weird creature shook its head and said that it must leave during darkness. Untombinde pleaded and at last the snake agreed that she could fetch his mother to speak to him. Untombinde hurried from the hut. When they returned, instead of a snake, a handsome man was waiting for them.

"Because of the bravery of Untombinde I am restored to my strength and beauty," said the man.

The mother of the heir wept with joy. She took the man to stand before the king, who was overjoyed at seeing such a handsome son. The marriage between the heir and Untombinde was arranged at once. There was much dancing and great feasting and in the course of time, the heir came to the throne with Untombinde as his queen.

The Horns of Plenty

Once, long ago, there was a great kraal with many huts. Women went about their work and happy children played on the veldt. However, there was one thin little boy who was not happy. The boy's mother had died a year before and he was hungry and unloved. No woman in the kraal wanted the trouble of feeding the orphan boy. He was turned away from hut after hut and no one listened when he wept. The boy's father still lived, but he went out each day hunting. When he came home tired in the evening, he had no time for the boy. The unfortunate little fellow became thinner and weaker.

Try as he might, he could please no one. One day he collected some firewood, hoping to please one of the kraal women and be given a meal, but the woman only complained that the bundle of wood was not big enough and beat the boy and turned him away.

"I will leave these cruel people and never return," vowed the boy.

As darkness fell, he went to the cattle pen and took one of his father's bulls. He scrambled on to its back and rode the huge creature far away across the veldt. At dawn the bull and the boy lay down to rest. However, they had not rested for long when they saw a cloud of dust approaching.

"That is a herd of cattle led by a strong bull," said the bull with the boy. "He will challenge me to a fight, but do not worry. I shall be the victor."

The thin, little boy watched with fear, as a mighty bull approached. It pawed the ground and breathed noisily through its huge nostrils. It tossed its huge head and sharp horns and challenged the boy's bull to fight.

A ferocious struggle took place. The two huge creatures, charged and locked horns and slashed and kicked at each other. At last the bull, which belonged to the boy, triumphed and their enemy hastened away with his herd.

Again the boy and the bull journeyed across the endless veldt. As night was falling another huge bull confronted them, pawing the ground and breathing forth defiance.

"Get down from my back," said the boy's bull. "I must fight this second bull, but now I am tired and I shall not win. However, feel no fear. When I am dead, take my horns and carry them with you. Strike them when you are hungry or in need and you will be given whatsoever you want."

The boy was terrified to think that his friend would be killed and he would be left alone, but he had little choice in the matter. He slid from the back of the bull and watched while a second fight took place. The bulls struggled until finally the friend of the boy breathed its last and slid to the ground dead.

The little boy wept, then remembering what the bull had said, he took its horns and carried them with him on his journey. Come what may, the boy was determined never to return to his own kraal.

127

As night was falling, the boy came to a hut, where he asked for shelter. The owner welcomed him indoors.

"I will willingly give you shelter," the man said agreeably enough, "but I can give you no food. There is famine in this land and I have but weeds to eat myself."

The boy smiled and touching one of the horns of his bull, asked for meat and drink to be set before them. At once food appeared in abundance and both the boy and the man ate well. The man expressed gratitude and amazement and then the two of them settled down to sleep. Realizing the value of the horns, the man determined to obtain them for himself. During the night, he hid the magical horns in a corner of his hut and replaced them with some old horns from one of his own dead bulls.

In the morning, the boy thanked the man for the night's shelter and went on his way. He walked for many hours and when he felt hungry, he touched one of the horns and asked for food. No food was set before him. The boy realized how he had been tricked. He walked wearily back to the hut where he had slept the night before. He listened outside the door and heard the man touching and striking the magic horns and ordering them to set food and drink before him, but the horns would obey only the little boy. Nothing was set before the thieving man, who became more and more enraged.

The boy entered the hut, and the heart of the man was filled with terror, for he feared the magical powers of the boy. The man fled and watched from afar and did not dare to return while the boy remained. So the boy touched the horns and asked for food. A fine meal was set before him. When he had eaten, he settled in the comfortable hut, where he slept well all night and in the morning he departed safely with the precious horns.

All morning the boy walked under the bright sun. At noon, he sheltered in the shadow of a rock and ate food set before him by the horn. Again he walked on and as night fell he came to another hut.

"Will you give me shelter for the night?" the boy asked the man in the hut.

The man looked at the dusty, dirty orphan.

"Be on your way!" he said. "I want no ruffians like you staying in my hut."

Wearily the boy walked on until he came to a river. He washed in the cool waters and again touched the magical horns.

"Bring me fine clothes and brass ornaments with which to adorn my arms and legs," he said.

At once these things were given to him. The boy put them on and, arrayed like the son of a chief, he approached a fine kraal. The headman hurried out to greet him.

"Welcome, oh mighty one," smiled the headman, bowing and calling for a feast to be prepared.

The boy stayed in this kraal for several years. Whatever he needed was brought to him by the horns of plenty. As the boy was so obviously wealthy, he was treated with great respect by his new friends. The beautiful daughter of the chief was given to him as a wife and for the rest of his life, the little orphan boy lived in happiness and plenty.

128

The Proud Princess

Long years ago, there lived a great king whose conquests stretched from horizon to horizon. His warriors were mighty and the stamping of their feet struck fear into the hearts of his enemies. One happy day, as the armies returned from yet another great victory, a daughter was born to the king.

"Because this girl has been born on the day when my enemies have fallen like grass before the scythe," said the king, "she will be the most loved of my daughters. When she grows to womanhood and comes of age, the celebrations will be such as have never before been seen. Cattle will be driven in from the north and from the south, from the east and from the west. The dust from their hooves will rise in a mighty cloud, big enough to blot out the sun. The cattle will be slaughtered and a feast prepared more generous than any feast ever set before any princess."

Victorious kings often spoke in such a way, the people expected it. Everyone knew that it was vain talk meant to honour the glorious victory of the soldiers, but everyone knew such boasts could not be fulfilled.

Everyone knew these things except the little princess. The girl was beautiful and her proud mother often told her of the fine words spoken by her father, the king. The mother knew that the king meant that he would provide a very handsome feast for his favourite daughter, but the little girl believed all the words about the dust from the hooves of the cattle rising up and blotting out the sun. The princess grew up with a big opinion of her own importance and she became proud. However, as she was indeed the favourite daughter of the all-powerful king, no one corrected her.

At last the day came when the proud princess was of age. As was the custom she left the village and stood on the veldt.

"Tell my father I am ready for him to drive the cattle before me, as he promised," she said to her attendant maidens.

The girls hurried away and the princess waited, expecting to see the cattle destined for her coming-of-age feast driven before her.

The mighty king ordered twenty oxen to be sent forth. Twenty oxen was a very generous present for one girl.

The proud princess, who had believed every word about cattle coming from the north and from the south, from the east and from the west, could scarcely believe her eyes.

"Cattle? Cattle? What cattle?" she asked, looking around and letting her eyes pass the twenty oxen as if they were not worth noticing. "I see nothing!"

The herdsmen returned to the king and told him of his daughter's words.

"It is right that a mighty king should have a daughter who knows her worth," said the king, through tight lips.

He ordered the men to drive forty more oxen before his daughter.

Again the proud princess was disappointed.

"I see nothing," she sneered.

By this time the king was furious, but he did not wish to be shamed, so he ordered a hundred oxen to be driven out from the kraals. Still the girl was not pleased. All her life she had expected to see thundering herds of cattle filling the veldt from horizon to horizon when she came of age, so she could not believe that these little groups of oxen were all she was to receive.

"Tell my father," she said to the herdsmen, "that the great, red sun is shining in the sky and until its light is hidden by the dust from the hooves of the cattle, I will not return home."

The king was again enraged at his daughter's words, but he would not be shamed by failing to provide his daughter with what she considered to be her due. He assembled his warriors and sent them to all the villages of his own tribe. From every kraal the king demanded a tribute of oxen. No one dared to refuse. Thousands of head of cattle were driven before the proud princess.

She looked skywards.

"I can still see the great, red sun," she said.

The king assembled an even greater army. He sent it to threaten the neighbouring tribes who, in fear, sent presents of cattle to stop the great king from destroying their homes. Still the princess was not satisfied. At last a band of warriors stumbled upon the entrance to a valley which none of them had seen before. To their amazement, they beheld grass greener and more luscious than any in their own land and, best of all, the valley was filled with plump, healthy cattle.

"We will drive these oxen back to our king," smiled the warriors. "Even the proud princess must be satisfied with the gift of so many fine beasts."

The warriors crept to the narrow end of the valley and then with shouts and waving of arms, they drove the cattle out to the veldt. Suddenly they heard a voice calling to them from the mountainside.

"Why do you think you have the right to drive away my cattle?" asked the voice.

Sitting amongst the bushes was a mighty, hairy monster, the Lord of the Cattle himself, the magical spirit of the oxen. The cattle in the valley were his own perfect herd.

The Zulu warriors feared nothing and no one, so they shook their spears at the monster on the mountain.

"These spears give us the right to do exactly as we please," they laughed. "What have you to say to that, old furry feet!"

The Lord of the Cattle, said nothing. He watched them go in silence.

The warriors drove the cattle across the plain and the dust from their hooves rose in a cloud that blotted out the sun. At last the proud princess smiled and was satisfied and the king was delighted because now he would not be shamed.

The cattle were slaughtered and a great feast was prepared. Only one thing was not done – the warriors did not tell the king about their words with the King of the Cattle and they felt uneasy. They did not wish to relate anything which might displease the king and spoil the celebrations.

130

After the meal, the proud princess went to the hut of her mother and sister. For a few days, all was well. Then, as the sisters were resting in the hut out of the heat of the noon sun, a mighty thundering shook the ground. The great, furry monster, the Lord of the Cattle, was at the gate of the kraal. He broke down the fence and, as the girls rose to their feet to see what was causing such commotion, two leaves blew into their hut.

"Go and fetch some water from the stream," the leaves said to the younger girl, but to the proud princess, they said nothing.

The younger sister went to the stream and filled a jar with water, but when she turned to walk away, she found that she could not move her feet as they were rooted to the ground by magic.

The proud princess was all alone.

"Go to a neighbour's hut and fill a jar with water," the leaves said to the proud princess.

She laughed at them.

"Fetch water yourselves, if you want it," she said.

The leaves repeated their order and something about them frightened the proud princess into obeying.

When the princess returned with the water, she was ordered to light a fire and grind corn and make bread. The proud princess was furious, she had never done such menial work in her life.

"My hands are not used to work," she protested. "Look! My nails are long. I cannot grind corn."

The leaves trimmed the long finger nails of the proud princess and set her to work. When the bread was baked, the leaves ordered the princess to carry it with a calabash of milk to the gate, where the monster was waiting. The princess was too frightened to do anything but obey. As she walked through the village, the leaves followed her, stealing all the food they could carry from the huts. At the gate, everything was given to the monster, who swallowed it at once.

He looked at the princess and said, "Put on your finest clothes. Wear your petticoat of beads. Put on your necklace of brass and your bracelets and your armlets."

The trembling princess did as she was commanded, then returned to stand before the monster.

"Climb on my back," he ordered.

Then he turned and lumbered away.

All this while, the younger sister had been standing by the stream, unable to move, but she knew in her heart what had happened. As the monster disappeared from sight, the sister's feet were freed. She ran screaming to her mother who was working in the fields. The mother ran to her empty hut, saw that the village had been robbed and told the other workers, who called the warriors. A band of soldiers grouped together and took up their weapons. They followed the trail of the great monster until they caught up with him.

"Give back the princess," the warriors shouted.

The Lord of the Cattle laughed at them.

"Do your feeble best to stop me," he jeered. "When you have done all you have to do, turn and go home."

He stood still while the men threw their spears at him, but no weapon could pierce his thick hide. Still laughing, the monster turned and crashed away through the bush towards his secret valley. The bravest of the men followed him, but at last they realized they were wasting their time and, weak with weariness, they went home. The proud princess was alone, riding on the back of the furry monster, the Lord of the Cattle.

On they went into the valley with the rich, green pasture, and up the mountain slopes, until they reached a bare, bleak cave. Inside were a pillow, a sleeping mat and bread and water.

"You will live here for a year and a day," said the monster to the princess. "No one will cook your food. No one will clean for you. You will learn not to be proud. Your father humbled me by taking my cattle, now you must become humble in return."

For a year and a day the proud princess lived a harsh, uncomfortable life. At the end of that time, the monster allowed her to walk back to her own home. How pleased the girl was to see the comforts of the village. After that, she was grateful for everything put before her and never again demanded enough cattle to blot out the sun.

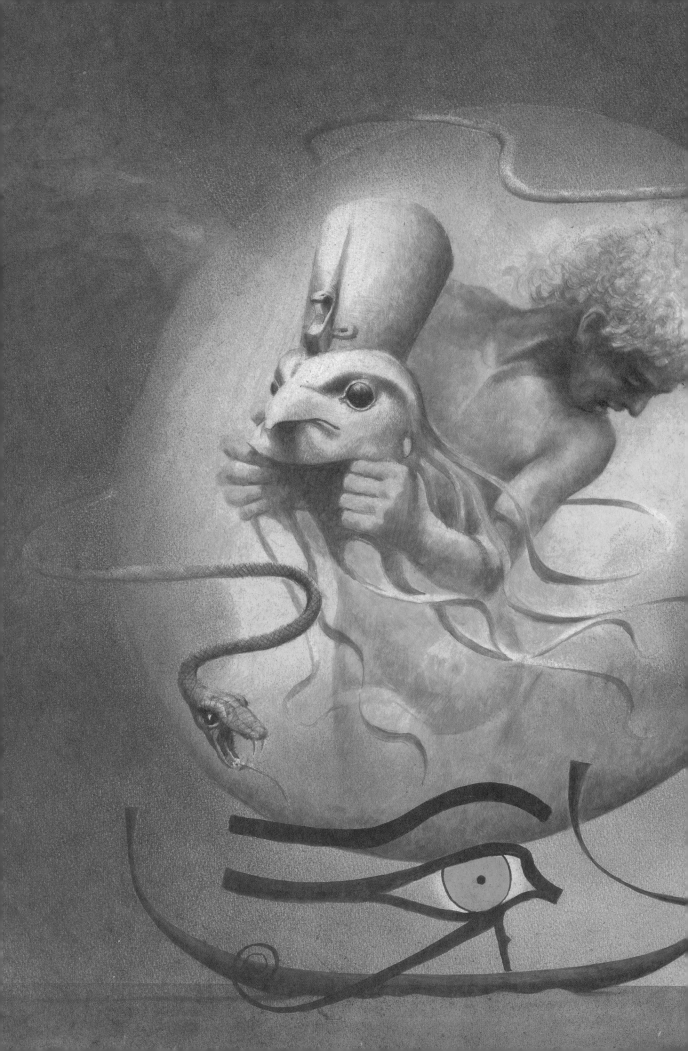

The Battles of Horus

Egypt lies at the north east of Africa, straddling the lucrative trade routes between Europe, India and the Far East. The legends of Egypt feature a bewildering array of gods. This is because at one time, each of the thirty-five or so local districts had its own 'company' of nine gods. As the land became more united, the rulers tried to reconcile all these local beliefs into one national religion. They said that each chief, or local god, was really the same great god, under a different name. Some districts went along with this arrangement and some did not.

So in some places we read that Ra, Horus, Tem, Harmachus and Khepera are names for the one Sun God while, in others, we are told that Horus is the son of Ra and that the other names refer to different Sun Gods of varying importance. Horus himself is a changeable character, sometimes he is himself; sometimes he is his own son and all this can be in the same story! In the following legend, Horus is quite clearly the son of Ra and the plot would appear to be a folk memory of ancient tribal conflicts.

Long ago, when the world was young, Horus was the god of the daylight sky. Horus the boy was young and eager, like the first rays of dawn. Horus the man had the strength of the sun at noon. Sometimes he appeared with the body of a man and the head of a falcon, sometimes he was a golden, raging lion. As the sun sank towards the west, so did the power of Horus wane. This was the time for the enemies of Horus to attack him. Set, the god of the night sky, was the enemy of the beautiful god of day. When night fell, it was wise for Horus to be wary.

Now Ra, the ancient god of the sun, was growing old. His enemies harried the borders of his kingdom, taking land here, stealing goods and horses there. Set was his greatest enemy, for Set was a cunning warrior and had many evil followers. In days gone by Set had slain Osiris, son of Ra and brother of Horus. Such a deed could never be forgotten, far less forgiven, for Osiris had been sweet and beloved by his family.

Ra journeyed with his army into the land of Nubia, where he was met by his son Horus, who was also at the head of a horde of men.

"Father," said Horus, "your enemies are marching against you. They will not disappear like water in the desert and they are cunning and bold."

The old man Ra, looked at his strong, golden son.

"Take your place at the head of our armies," he said. "Go forth and trample our enemies into the dust."

Horus smiled. He was not without cunning of his own.

"There is more than one way to defeat an army," he said.

Leaving his men in hiding, Horus went to consult the god, Thoth. Thoth knew many magical things and he gave Horus a glittering disc in which to fly. The disc shone like the sun and had great wings on either side. Horus

136

flew into the sky and hovered over the armies of his enemies, glaring down at them, so that the minds of the soldiers became confused. They did not know where they were, or who they were, and they picked up their swords and slew each other. Only a handful of Set's men staggered alive from the field of slaughter. Gradually they regained their wits and wondered why they had behaved in such a fashion.

Still in his golden disc, with the wings on either side, Horus flew low over the slain and dying, looking for his enemy Set, but he was not there. Fortunately for Set, he had been away in the north, as he had not thought that battle was about to begin.

Horus returned to Ra and the goddess Astarte and told them of his defeat of the army of Set. They were amazed and could scarcely believe his words, for they knew that their own armies had not unsheathed a single sword. Horus led Ra and Astarte into the golden disc and flew with them over their slaughtered enemies. The heart of the old man was glad.

"Now I am safe," he smiled.

Ra invited Horus to take a boat ride with him and his court on the cool waters of the Nile, but Horus and Ra were rejoicing too soon. Set was still alive and he had more followers eager to overthrow the power of Ra.

"Horus is not the only one to know the ways of the cunning ones," said Set.

He turned his followers into crocodiles and hippopotamuses and sent them into the River Nile.

"Turn over the boats and swallow Ra and Horus," he ordered. "No harm will come to you. Your thick hides will protect you."

The followers of Set slipped into the river ahead of the boats of Ra and Horus, but the god Thoth sent a warning to his friends. He also sent more of his magical weapons, equipping Horus and his men with spears and chains of glittering metal.

With a mighty churning of water, the army of crocodiles and hippopotamuses charged at the oncoming boats. Horus spoke the words taught to him by Thoth from his Book of Magic, while his men stabbed into the water with their glittering, magical weapons. Many crocodiles were killed. Many hippopotamuses were captured. Many more fled. The creatures which fled to the north escaped, but Horus pursued those which swam southwards where he overtook them and, after another great battle, slew even more of the followers of Set, the god of night.

These great victories pleased Ra, but still the old man was frightened.

"I shall never be safe while Set and his followers live," he said. "Horus, climb into your golden disc with the huge wings on either side and slay the rest of my enemies."

Horus, the mighty warrior, was eager to obey the instructions of his father. He entered the golden disc and this time the goddesses Nekhbet and Uaszet flew on either side of him. Thoth, the maker of the disc, joined Ra in the boats and they sailed north, while Horus and Nekhbet and Uaszet flew above them. They scanned the water, but the crocodiles and hippopotamuses had learned a bitter lesson and stayed under water, out of sight.

For days Ra and Horus searched for their enemies. The goddesses Nekhbet and Uaszet twisted and curled through the sky in the shape of great snakes. At last they spied the crocodiles and hippopotamuses lurking beneath the surface of the river and, calling Horus in his golden disc, the goddesses glared down at the creatures under the waves and those which did not flee were destroyed. Ra watched from his boat and rejoiced.

Horus called for his soldiers and drove the remnants of the army of Set from the land. Throughout all the battles, Horus searched for Set, wishing to fight him with his own hands in revenge for the killing of Osiris. It was not to be. Set escaped. Time passed. Ra and Horus thought that all danger was finished until one morning, as the boy Horus came up with the dawn and grew to manhood at the noontime of the day, Set stepped forward and challenged him to mortal combat.

It was agreed that the fight should take place upon the River Nile. Isis, the grieving widow of Osiris, gave Horus a magical boat. This lovely craft was not only decorated from stem to stern, it was also protected by ancient spells so no harm could come to anyone who sailed in it.

Set was employing cunning of his own. He took the shape of a great, red hippopotamus and slipped into the water and lay in wait, then he called up a great storm to rage along the river. Huge waves lashed the boats of Horus and his followers, only the magic of Isis saved them from foundering and all the while Set lurked on the bed of the river, waiting to swallow the sinking bodies of his enemies.

Realizing that the power of the storm was not enough to fulfill his plans, Set, the god of the night, caused darkness to fill the sky.

"Now will the power of Horus falter," he smiled.

However, the courage of Horus did not fail, he grew to the size of a giant. He knew no fear, for again he had the weapons of Thoth to help him. A great light like the sun shone from the prow of the boat and cut through the darkness, while Horus peered out into the storm looking for his enemy. He raised another magical weapon – a great harpoon sharp enough to pierce the strongest defence.

Set, disguised as the red hippopotamus, lurked beneath the surface of the water, waiting impatiently for the ship to sink so that he could swallow Horus, his enemy. At last, puzzled to know why the ship stayed afloat, Set raised his head into the light beaming from the prow of the magic craft of Horus. One glimpse of his enemy was enough for the mighty warrior of the sun. Horus threw the harpoon and it entered the head of Set and killed him.

The storm ceased to rage. The river became calm. Horus and his companions sailed back to stand before Ra, the mighty god.

"Father," said Horus, "Set, your enemy, is killed. The murder of Osiris is avenged."

Then there was great rejoicing throughout the land and songs were sung in honour of Horus, the mighty warrior.

138

The Cunning Man

Malawi is an African republic, which lies south of the equator. It is a landlocked country, bordering the enormous Lake Malawi which is five hundred and fifty kilometres long. The main crops of the land are maize and tea. The official language is English and old stories from this land can be found recorded by early English settlers.

Once, long ago, there was a great famine in the land and a certain cunning man decided to save himself from hardship. He went out into the forest and picked some wild figs. He walked on until he found a man so hungry that he was eating grass.

"Would you like to eat these figs?" asked the cunning man.

"Yes, indeed," replied the other man, eagerly taking the fruit and eating it.

When all the figs were gone, the cunning man asked, "What are you going to give me in return?"

The hungry man looked at him in surprise. "I thought the figs were a gift because you felt sorry for me," he said. "I did not know I had to give anything in return."

"Come, come, what nonsense!" shouted the cunning man, standing up tall and glaring down. "Of course you have to give me something. Why should I give a gift to a complete stranger? This was a trading arrangement. Do not try to escape your part of the bargain now, you cheat!"

The man who had been eating grass was so distressed by all the shouting and unpleasantness, that he gave the cunning man a fishing net to appease him.

The cunning man went on his way along the side of the great lake. Presently he came upon some people who were trying to catch fish with their hands without success.

"Why are you doing such a foolish thing as to try to catch fish with your hands?" asked the cunning man.

"Because we are so poor we have had to sell our fishing nets," replied the people.

At once the cunning man held out the fishing net he had taken from the man who had been eating grass. "Would you like to use this net?" he asked.

"Thank you," said the people, and eagerly taking the net, they caught a good supply of fish from the lake.

No sooner was this done, than the cunning man said, "Half those fish are mine. You must give them to me in return for the use of the net."

The fisher people were amazed. "We thought you lent us the net because you felt sorry for our plight," they said.

"How ridiculous! Business is business!" shouted the cunning man. "What sort of thieves are you that you try to cheat me of my dues? Why should I, a

139

stranger, give you something for nothing? You must have known from the beginning there would be a price to pay for using the net. Do not try to go back on your bargain now!"

The fisher people were so upset at being accused of bad faith, that they gave half the fish to the cunning man. He then walked on his way until he came to a village where the people had porridge to eat, but nothing to give it relish.

"Porridge with no relish is dull fare," said the cunning man. "Would you like some of my fish to cook?"

"How very kind," smiled the people of the village, thinking that the stranger was willing to share his food with his fellow men in their time of trouble. No sooner had the fish gone down their throats, than the cunning man held out his hand.

"What are you giving me in return for my fish?" he asked.

"We did not know we had to give anything?" said the village folk in surprise.

"Don't try those tricks with me," shouted the cunning man. "A man gave me a fishing net in return for some figs. The fisher people gave me half their catch of fish in return for the use of the fishing net. Why should you not give me something in return for those fish you have eaten? What is so special about you that you should have something for nothing?"

He made so much commotion that the village folk gave the cunning man a supply of millet, with which he happily made off along the road. Further on his journey he came upon some men who were eating white ants.

"Ants are not food for decent folk," said the cunning man.

"We know that," replied the men, "but we have nothing else."

"Would you like this millet?" asked the cunning man and the men at the wayside gladly accepted it and ate it. Immediately the cunning man asked for something in return.

"A man who was eating grass gave me a fishing net. Some fisher people gave me half their catch of fish in return for the use of the net. Some village people gave me millet in return for fish. What are you going to give me in return for the millet?" he shouted.

When they heard what other people had given to the cunning man, the men at the roadside dared not refuse him and they gave him some fine guinea feathers of great value. Feeling pleased, the cunning man continued on this way until he met some men decorated with the leaves of a maize plant. They saw the guinea feathers in his hand and asked for them.

"Those feathers will give a fine finish to our grand outfits," they said.

The cunning man agreed to hand the feathers over in return for a goat, which he drove on before him to the next village. By this time night was falling and the cunning man asked for shelter for himself and his animal. The kind folk of the village allowed the cunning man to pen his goat in with theirs and to sleep in one of their huts. During the night, the ungrateful fellow arose and killed his goat. In the morning he made a great fuss, shouting and wailing at the loss of his fine animal.

"Your animals trampled it in the night!" he shrieked. "You should have warned me that your goats were bullies. Now you owe me something in return."

To rid themselves of such a trouble-maker, the folk of the village gave him an ox, which pleased the cunning man. He drove the ox to his own home, where he slew it, and taking the tail, he hurried to another lakeside village, where he planted the tail in the mud. He set up a great wailing and shrieking until the men of the village came running to see what was the matter.

"My ox! My ox!" wailed the cunning man, pointing at the tail sticking up out of the mud. "I was driving it along this path, when it slipped into the mud and sank. If it is you village folk who made this path, then you are in great trouble. Fancy building a path through such a dangerous place! It is your fault that my ox is lost."

When they heard those words, the men of the village grasped the tail of the ox and heaved and pulled, doing their best, as they thought, to pull the unfortunate ox out of the mud. Of course the tail came away in their hands.

"Fools! Fools!" screamed the cunning man. "Now you have pulled the tail from my ox, all hope of saving it is lost. Oh you wicked bunglers! What are you going to give me in return for a creature of such value?"

The simple village folk were so upset at such dreadful accusations that they gave the cunning man twenty cattle in return for the one ox, which, in fact, had not been lost at all.

The cunning man drove the cattle home, feeling happy, as well he might. He had made a handsome profit from picking a few wild figs from the forest.

The Clever Monkey

This and the following story, TRICKY MR RABBIT, come from the west coast of Africa and are much more light-hearted than the Zulu stories. Anyone who reads many of these tales is tempted to see in them the roots of the Brer Rabbit stories told by the negroes of the United States.

Once there were two cats who were very fond of eating cheese. On a fine day when the women were busy talking together, the cats stole some cheese. Then came the problem of dividing it into equal shares. The cats eyed one another with suspicion each thinking that the other would take the bigger portion.

At last one cat said, "Let us ask a monkey to divide the cheese for us."

The other agreed willingly and they approached a monkey, who just as willingly took the cheese.

"Fetch some scales," the monkey said to the two cats.

When the cats returned, the monkey took a knife and cut the cheese into two pieces. However, one piece was clearly much bigger than the other.

"Dear me!" said the monkey. "This will never do. I will eat part of the big piece of cheese to make it weigh the same as the other."

Before the cats could object, the monkey ate part of the cheese and, of course, he ate too much.

"Dear me!" he said. "Now this piece is smaller. I shall have to eat some of the other cheese to make the two pieces the same size."

By this time the cats realized that the monkey intended to eat all the cheese.

"Please do not bother with our affairs further," they said. "Give the cheese back to us and we will divide it ourselves."

The monkey continued to nibble at the cheese.

"I could not do that," he said. "You would start quarrelling again for sure. Then the king of all the animals would blame me for the conflict between you. No, I must continue to bite first this piece of cheese and then that piece, until they are exactly the same weight. If in the course of my efforts all the cheese is eaten, then that is fate and you must accept it."

The cats saw that the cheese would never be returned to them and turned away. The monkey laughed and called after them, "You have learned a lesson. Never let greed lead you into foolishness."

He finished enjoying the cheese.

Tricky Mr Rabbit

Once, long ago, there was a cunning rabbit who enjoyed playing tricks on the other animals. The bigger the other animals were, the more Mr Rabbit enjoyed the joke.

One day Mr Rabbit was walking near the sea, when he saw Mr Elephant.

"How big you are Mr Elephant," said Mr Rabbit. "How big your feet are. Why I declare I have never seen such big feet on any other creature."

The rabbit trotted round the feet of the elephant pushing and prodding at them.

"Clumsy feet some people would call them," laughed Mr Rabbit. "How do you avoid tripping over with huge feet like that at the end of your legs? I feel sorry for you, Mr Elephant, having big, clumsy, awkward feet like that!"

Mr Elephant did not care to hear such talk.

"You are an impudent creature, Mr Rabbit," he said. "I feel like giving you a good spanking."

The rabbit laughed and ran in circles round the elephant.

"I feel like tying a rope round your middle and dragging you into the sea. That's what I feel like doing," jeered the rabbit.

This talk from a small rabbit made the elephant really angry.

"What, you! Tie a rope round a big fellow like me and drag me into the sea!" he trumpeted. "You could not possibly do it. What nonsense!"

The rabbit took a coil of rope from his back.

"Let me tie this rope round you," he said, "and if I cannot drag you into the sea, then you have my permission to give me a good beating. I will stand still while you do it."

"Agreed," laughed the elephant, allowing the rabbit to tie the rope round his waist.

Then the rabbit ran to the seashore with the other end of the rope and spoke to a whale.

"Mrs Whale," he said. "You are big and I am little, but I bet that I can tie this rope round your middle and drag you up on to the land."

The whale roared with laughter.

"Indeed you cannot," she said. "Why, what a big opinion you have of yourself, you little bundle of fur, but you can try if you wish. I have nothing else to do this fine afternoon."

The whale kept still as the rabbit tied the rope round her middle.

"Now," smiled the rabbit, "you pull hard on this end of the rope and I will go and pull on the other end of the rope."

The whale started to swim out to sea, as the rabbit hurried back to the elephant.

"Mr Elephant," called the rabbit. "I am starting to pull you into the sea. Stop me if you can."

144

The elephant felt the strong tug on the rope as the huge whale swam out to sea. He was amazed at the strength of the rabbit, as he thought, and pulled with all his might to stay in the same place. Meanwhile, in the sea, the whale was astonished to find herself being held back.

"How can that tiny rabbit stop a mighty whale like me from swimming forward?" she gasped. "What shame to be outpulled by a rabbit!"

Mrs Whale flapped her huge tail from side to side and heaved forward in the water.

The elephant felt himself being dragged towards the beach. Step by step he was pulled to the very edge of the water and all the while the rabbit was hiding behind a bush and laughing fit to split his sides.

When his feet were splashing in the sea, the elephant saw that the other end of the rope was tied round a mighty whale.

"Mrs Whale!" he called. "Have you been speaking to a rabbit?"

Mrs Whale looked round and was amazed to see an elephant pulling at the other end of the rope.

"Indeed I have," she said. "Tell me, why are you pulling at the rope? The rabbit should be pulling."

"We have both been tricked," shouted Mr Elephant. "Come near to the shore and let me untie this rope."

While Mr Rabbit was having a great laugh, the elephant used his trunk to untie the rope from himself and Mrs Whale. Mr Rabbit, being no fool, ran away before the rope was completely undone. At last Mr Elephant threw off the rope and looked round.

"I will catch that rabbit and give him a beating no matter how far ahead of me he is," vowed the elephant.

He set off after the rabbit and soon he was gaining on him. The elephant was very cross as he ran with long strides of his big feet following the rabbit. Realizing that soon he would be overtaken, the rabbit hid in the skull of a horse. The elephant came panting along and said, "Mr Skull, have you seen a rabbit running this way?"

"Indeed I have," the skull seemed to reply, but of course it was really the rabbit calling from within the skull. "Indeed I have," went on the skull, "only then I was a horse. That rabbit spoke to me cheekily and I was about to give him a kick, when he stared at me with burning eyes and pointed a finger at me and in a second turned me into what you see before you."

The elephant stopped and stared at the skull. He gulped and turned for home.

"Well," he said, "if that rabbit ever comes this way again do not tell him that I was chasing him. Do not even tell him that you saw me. I have decided I do not want to catch him after all."

As soon as the elephant was out of sight, the rabbit crawled out of the skull and ran towards his own home, laughing all the way.

146

Asia

ASIA

Momotaro or the Peach-boy   150

The Son of the Ogress   156

Baba Yaga and the Stepdaughter   161

Baba Yaga and the Brave Youths   164

The Prawn that Caused Trouble   168

The Leather Bag   173

The Deceitful Pelican   178

Into the Jungle   182

The Bridge of Magpies   187

Momotaro or the Peach-boy

This is an old folk story from the islands of Japan. Buddhism and Shintoism were the main religions of the time. The military tradition of the Samurai was the admired ideal. Fulfilling one's family duty and knowing one's status in society were expected virtues. They can all be seen in this story.

It was the springtime of the year. The fields were freshly green. The branches of the willow trees shook their catkins across the rivers. The harsh winter air had turned soft, ready to welcome summer.

An honourable old woman knelt where the river eddied into a shallow backwater. She was washing clothes and amusing herself by watching the antics of the little minnows as they darted through the clear water. Suddenly a peach, more enormous than the honourable old woman had ever seen in her life, came rolling down the river.

"I am sixty years old," gasped the honourable old woman, "this is the first time I have ever seen a peach as large as this. What a fine supper it would make for me and my husband."

The peach was in deep water where the honourable old woman could not reach it. Leaning towards the huge fruit, she called softly:

"Cold are deep waters, but the shallow are warm.

Leave the cold and come to warm."

At the sound of her voice, the peach ceased its tumbling over the strong spring currents which came from the melted snow of the mountains. It bobbed into the backwater over the heads of the minnows and rubbed against the hand of the honourable old woman. Eagerly she picked it up and took it home on top of her pile of washed clothes.

At supper time, the honourable old man came home from where he had been cutting grass in the mountains. The honourable old woman ran to meet him and show him the peach.

"That is wonderful," he said, "and I am hungry. Let us eat it at once."

The honourable old woman took out a chopping board and a knife and was about to cut the luscious peach, when the voice of a child called out, "Honourable old woman, wait!"

The peach fell apart and a fine, strong little boy jumped out.

The old couple were amazed and fearful.

"Do not be alarmed," laughed the boy. "You have often lamented to the gods that you have no child. At last they have taken pity on you and sent me down to be your son."

The old couple were delighted and as the boy had come to them in a peach, they named him Momotaro or Peach-boy.

The years went by and Momotaro grew up to be handsome, brave and immensely strong.

One day he stood before the honourable old man and said, "Father, my gratitude to you is higher than the mountains on which you cut grass and deeper than the river where the honourable old lady washes clothes. How can I ever repay my debt to you?"

"Do not thank us for doing our duty. Honourable people could do no less," replied the old man. "When we are old you will look after us, as is your duty and you will owe us nothing."

"It distresses me to leave you before my duty to you is done," said Momotaro. "Honourable Father, will you give me permission to go away for a short while?"

The old man was surprised.

"Why should you want to leave your home? Where could you find more happiness in performing your duty than here?" he asked.

"In the north of Japan, separated from the mainland by a stretch of sea," said Momotaro, "is an island inhabited by demons. They do not obey the gods of Japan, but go their own wicked ways. They steal people and goods, but I hope to crush them at a blow and bring their stolen riches back here. That is why I wish to leave you."

The honourable old man was astonished at this request. After deep thought, he realized that as Momotaro had come from the gods, it was unlikely that they would let harm befall him. He gave the young man permission to make the journey.

"If the demons are enemies of Japan, the sooner you kill them the better," he said.

The honourable old lady prepared Momotaro's clothes and made him a supply of millet dumplings. He was ready to go. The two old people waved goodbye to him with tears in their eyes.

"Return victorious!" they called.

Momotaro walked swiftly along the road, eager to be about his business. At midday he sat at the side of the road to eat some of his dumplings. The scent of the food brought out a fierce dog which barked at his legs.

"You are on my territory. Give me some of your food or I will eat you alive!" it said.

Momotaro kicked it aside.

"Get away from me, you miserable cur," he shouted. "I am on my way to kill the enemies of Japan, but if you hinder me, I will kill you first."

The dog cowered with fear.

"I see you are the mighty Momotaro," it whimpered. "I humbly beg you to forgive me. Please allow me to go with you to slay the enemies of our country."

"I have no objection," said Momotaro and gave the dog a dumpling.

When they had finished eating, they went on their way through the high mountains. After many a mile, a strange wild creature leapt down from a tree and stood in Momotaro's path.

"I hear you are the mighty Momotaro, marching to slay the foes of Japan," it said. "Please allow me to go with you."

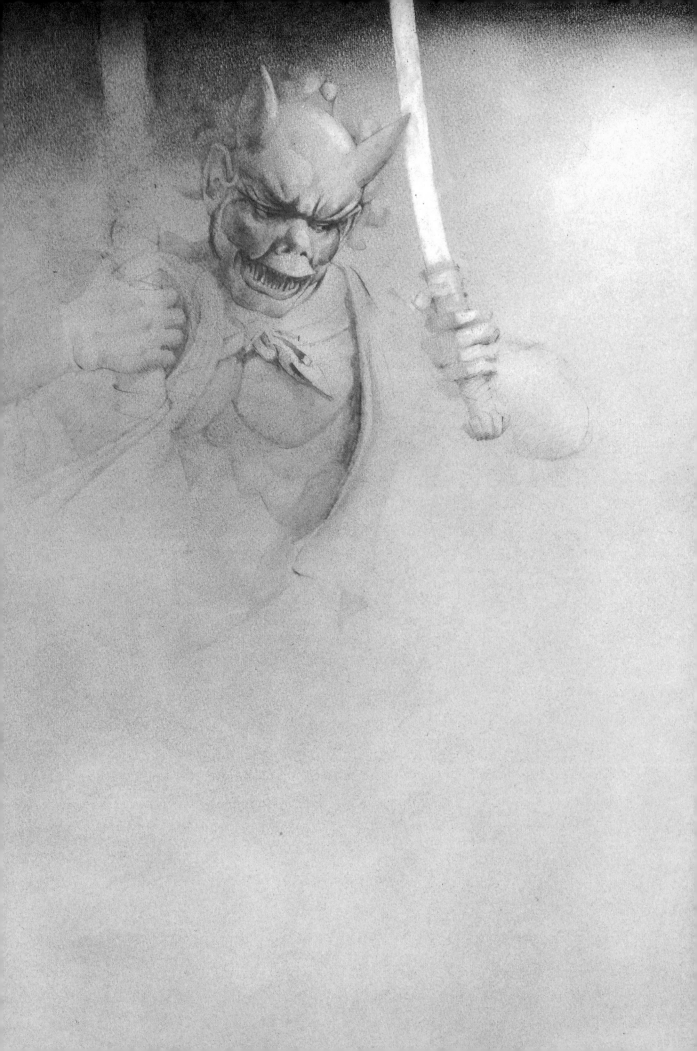

At this the dog hurried forward in a rage.

"What insolence!" it growled. "How dare a mountain monkey like you seek to go to war in the company of Momotaro? I alone am worthy to go with him."

Naturally, this speech made the monkey furious. It made as if to draw a sword, but as monkeys do not carry swords, it made do with baring its teeth and sharpening its claws. It seemed that nothing could stop the two from attacking each other, until Momotaro stepped forward.

"Do not be hasty," he said to the dog. "This monkey could be useful. I want to take it with me to be my vassal."

He gave the monkey half a dumpling and when it was eaten, gave the order to move forward. However, the monkey and the dog would not stop squabbling. There was no peace until Momotaro gave the monkey his standard and told it to march along the road ahead. Momotaro then gave his sword to the dog and ordered it to walk behind. Momotaro himself held up his iron war fan and walked between the two of them.

So the war party marched on through valley and wilderness until a wonderful bird sprang from the ground. The dog leaped joyfully forward, thinking to eat the bird.

Momotaro stopped him and said to the bird, "If in your insolence you seek to hinder my journey, then my dog shall bite off your head. If you will submit to me, then you may become my vassal."

The bird bowed deeply and said, "If you are the mighty Momotaro, whose fame has filled the land, then may I, a humble pheasant, go with you to kill the enemies of Japan?"

The dog growled in its throat.

"Are we to be dishonoured by the company of this worthless fellow?" it grumbled.

"That is no decision of yours," replied Momotaro. "I say that the pheasant shall come with us and I warn all three of you now, that if there is one word of quarrelling, I will send you home. We shall never overcome our enemies if there is dissent amongst ourselves."

The three animals listened humbly and promised to obey Momotaro implicitly. The pheasant ate half a dumpling and became a vassal to Momotaro and they all went forward together. At last they came to the sea. They peered across the heaving waters but could see no island. The sea voyage would obviously be long and rough and the three land creatures stood and shivered.

Momotaro was disgusted.

"You cowards!" he shouted. "Do you fear the ocean? What companions I have brought with me! I should have been better off alone. I will get rid of you now, as I should have done before. Go home!"

The three animals clung to Momotaro and begged to be allowed to stay. Believing that they had found some courage after all, he consented to their helping him build a boat and soon they were sailing out across the wide ocean. The waters rose and fell. The animals felt ill and to take their minds

154

from their troubles each animal showed off in its own way. The dog begged. The monkey performed tricks and the pheasant sang a mournful song. In no time they were at the island.

It was a fearsome sight. The path ashore was blocked by a gate of iron. The many houses were crowded together and protected by iron roofs, while flags flew defiantly in the wind.

Momotaro turned to the pheasant.

"Make use of your wings," he said. "Fly over the gate and see what these demons are doing on their fine island."

The pheasant obeyed instantly and found the demons all sitting on their roofs. It called down to them, "He, who was sent by the gods, has come to destroy you. If you wish to save yourselves, surrender at once."

"What vanity!" jeered the demons. "Feel the edge of our weapons, pheasant, and give us no more talk of surrender!"

Rising up into the sky, the pheasant swooped strongly down and pecked off the head of a red demon. After a mighty struggle the pheasant burst open the iron gate and the dog and monkey charged in. The demons were startled, for they thought they were fighting one bird, believing the pheasant had meant itself when it spoke of one sent by the gods. Their alarm made them fight all the more fiercely. The pheasant, the dog and the monkey were soon engaged in a fearful combat with red and black and blue demons, and their screams drowned the sound of the waves on the rocks.

At last only the leader of the demons was left. Seeing all his comrades slain, he threw down his weapons and broke off his horns as a sign of surrender. He knelt before Momotaro and offered him all the treasure on the island.

"Spare my life," he begged, "and I will never do wrong again."

Momotaro laughed in derision.

"You coward!" he cried. "For years you have killed and robbed and now you talk of being spared. I will take you to Japan where your head will be cut off and stuck on a stake that everyone may see your reign of terror is over."

So the monkey led away the chief of the demons as a prisoner. All the riches of the island were loaded onto the boat and Momotaro and his band returned to Japan.

Great was the rejoicing of the honourable old man and the honourable old woman when Momotaro returned to them victorious. They all lived in wealth and happiness for the rest of their lives.

The Son of the Ogress

The highways of old India were more dangerous than most. Not only were there tigers and other large or poisonous creatures for an unwary traveller to contend with, but also bands of Thuggees who used the roads as their hunting grounds. These worshippers of Khali, the goddess of death, made friends with travellers, offering to ride with them as a protection against bandits. Then at a chosen spot, the Thuggees would strangle their victims, rob the bodies and bury them without trace. In these circumstances, it is hardly surprising that legends grew up of monsters that lay in wait by the roadside.

The land of India is vast and its roads are long and lonely. In the olden days travellers were right to be fearful because robbers and bandits lay in wait at the sides of the dusty highways, while ogres and angry spirits lurked in the forest glades and the mountain passes. Prudent travellers journeyed in groups in the hope of protecting one another. The man who walked the roads alone, did so anxiously, and forever glanced over his shoulder.

In those distant, dangerous days, a Brahman priest, though necessity, had to travel alone towards Benares. Living in a cave near the side of the road was a creature known as a Yakka. She had the body of a woman, but the head of a horse. She was wild and greedy and powerful and lived by eating human flesh.

This terrible Yakka, seized the Brahman and carried him to her cave, intending to eat him, as she had eaten so many other unfortunate people. However, the man was young and very handsome and the Yakka fell in love with him. She said she would spare his life, if he would marry her and live with her in the cave. The Brahman chose what seemed to be the lesser of two evils and agreed to marry the dreadful creature.

"Surely, soon, I shall find a way to escape," he thought, "and this nightmare will be over."

The Yakka was cunning and cautious. She never left the cave without rolling a huge boulder to block the entrance. The Brahman was a prisoner for several years, shut in the dark and the damp and yearning to return to the life of the town. It was true that the Yakka made every effort to improve her behaviour. Under the influence of the gentle Brahman, she gave up eating human flesh and ate fruits and grain in its place. She drank wine instead of drinking human blood. However, she still lurked at the side of the road and obtained what she wanted by robbing the caravans of travellers. She and the Brahman continued to live in the rough cavern, its walls dripping with water, far away from the pleasant company of human folk.

157

A baby was born to the Yakka. He was a beautiful boy, fortunately, like his father and both the Yakka and the Brahman loved him dearly.

One day, when the Yakka was out hunting, the boy said to his father, "Why is my mother's face so different from ours?"

"Because your mother is an ogress and we are human men," replied the Brahman.

The boy asked, "Why do we stay continually in the dark of this damp cavern when the yellow sunlight shines outside?"

"Because your mother is strong and will not let us leave and when she is away, she rolls that huge boulder across the mouth of the cavern," replied the Brahman.

"Why do you not push the boulder aside that we may escape?" asked the boy.

"The boulder is huge and I am not strong enough to move it," replied the Brahman.

At that the boy smiled and getting up, put his young shoulder to the stone and rolled it aside with ease. He was, after all, the son of his mother and had her strength.

Taking his father by the hand, the boy led the way out into the sunlight and the two of them hurried as fast as they could towards Benares. However, the sunlight dazzled them, after their life in the darkness of the cavern. They stumbled and even the boy felt weak. Before long they heard the thud of the Yakka running behind them. She seized them both.

"My dearest son and my beloved husband," she wept. "How could you wish to leave me? Do I not work and fight every day to give you everything you need? Do I not collect soft moss and ferns for your beds? Do I not bring wine and dates for you to eat? Oh thankless ones, why do you run away?"

"Mother," replied the boy. "It is true you bring us many delightful things, but we need light and air. Living in the dark is terrible for us."

"Very well," agreed the Yakka, "return with me and I will break the boulder at the mouth of the cavern. You may both walk in the sunshine and wander beneath the trees."

In truth, having little choice, the boy and the Brahman returned with the Yakka. She kept her promise and from that day on, the man and the boy enjoyed the fresh breezes and the sunshine whenever they wished. If they ventured too far from the cavern, they heard the heavy thudding of the Yakka's feet behind them and they were dragged back to live obediently under her gaze.

The boy, being the son of his mother, was able to learn her secrets. As he grew older, he came to know that the power of the Yakka spread only as far as the river in one direction, and three leagues to the mountains in the other direction.

"Father," whispered the boy one evening, "do as I say and tonight we will escape. I can no longer live in this loneliness, away from the voices of people."

When night had fallen, and the ogress was in her deepest sleep, the boy led

158

the Brahman out of the cave. They ran their fastest and were at the side of the river before they heard the Yakka in pursuit behind them. The Brahman was exhausted, but the strong young son picked up his father and carried him across the river to safety. Only then did he turn his head to look back.

The Yakka stood on the far bank and wept.

"How shall I live without you?" she cried. "Come back to me!"

"Never!" called the boy. "We are going to live in the land of humans."

Then realizing that she had lost them for ever, the Yakka called across the flowing river, "My dear child, take this talisman to help you on the hard way through life. Hang it round your neck. Through its power, you will be able to see footsteps made by men even after twelve years."

She threw a necklace with a stone pendant across the river. The boy picked it up and put it on. He thanked his mother and said goodbye to her. Then he and the Brahman turned their backs and saw her never again.

Happy in their new freedom, the father and son walked into Benares straight to the king's palace. There they asked to see the grand vizier.

The son of the ogress bowed and said, "I have the power of seeing footsteps. Set me to guard the king's treasure house. If any robber breaks in, I shall be able to follow his footsteps and retrieve the treasure. The king need fear thieves no more."

The grand vizier gave this news to the king, who showed great interest and sent for the Brahman and his son to stand before him.

"What do you want for guarding my treasure house?" he asked.

"He desires a thousand rupees a day," replied the grand vizier.

The king hesitated. It was a high sum. However, the treasure house was full of gold and jewels and the world was full of thieves.

"Very well," agreed the king.

For some months the boy and his father lived happily at court, enjoying the company of men and the luxuries of palace life. No thief went near the treasure house, for talk of the boy who could see footsteps had spread through the land.

Then, one hot day as he sat longing for the touch of a cool breeze, the king said to the vizier, "I am restless at paying so much money to that boy. How do we know he really can see footsteps? He may be an imposter. Let us rob the treasure house ourselves tonight and see if the boy has the powers he claims."

The vizier agreed. That night he and the king broke into the treasure house, took several bags of gold and jewels, walked three times round the gardens and put the sacks in a tank of water.

The next morning they sent for the son of the Yakka.

"Boy," said the king. "The royal treasure house has been robbed. Now let me see you follow the footsteps and retrieve my riches."

"Certainly, my lord," smiled the boy and wearing the necklace with the stone pendant given to him by his mother, he walked to the treasure house.

There on the ground, he clearly saw the footsteps of two men. He followed them three times round the gardens and stopped at a tank of water.

"Send a man in here," he said, "and you will find the missing riches."

This was done and the watchers murmured with wonder and clapped their hands as the sacks were taken from the bottom of the tank.

However, the king was still displeased. He no longer wished to pay large sums of money to the boy.

"This is all very well," he blustered, "but anyone might have guessed that the tank of water was a good hiding place for stolen jewels. Can you find the thieves, my boy? That is the real test."

As it happened, the son of the Yakka had already recognized the footprints as those of the king and the vizier, who naturally wore shoes finer than those worn by anyone else in the land. The boy hesitated to say who the thieves were, as it was shameful that two such noble men should be thieves and deceivers.

"Does it matter who the thieves are?" he asked. "The treasure is regained. Surely that is the important thing?"

At this the king felt sure that the boy really had no magic powers and indeed did not know who had taken the treasure. Feeling secure and hoping to expose the boy as a fraud and thus avoid paying him, the king insisted. "Find the thieves. They deserve to be punished. If you cannot follow the footsteps of the thieves and say who they are, I shall no longer pay you."

Still the son of the Yakka hesitated, for it is unwise to offend kings.

"The names!" jeered the king. "Give me the names of the thieves or I shall have you declared a fraud."

At that the boy pointed towards the king and the grand vizier.

"You are the thieves," he said. "The footsteps lead to you."

All the onlookers were shocked to learn that their respected ruler and the chief of his ministers could stoop to such trickery. Word spread through the city that the king and the vizier were not fit to occupy positions of trust and honour. They were deposed and exiled and the throne was given to the boy who was the son of an ogress.

Baba Yaga and the Stepdaughter

Vast as it is, Russia is but a small portion of the modern U.S.S.R., which includes the Ukraine, Georgia, Tartary and many other old kingdoms, as well as the endless reaches of Siberia. Russian folk tales were an oral tradition, as the written word in Russia was devoted almost exclusively to church matters. It is said that Ivan the Terrible had three storytellers, who sat at his bedside and took turns to relate tales, until he fell asleep. It was not until the nineteenth century that the Russians themselves wrote their folk stories down, when a man named Afanas'ev made a great collection of all he could trace. These are two of them.

Once there was a peasant girl, named Karen, whose mother died and whose father married again. The new wife hated her stepdaughter. After a few months the father went away visiting friends and the new wife saw her chance to get rid of her stepdaughter, Karen.

"Run an errand for me," said the wife. "Go to visit my sister, who is now your Aunt Irena. Ask her to give you a needle and thread to make a shirt."

However, instead of giving the girl directions to the house of Irena, the wife told her the way to the house of Baba Yaga. Suspecting that her stepmother intended harm to come to her, Karen went first to the home of her real aunt.

"Hallo, my little petkin," smiled the aunt. "Why have you come to visit me?"

"My stepmother has sent me to visit her sister, Irena, to ask for a needle and a thread to sew a shirt, but I fear that evil will befall me," replied Karen.

The aunt asked what directions the stepmother had given to Karen. When she heard them, she said, "Dear little niece, in that fearsome place, a birch tree will lash your face, here is some ribbon to tie it with. Some gates will creak at you, here is oil for their hinges. Dogs will seek to tear you limb from limb, here is bread to throw to them. A cat will try to scratch out your eyes, you must give him this ham."

"Thank you, little Auntie," said Karen and walked on her way to what she thought was the home of Irena, but was really the house of Baba Yaga.

"Good day, Auntie," said Karen, to the skinny-legged creature she found sitting inside the house. "My stepmother has sent me to ask for a needle and thread to make a shirt."

Baba Yaga, seeing a plump girl, who would make a tasty supper, standing before her, had no desire to say anything to drive her away.

"Did she, dear? Then come in and sit down," smiled Baba Yaga. "I will give you the needle and thread by and by, but first you must do a little work for me."

161

She told Karen to commence weaving at the loom which stood in the corner, and Baba Yaga hastened out to her maid.

"Heat the water and wash my niece who has arrived on a visit. Wash her well, because tomorrow I wish to eat her for my breakfast."

Karen heard these words and shook with fright, but she kept her wits about her. When Baba Yaga went out, Karen spoke to the maid and said, "You are burning too much wood. Pour some water over it to cool it down, but do not bring the water so quickly that you put the fire out. Bring the water in a sieve."

Karen gave the maid her scarf as a present and as no one had ever given her a present before, the maid obeyed Karen and went about her work with endless slowness.

A cat came spitting and scratching into the room. Karen gave him the ham and asked, "Is there no escape from this place?"

The cat gave Karen a towel and a comb.

"Go through the door and run away," it said. "Baba Yaga is sure to pursue you, so keep putting your ear to the ground. When you hear the thud of her footsteps, throw down the towel and a wide river will appear. If Baba Yaga is very hungry, she will cross the river and continue to pursue you. Therefore you must continue to put your ear to the ground. When you hear the thud of her footsteps for the second time, throw down the comb between you and her. A thick forest will spring up and Baba Yaga will cease the chase and return home."

Karen thanked the cat and taking the towel and the comb ran out of the house. The dogs in the yard barked at her heels, with lolling tongues and staring eyes and seemed about to tear her to pieces. Karen threw them the bread given to her by her aunt and the dogs let her pass. Next she came to some gates, which gripped themselves tight shut. Karen poured oil onto their hinges and they swung open and let her through. Across the path in front of her, a birch tree lashed its branches to and fro in a fierce wind. Karen took out the ribbon she had brought from her auntie's house and tied back the birch branches and walked safely forward.

Meanwhile Baba Yaga returned home. She stood by the door and called, "Dear little niece, are you working hard at the weaving?"

The cat, which had been pleased with its gift of ham, tried to help Karen. It pushed and pulled at the loom and replied, "Yes, little auntie. I am working hard."

Baba Yaga was not to be fooled so easily. The loom was not making the correct noise and the voice of the cat was harsh, not soft like Karen's. Baba Yaga rushed into the room and seeing that Karen was gone, beat the cat and shouted, "Why have you turned against me?"

"In all the years I have served you, you never gave me ham, but that girl did, so I helped her," said the cat.

Flinging the cat into the corner of the room, Baba Yaga ran into the yard and started to whip the dogs, shrieking, "The girl must have run through this yard. Why did you not tear her to pieces?"

162

"In all our lives, you have never given us so much as a burned crust," snapped the dogs, "but that girl gave us fine bread, so we helped her."

Next Baba Yaga commenced to kick the gates.

"You let a fine breakfast through," she screamed. "Why did you not keep the girl locked in?"

The gates swung easily on their comfortable, oiled hinges.

"You let us rust, but she gave us oil, so we let her through," they murmured.

Baba Yaga ran between the gates and glared at the birch tree, preening itself in its pretty ribbon.

"Such vanity!" she snarled. "I suppose that wretched girl gave the ribbon to you."

"Indeed she did," rustled the birch. "Is it not beautiful? You have never given me so much as a piece of string to stop my branches from blowing into tangles. Of course I let the charming girl through."

The maid leaned from a window of the house and shouted, "And the girl gave me this pretty scarf and I helped her too. You should treat us better, if you want us to be faithful."

"A pretty trouble-maker that so called niece has turned out to be," screeched Baba Yaga. "She must not live a day longer."

Baba Yaga ran along the road in Karen's tracks. Far ahead, Karen put her ear to the ground and heard the thud of the furious creature's footsteps. The girl took the towel given to her by the cat and cast it on the ground between herself and Baba Yaga. At once a broad river foamed across the land.

Karen fled onwards, hoping that she would hear no more footsteps, but Baba Yaga's wrath was so great that no river could stop her. She stepped into the water and the heat of her anger turned it to steam and she walked easily to the other side.

Again, with her ear to the ground, Karen heard the thud of footsteps. She threw down the comb and as the cat had said, a thick forest sprang up between Karen and Baba Yaga. This time Karen was able to hurry safely on her way, for Baba Yaga spent so much time trying to push and break her way through the forest, she quite forgot who she was pursuing and why she was so angry. After several hours, she went home and thought no more about the matter.

Meanwhile Karen arrived at her home to find her father had returned from his journey. She told him all that had befallen her and he was so angry with his second wife, that he turned her out of the house. Karen never saw her stepmother nor Baba Yaga again, but married a nice young man and lived happily ever after.

Baba Yaga and the Brave Youth

Once upon a time, a cat and a sparrow and a brave youth lived together in a hut in the forest. One day they ran short of firewood and the cat and the sparrow went into the forest to cut logs.

Before they left, they said to the brave youth, "If Baba Yaga comes to count the spoons, keep quiet, or she will get you."

"Very well," agreed the brave youth.

A little later on, when the brave youth was dozing on the stove behind the chimney, Baba Yaga came into the hut and started to count the spoons.

"This is the cat's spoon and this is the sparrow's spoon and this spoon belongs to the brave youth," she said.

The brave youth roused from his sleep and feeling indignant that Baba Yaga was meddling with his spoon, forgot his promise and shouted out, "Baba Yaga, leave my spoon alone."

At once Baba Yaga seized the youth, mounted on the kitchen mortar as if it were a steed, urged it on with its pestle, and rode out of the hut and through the forest. Baba Yaga even thought to snatch up a broom from the threshold of the cottage and used it to sweep away her tracks as she rode along.

The brave youth shrieked at the top of his voice, "Cat run! Sparrow fly! Save me from Baba Yaga!"

Hearing his cries, the cat ran to scratch at Baba Yaga's legs, the sparrow ran to peck at Baba Yaga's eyes and so the brave youth was saved.

The next day the cat and the sparrow again went into the forest to cut wood.

"We are going far away today," they said to the brave youth. "If Baba Yaga should come, be sure to keep quiet, for we shall not be here to save you."

"Very well," agreed the brave youth and sat down to keep warm on the stove behind the chimney.

Almost at once Baba Yaga entered the hut and started to count the spoons.

"This is the cat's spoon," she said. "This is the sparrow's spoon and this spoon belongs to the brave youth."

Once more the brave youth was so cross that Baba Yaga was touching his spoon that he could not stop himself from calling out, "Baba Yaga! Leave my spoon alone!"

Seizing him from the top of the stove, Baba Yaga started to drag the youth away through the forest, but he screamed, "Cat run! Sparrow fly! Save me from Baba Yaga!"

Fortunately the cat and the sparrow had not gone far on their way. They heard the brave youth and returned and scratched at Baba Yaga's legs and pecked at her eyes and saved the youth, as they had done the day before.

On the third day the cat and the sparrow again left to cut wood in the forest. Before they left they once more warned the brave youth that if Baba Yaga came into the hut to count the spoons, the youth must keep silent.

"We are going far, far away today," they said, "and if Baba Yaga gets you, we shall never hear your cries for help."

When the cat and the sparrow had left the hut, the brave youth again sat on the stove behind the chimney to keep warm. There was no sound of Baba Yaga for an hour or more, but at last she came into the hut and started to count the spoons.

"This is the cat's spoon and this is the sparrow's spoon and this spoon belongs to the brave youth," she said.

Although the brave youth was furious that Baba Yaga was touching his spoon, he kept silent, for he knew that the cat and the sparrow were too far away to help him.

Again Baba Yaga counted the spoons, saying, "This is the cat's spoon and this is the sparrow's spoon and this spoon belongs to the brave youth."

The brave youth burned with rage, but still he said nothing.

A third time Baba Yaga counted the spoons.

"This spoon belongs to the cat," she chuckled, "and this spoon belongs to the sparrow and this spoon belongs to the brave youth and a very nice spoon it is too. I think I will take it and use it to eat my soup."

At that the brave youth could hold his tongue no longer. Jumping down from the stove, he shouted, "Baba Yaga! Leave my spoon alone."

Immediately Baba Yaga seized the brave youth and dragged him through the forest and although he called, "Cat run! Sparrow Fly! Save me from Baba Yaga!" no one came to his aid.

Baba Yaga took the brave youth to her home, locked him in the wood shed and said to her eldest daughter, "I am going to Moscow to visit friends. While I am gone, cook the brave youth for my supper."

"Very well," replied the eldest daughter and lit the stove to heat the oven.

When the oven was hot she fetched the brave youth from the shed and told him to lie down in the roasting pan. He lay down with one foot on the floor and the other jammed against the ceiling, so that he could not be moved.

"Not like that," said the eldest daughter.

"How then? Show me!" said the brave youth.

He stood up and the eldest daughter lay down in the roasting pan, curled up neatly to fit into the oven.

"Like this," she said.

At once the brave youth pushed her into the oven and went back to the wood shed. After a while Baba Yaga returned, licking her lips and saying how much she was going to enjoy her supper.

"Only if you enjoy the taste of your own daughter," shouted the brave youth.

166

When Baba Yaga saw the brave youth uncooked in the wood shed, she was furious and called her second daughter to her.

"Roast this brave youth for my supper," she ordered and once more went out to visit friends in Moscow.

The second daughter built up the fire in the stove and when the oven was hot enough, she fetched the brave youth from the wood shed and told him to lie down in the roasting pan. He lay down with one foot on the floor and the other jammed against the ceiling, so that he could not be moved.

"Not like that," snapped the second daughter.

"How then? Show me!" said the brave youth, getting up and making way for the second daughter to lie in the roasting pan.

"Like this, stupid!" jeered the second daughter, curling up in the pan, neatly ready to fit into the oven.

At once the brave youth pushed the second daughter into the oven and sat down to await Baba Yaga's return. Presently she came rushing in, laughing and calling, "Set my supper on the table. Some slices of roast brave youth is what I long for."

"Then you will be disappointed," called the brave youth, "for roast second daughter is all that can be set before you."

"You wretch!" screeched Baba Yaga. "I will eat you yet."

She handed him to her third daughter and told her to cook the brave youth for her supper. The brave youth outwitted the third daughter in the same way as he had tricked her sisters. He stretched out in the warmth of the kitchen and waited for Baba Yaga to return. Her rage knew no bounds.

"To think that with three daughters, I have been brought to cooking my own supper!" she shouted. "Oh well, if you want a thing done do it yourself, as the old saying goes. At least if I cook the brave youth myself, I know he will be correctly cooked to my liking. I suppose this is all for the best."

She built up the fire in the stove and when the oven was hot enough, she took out the roasting pan and told the youth to lie on it. He lay down with one foot on the floor and one foot jammed against the ceiling so that he could not be moved.

"Not like that, imbecile!" screeched Baba Yaga.

The brave youth got up from the roasting pan.

"How then?" he asked. "Show me!"

"Am I the only one who knows how to do anything correctly?" asked Baba Yaga, lying down on the roasting pan, neatly curled and ready to fit into the oven.

"No," laughed the brave youth. "Your daughters knew as well."

He pushed Baba Yaga into the oven and ran home. He told the cat and the sparrow what he had done.

"I know how to deal with Baba Yaga," he laughed. "I am a brave youth."

The Prawn that Caused Trouble

Burma lies on the eastern side of the Bay of Bengal. It borders India, Bangladesh, China, Laos and Thailand, and is dominated by the mighty River Irrawaddy which drains south to a vast delta on the Andaman Sea.

Once, long ago, a man named Chemchongsaipa was standing on the banks of the river sharpening his weapons. A prawn, irritated by the stomping of the man's big feet as he moved around, bit him in the leg.

"That will teach him to come trampling about near me!" thought the prawn, satisfied with his actions.

The tall man could not see the small prawn, so in his anger at the stinging of the bite, he lashed out at a nearby tree and cut it.

The tree was indignant.

"Why strike me, an innocent bystander?" it complained.

The tree, intending to hit the man, dropped a piece of fruit as big as a melon from one of its branches, but it missed. The fruit landed not on the man, but on a cock which was unfortunate enough to be walking by.

The cock was not pleased, but he was afraid to attack the mighty tree so he scratched at a nest of ants.

"Everyone says you like work!" he squawked. "Well, work to fix this damage. That should please you." The ants had enough work to do already and they resented the cock's sneering.

"Because we are good workers, everybody attacks us," they complained. "How terrible it must be, to be jealous!"

Despite their attitude, the ants wanted to vent their anger, so they stung a passing snake.

"Dear me! Dear me! In the wrong place at the wrong time!" sighed the snake. "That is the story of my life!"

He opened his mouth and darted his tongue forward to sting a boar.

"Why did you do that?" asked the boar.

"For the same reason that the ants stung me," replied the snake, "because you were there."

Very few creatures care to argue with a snake. The boar hurried off and took out his fury by rooting up a plantain tree. In the plantain tree lived a bat, which was not at all pleased at having its home flung to the ground.

"Someone will pay for this," squeaked the bat, blundering about in the sunshine, until it flew into the ear of an elephant, and promptly bit it.

The elephant trumpeted with pain and kicked over a mortar, which was used for pounding rice. The mortar rolled down the hill and knocked over a house which belonged to a little old lady. She was surprisingly fierce.

"Pay me the money to rebuild my house!" shouted the little old lady.

"Why should I?" screeched the mortar. "It was the elephant who kicked me down the hill. He should pay for your house, which in any case should not have been in my way. You are lucky I do not ask you to pay me because of my bruises."

The little old lady ran up the hill and confronted the elephant.

"Pay for my house to be rebuilt," she demanded.

"Not I," snorted the elephant, shaking the bat from his ear. "Blame this bat, it is all his fault."

"My fault! My fault!" squeaked the bat. "What a travesty of justice! Can I help it if my home falls to the ground? Everyone should be rushing to my aid. If you have any complaints go to that unreliable plantain tree."

The plantain tree lay on the ground feeling very poorly.

"Blame the boar, not me," he groaned. "My roots are shrivelling up in the air and my head aches from my fall. Will you not stay to comfort me?"

"We all have our troubles!" snapped the little old lady. "And I do hate to hear people whining. Stand up for yourself or be quiet!"

She chased after the boar.

"Give me the money to rebuild my house," she said.

"Certainly not," replied the boar. "The fault lies with the snake who bit me."

The little old lady took a forked stick and pinned the snake to the ground.

"Pay for my house to be rebuilt," she said.

"Never," spat the snake. "I am completely innocent. I was harming no one until those ants stung me."

"You snakes are untrustworthy," said the little old lady. "I will keep you prisoner until I have spoken to the ants."

The ants admitted to stinging the snake, but said it was the fault of the cock, which had driven hard-working folk beyond endurance with his persecution.

"Rebuild my house," said the little old lady to the cock.

"Take your request to that tree, madam," replied the cock. "He dropped a large fruit on my head for no reason at all."

"In this correct?" snapped the little old lady to the tree.

"No reason at all!" gasped the tree, shaking with indignation. "That man slashed me with a sharp weapon. How much provocation am I supposed to endure?"

The little old lady felt quite cheerful. The man would be able to do a fine job of rebuilding her house. In any case he was her son and she was sure that he would help her.

"Rebuild my house," she said to the man.

"Very well, honoured mother," he replied, "but not before vengeance is taken on this prawn, the cause of all the trouble."

The prawn looked around him, but could see nobody else to blame. He was indeed the cause of all the commotion.

The man, the tree, the cock, the ants, the snake, the boar, the plantain tree, the bat, the elephant, the mortar and the little old lady all stared down at the prawn.

"You deserve to die," they said. "Do you wish to die in cold or hot water?"

"In cold," said the prawn and slipped away to the bottom of a pool, where it felt safe and happy.

"I fooled them!" he laughed.

He was not to enjoy the last laugh.

All the offended creatures gathered round the pool and told the elephant to suck it dry. They seized the prawn and gave it to a toad to make into soup for their dinner. The toad cooked busily and duly called the others to enjoy the feast. They began to eat, but after a while, they looked at each other.

"This is water!" they complained. "There is no taste of prawn."

"Yes, well I am sorry about that," sighed the toad, "but as I was preparing the soup, I thought I would taste the prawn, to make sure it was truly delicious and, somehow, I swallowed it. Accidents will happen."

All the other creatures were so cross that they pinched the toad all over his back and that is why toads have warts on their backs, even to this day.

The man rebuilt the home of the little old lady and replanted the plantain tree. Everyone agreed that although the soup had been a disappointment, it had nevertheless been an interesting day – for everyone except the prawn. No one asked his opinion.

A tale from Korea

The Leather Bag

The Korean peninsula extends south from the land mass of Asia. To the east lies the Sea of Japan and Japan itself, while to the west, across the Yellow Sea, is China. Korea is a mountainous country of forest and scrub with agricultural land near the coast and in the river valleys. In the early days, when this story was set, agriculture was prosperous and rich men were able to employ many servants.

Long ago, in the land of Korea, there lived an only son of rich parents. The boy loved listening to old tales and ancient fairy stories. Every evening when the boy went to bed, a servant would sit in his room and tell him another exciting legend. Many of the stories were of fierce dragons and tigers, others were about bad fairies or the ferocious fox-spirits and some were about good fairies and lovely maidens and gallant heroes.

Hanging on a hook on the boy's bedroom door, was an old leather bag which had a tight drawstring round its neck. As the servants told the stories to the boy, the spirits from the story had to go into the bag and stay there. They could come out only when the boy told the same story to someone else.

Unfortunately for the story spirits, the youngster was rather selfish. During the day, when the boy played with children of other families, they would say, "We know your servants tell wonderful stories. Please tell some of them to us."

The boy would not. He kept all the tales to himself.

As the years went by, the old leather bag, which hung on the hook on the door, became more and more crowded. The story spirits, good and bad, were squashed in together until there was hardly any room to move. They became angry, discontented and also bored.

The boy grew into a youth. Only one storyteller was left to him, a faithful old servant, who knew every ancient tale in the land. Although the boy was now almost a man, the servant still told him a new story every evening. Then, yet another story spirit had to squeeze into the leather bag, hanging on the hook on the bedroom door.

"No room! We are squashed already," shouted the spirits in the bag, but to no avail, into the crowded darkness the new story spirit had to go.

Friends still asked the youth to tell them some of the many stories he knew and still the selfish boy refused.

The youth became a man. His parents died, but he had a kind uncle to watch over his affairs. As the young man was rich, the uncle had no difficulty in arranging a good marriage for him. All the preparations were made and the day arrived, when the young man was to set out in procession for the house of his bride. The old servant, who was the storyteller, was about to enter the bridegroom's bedroom when he heard angry voices. He stopped in puzzlement because he thought the room was empty. Had thieves entered? He crept forward quietly to listen.

"He's getting married today, you know," said one voice.

"Yes," added another. "He is dressing up in grand clothes and going to a fine feast, but we are left in this crowded bag as usual."

"It isn't good enough. We have been here far too long," barked the unmistakeable sound of a fox-spirit. "Let us kill this selfish young man and when he is dead we shall be released from this bag."

"What a good idea."

"Yes, we will do that," agreed many other discontented story spirits.

The old servant carefully pushed open the bedroom door and peeped in the old leather bag, hanging on the hook. To his surprise it was bulging and moving about, as the story spirits shook their fists and talked in angry voices. The spirits of the good fairies and lovely maidens and gallant heroes said nothing. They were afraid of the other spirits.

Fortunately for the selfish young man, the old servant loved him. He stood listening quietly as the story spirits went on with their plotting.

"It is a long ride to the house of the bride," said a tiger spirit. "The young man will become hot and thirsty. The spirit of the water is a friend of mine, I shall ask him to lurk in a well at the roadside and place a handsome gourd to float on the cool water. The young man will drink, then the spirit of the water can make him ill and choke him."

"Wonderful!" laughed a fox-spirit. "If, by any chance, that should fail, I will ask my friend, the fairy of the strawberries, to sit in a field at the side of the road. If the young man passes the well without drinking, he is sure to want to eat some ripe, sweet strawberries. My friend will jump down his throat with the red berries and choke him."

The leather bag swayed as the other spirits clapped and murmured approval.

Next the squeaky voice of a bat-spirit spoke, "I know something about weddings," he said. "I know that when a bridegroom dismounts in the courtyard of the house of the bride, a bag of rice husks is placed beneath his feet so that he may descend comfortably from his steed. I will arrange for a red hot poker to be amongst the husks so that the young man is burned."

"Oh, very good!" approved all the other voices.

Then a snake spirit hissed its contribution.

"I will ask a cousin to hide under the mat in the bedroom of the bride," he said. "If everything else fails and the bridegroom joins the bride, my cousin will slip out from under the mat and bite him. That will be the end of all our problems."

"Good! Good!" laughed the voices of the story spirits.

Then there was silence and the bag became still.

The old servant was horrified. He loved his master and wished no harm to befall him, however, he knew that if he told this tale of story spirits in the leather bag on the hook on the bedroom door, no one would believe him. They would think that his mind had become unhinged.

"I must save my master by cunning," thought the servant.

174

He went to see the uncle and asked permission to lead the young man's horse on the procession to the house of the bride.

"Of course not," replied the uncle. "You are too old, the journey would be too far for you."

"Please, please," begged the old man. "I have cared for my master for so long, I should like to take him to his wedding, then I will retire in peace."

"Very well," sighed the uncle. "You may lead the horse."

The wedding procession set out with the old servant holding the bridle of his young master's mount. The horse had a splendid saddle, with tassels. The bridegroom wore magnificent clothes. There were attendants on foot. At the rear of the procession rode the uncle, also on a splendid horse which was led by a groom. Other servants carried a beautiful palanquin in which the bride would ride on the return journey.

The sun shone down and after journeying for some distance, the bridegroom grew thirsty. At that very moment he saw a cool well with a handsome gourd floating on the water.

"Fetch me a drink," he ordered the servant.

The old man gripped the horse's bridle and hurried onwards.

"Now, young master," he said, "you must not stop for a drink. You know drinking in the bright sun will make you sweat and that will never do in your fine wedding clothes."

The other attendants were amazed to hear the old servant defy his master in such a fashion, but the procession went on. Next they came to a field of strawberries.

"I am still thirsty and hungry too now," said the bridegroom. "Fetch me some strawberries."

"Now, master, you don't really want strawberries," said the old servant, hurrying ever forward. "You will only drop juice down your fine outfit. You know that your dear and lamented mother never allowed you to eat while you wore your best clothes."

The other attendants could scarcely believe their ears. They sent word back to the uncle that the mad old servant was refusing to obey his master. The uncle hurried forward.

"What is going on?" he asked. "Is it true that this servant has refused to fetch a drink of water or any strawberries?"

"Yes, yes," replied the bridegroom, "but let there be no fuss. He is a faithful old servant."

"There will be no fuss now," fumed the uncle, "but after the wedding, he will have a good beating."

So the old servant took his master safety past the first two traps set by the story spirits and in due course the procession arrived at the house of the bride. A great feast had been prepared and a large tent set up to shelter the guests. In the courtyard a sack of rice husks was placed at the side of the bridegroom's horse. As the young man dismounted the old servant snatched the sack away.

"Have you really gone mad, old friend?" asked the young man, as he missed his footing and fell over.

Again the uncle was furious and promised the servant a double beating, as soon as the marriage ceremony was over. The servant said nothing. He had saved his master from the third hazard.

The ceremony began. A cock and a hen, dressed in fine robes and tied to goblets of wine, were placed on an elegantly carved wooden table and near the table was a lovely screen embroidered with dragons for good luck. The bridegroom stood to the east of the table. The bride, dressed in embroidered clothes and attended by two maidens, walked in from the west. The bride and groom bowed to each other. The ceremony continued. Sips of wine were taken from the goblets to which the cock and hen were tied and the formalities were complete.

There was great feasting and much talking and visiting together of relatives. At last the time came for the bridegroom to retire with the bride to her chamber. Here was where the last attempt would be made by the story spirits to kill the young man. The old servant followed the procession to the bride's chamber door then, to everyone's astonishment he pushed forward, drew a sword from within his clothes, lifted the rug and chopped to pieces the snake which lay beneath.

Such fuss and commotion had never been seen in the household before. When the snake was dead the old servant sighed with relief. All the plots to kill his young master had been foiled. He told the whole story of the spirits in the leather bag. The young man believed what he heard and repented his selfishness in keeping the story spirits squashed in the bag for so long.

"From now on I will tell to others the stories I have enjoyed so much myself," he said.

In the course of time, children were born to the young man and his bride. Every evening the young man sat with them and told them stories. They thought they had the best father in the world. One by one the story spirits were released to freedom and no more grumbling nor evil plot-making was heard.

As for the old servant. He was not given a beating, but lived out his old age in a comfortable room next to the nursery.

The Deceitful Pelican

The Malay Peninsula stretches south from Thailand. To the east is the China Sea and to the west is Sumatra. People of many races came to trade and settle in Malaya, bringing their folk tales with them. The Chinese told the stories of their ancient land, the British brought adventure stories from a cold country half a world away and the Polynesians brought legends from the vast reaches of the Pacific Ocean. The peasants of Malaya sat in their villages in the half light of the jungle, listening to the animal stories which had been told by the village storytellers for as long as anyone could remember.

The river tumbled from the mountains and slid over the edge of the rocks into a deep pool. The noise and turmoil made by the falling water was endless, or so believed Ruan the fish. Ruan did as his father had done before him and as his grandfather had done before that and as his great-grandfather had done before that. Ruan could think no further back than the days of his great-grandfather. He was not clever. Few fish are. When he was not eating, Ruan lay in the cool water at the bottom of the pool and tried to look like a mottled, brown stone. His father had told him to behave so. His grandfather had told his father to behave so and his great-grandfather had told his grandfather to behave so. None of them had ever wanted to do anything different. Fish are like that.

One morning a pelican came to stand by the side of the pool. The great pouch under its large beak was empty. For days the pelican had had little luck with its hunting. It was tired and hungry. It stared down into the pool and saw Ruan the fish lying on the bottom, pretending to be a mottled, brown stone. The pelican was a solitary creature and liked to stand by itself and think. That day its thoughts were all of deceit and plotting.

The pelican tossed its head and said, "Truly the creatures of this pool live in days of dreadful danger. How I admire their courage."

At once Ruan the fish hurried up from the bottom of the pool, filled with curiosity. He forgot all the words of his father and grandfather and great-grandfather about pretending to be a mottled, brown stone. Fish have few brains.

"Dear me! Dear me! What is this talk of danger?" he flapped. "I have a young family to consider. Tell me what is wrong?"

The pelican looked down at Ruan with interest.

"You have a young family?" he asked. "Little, tender fishlings are they?"

"Oh, indeed, indeed!" agreed Ruan the fish. "I have many sweet babies. Tell me what danger threatens."

"A terrible drought has stricken the country," said the pelican. "Soon no more water will flow from the mountains. The waterfall will cease to tumble

178

and this pool will dry away to nothing. Then, I sorrow to be the one to tell you, you and your young ones will perish."

Ruan the fish was alarmed and distressed at this news. He did not stop to think that the waterfall was tumbling as strongly and as noisily as it ever had. He did not consider that, if indeed there had been a drought, the flow of water would already be slowing.

He swam in circles and wailed, "What will become of my dear children? What will become of my loving wife? What will become of me?"

"How can I ignore the cries of such a dutiful parent!" sighed the pelican. "I will help you, if you wish."

"Can you? Will you? My eternal gratitude will be yours," puffed Ruan the fish.

"I have travelled the world," said the pelican. "I know many things. I know the way to a pool, which is fed by a deep spring. In the worst drought that pool never runs dry. I will carry you and your family to this haven of safety. You can see that my beak is large and comfortable. Will you snuggle into it and make this journey?"

"Oh, indeed, indeed we will," gasped Ruan. "Truly such a friend as you is beyond price."

"I will take you first to show you the beauty of your new home," said the pelican and opening his mouth, he waited for Ruan the fish to jump in.

Eagerly Ruan flipped his tail and leaped out of the water. His head spun as he swayed to and fro in the suffocating darkness of the pelican's beak. The pelican walked a few paces round a corner of the hillside to a pool further down the same river. It could have been a journey of a hundred miles for all Ruan knew in his flurry and excitement.

FLOP! The pelican opened its mouth and let Ruan slide into the cool water.

"Wonderful!" gasped the fish, when he had recovered his senses, such as they were. "You have found a new home of exquisite beauty for me and my wife and little ones. Please have the kindness to take me back to them, that I may prepare them for the journey."

Once more the pelican opened its beak and then carried Ruan the fish the few paces to his old home.

"Hurry! Hurry! Prepare for a mighty journey," called Ruan, twisting through the water and calling his family away from where they were safely feeding. "Soon this pool will dry up. Our lives are in terrible danger, but a wonderful new friend will carry us to a beautiful new home."

His wife and young ones fell into terrible confusion at this startling news, but after a while they gathered their thoughts together and swam up to the edge of the water.

"I will go first and wait for you in the new pool," said Ruan.

"Of course! Of course!" replied his wife and children. "Be seeking out the best places for feeding. Find where the shadows fall that we may keep out of the sun."

Such excitement had never been known before.

The pelican bent down and catching Ruan in its beak, carried him to the pool around the corner of the hillside. Ruan saw the pelican no more. He sought out good places for feeding and found where the shadows fell across the new pool. He waited at the edge of the water for his family to join him, he was disappointed. No one came. He flapped anxiously from side to side, asking the fish in the new pool if they had seen any youngsters arriving. They had not, and nor had they heard talk of any drought. Ruan began to have the most terrible doubts.

Meanwhile the pelican was taking Ruan's little ones, one by one from the old pool under the waterfall. Instead of carrying them to the new pool round the corner of the hillside, the Pelican was swallowing them into its pouch.

"Who is next?" called the pelican each time it returned to the waterside.

"Me! Me! Take me next!" called the baby fish, pressing eagerly forward and showing that they were true children of their father.

When all the fish were in its pouch, the pelican turned its eyes towards the crabs, which lived in the same pool by the waterfall. He told them the same story about the drought and how the pool would soon by dry.

"Really! How very interesting!" said the oldest, biggest crab. "Bend down and tell me more."

Now crabs are quite different from fish. They can walk from the water to the land and back again. They travel the world and they see things and they learn from what they see. The oldest, biggest crab had already surmised that if the water was still pouring over the waterfall as strongly as ever it had, then the story of the drought could not be true. He had also decided that the pelican was a creature that the inhabitants of the pool could well manage without.

The pelican bent down to tell the crab about the wonderful pool fed by the ever-flowing spring to which he could carry him. Before the pelican could utter any more of his lies, the crab seized him round the throat and squeezed with his pincers until the pelican was dead. The bird's beak fell open and all the little fish and their mother swam out to safety in their old pool.

The only person to suffer any harm from the whole affair was the pelican itself. Even silly Ruan one day thought to swim out of his new pool and back up the river to his old pool. There he was reunited with his family and went back to pretending to be a mottled, brown stone.

Into the Jungle

The Malay peninsula swings southeast into the China Sea and breaks up into a necklace of islands – Sumatra, Java, Bali, Sumbawa, Sumba, Timor, Tanimbar, Kepulauan Aru and so east to New Guinea and the Pacific Ocean. In some areas the islands are densely populated, and it is from these beautiful lands that many tales of princes and princesses have originated.

Long ago there lived the beautiful Princess Scri and the handsome Prince Sedana. They were cousins and they were in love. Prince Sedana lived in the palace of his uncle, the father of Princess Scri. The young people believed that when they grew up, they would marry each other.

When Prince Sedana was approaching manhood, he was sent into the jungle, as was the custom, to dwell with a holy man. The prince was to learn the wisdom of the ancients, acquire humility and come to understand man's insignificance in the face of eternity. He was also to learn that he must accept fate.

Prince Sedana walked into the jungle and silence was his only message home. Meanwhile, news of Princess Scri's beauty spread throughout the land. Many kings wished to marry her, but no marriage was arranged because Princess Scri was waiting for her beloved Prince Sedana to return from the jungle. Princess Scri's father approved of the match with her cousin and so the happiness of the young people seemed assured.

One day, the great and warlike King Pulagra heard of the beauty of Princess Scri. At once he decided to marry her.

"I am the greatest king in the land," he roared. "I must marry the most beautiful princess."

He sent his ferocious and favourite warrior, Kalendra, to ask on his behalf, for the hand of Princess Scri in marriage. Kalendra strode into the palace of the father of Princess Scri, his sword clanking at his side and a bodyguard spreading terror at his heels.

"I am sorry," said Princess Scri's father, "but the princess is already betrothed."

"Break the betrothal," said Kalendra, in a soft voice, and with a sweet smile. So terrifying was his appearance that he did not need to raise his voice.

The king, Princess Scri's father, shook with fright as he walked to the rooms of the ladies of the court. Ashen-faced, he sat down and spoke to his wives and daughter.

"There is a madman with a sword standing in front of my throne," he gasped. "He wants Scri to marry King Pulagra."

He turned to the princess.

182

"Pulagra is a great and wealthy king, he is a good match. Consent to marry him and save all our lives."

Princess Scri hesitated.

"What is King Pulagra like?" she asked. "Is he young? Is he handsome? Is he good-natured and agreeable? Is he anything like my dear cousin, Prince Sedana?"

"He has a big army," replied her father. "That is all that need concern us."

The king knew, as did his wives, that King Pulagra was old and grey, with grown-up children. Princess Scri shook her head.

"I do not wish to marry anyone but Prince Sedana," she said. "I will wait for him to return from the jungle."

No matter how her father and his wives begged, Princess Scri would not change her mind. The king was furious.

"You have no choice," he said. "I have no choice. Even if Prince Sedana came back from the jungle he would have little chance against this warrior Kalendra, who is in our palace with a drawn sword in his hand. We cannot say no."

The king went back to Kalendra.

"The honour of the proposal has overwhelmed Princess Scri," he said. "Please rest for the night and we will speak again in the morning."

During the night, the Princess escaped from the palace and ventured into the jungle, looking for her dear Prince Sedana.

"Ungrateful girl!" quavered her father. "All I can do now is try to save those of us she has so callously left behind."

Too frightened to face the ferocious Kalendra himself, the king sent a message by his chief courtier.

"My dearest daughter, whom I willingly grant as wife to the King Pulagra, is too young to realize what is best for her," he said. "She has fled into the jungle. The paths of the jungle are many and I do not have the skill to find her. If the unchallengeable warrior Kalendra wishes to use his renowned skills to find her, he has my permission to take her back to the court of King Pulagra for the marriage to take place."

The obsequious message had its desired effect. Kalendra left the court without killing anyone or destroying anything, and he journeyed into the jungle to look for the Princess Scri. The princess had many hours start and had walked for a long, long way. She had asked for shelter at the home of a worthy old man and his wife, who grew rice for a living.

The distance was nothing to Kalendra. He strode swiftly along the trail of the princess until he came to the home of the rice farmers. He kicked the door off its hinges, strode into the middle of the room and held up his sword, letting the sunlight glint on its razor sharpness.

"Where is the princess?" he asked with his sweet smile.

The poor old farmer and his wife were loyal to their princess and denied any sight of her. They said they would not know a princess if they saw one and that in any case, the well-dressed young lady had told them quite clearly that she was not a princess. Kalendra tied the old man to one of his own jack-fruit

trees and searched the house. He did not find the princess. She had slipped out through the back door as the warrior had kicked his way in through the front.

Meanwhile, the gods in heaven were disturbed by all the noise. The great god Batara Guru sent his brother Nerada down to earth to help Princess Scri.

"Show her the way to Prince Sedana," he said.

This was done, and Princess Scri ran towards the humble hut where her cousin was living and studying. He was surprised at her arrival and amazed at her distress. When she told him her story he looked doubtful.

"Perhaps it is better that you should marry King Pulagra," he said. "Perhaps it is not fate that we should be together. How can we be sure of anything in the face of the mysteries of eternity?"

This was not the greeting the princess had expected.

"Of course we should be together," she snapped, "it was Nerada, the god himself, who guided me to your hut. Now, prepare yourself for battle because soon Kalendra, the mighty warrior, will be upon us."

Hardly had she spoken, than the door was flung back and the light came blazing into the dim hut. There stood Kalendra. He seized the princess by the arm, and told Sedana that he had the permission of the princess's father to take her to be married to King Pulagra. Drawing himself up to his full glittering height, he smiled down at Sedana.

"Everything has been done correctly," he said. "Surely you do not wish to make trouble!"

In the hut of the holy man, Prince Sedana had been taught to think wisely and to consider every man's opinion in due fairness. He hesitated for he could see no flaw in the reasoning of Kalendra. He looked at the beauty of his cousin and found the resolution to fight.

Luckily the gods in heaven were still watching. Once more Nerada was sent to earth, this time with a magic arrow which he thrust into the hands of Sedana and, with its help, Kalendra was put to flight. Only with the help of the gods could the mighty Kalendra be defeated.

Still Prince Sedana could give no comfort to his cousin.

"We have defeated that monster of violence," he said, "but what shall we do now? If we go to live with your father, King Pulagra will send his army to attack. If we seek shelter with anyone, that person will be attacked."

"We must live in the jungle on our own," replied Princess Scri. "We can grow our own food as the land is fertile."

"You mean work like farmers?" gasped Prince Sedana in dismay. "When shall I have time to learn? The mysteries of the universe have not yet been revealed to me. I must spend many more hours gazing into my inner soul before I attain peace with myself."

"The gods are with us," replied Princess Scri. "There will be time for all things."

The prince and princess cleared the land. They obtained seeds and tools from friendly farmers and built a garden and a home for themselves in the jungle. The Princess Scri remembered the old man and woman who had helped her on her flight and she sent Prince Sedana to see if they were all right. He found them in a sorrowful plight, so he invited them to live with him and the princess in their new home.

"Give your own land to your children," he said. "Come and help me grow food in our new home, far in the jungle."

The old couple went with him and they all prospered.

Meanwhile, Kalendra had recovered from the confusion wrought in him by the arrow of the gods, and he went back to King Pulagra and told him what had happened. At once the king gathered together an army and marched in search of the prince and princess. On the way, his army plundered and destroyed everything in its path, as a warning to others never to oppose the greatest king in the land.

The gods in heaven were once more disturbed.

"All that noise and dust and shouting!" groaned the great god, Batara Guru. "It is frightful!"

He glanced at some of the lesser gods.

"Go down to earth and stop this turmoil at once," he ordered, "and arrange matters so that it does not start again."

Five gods snatched up their weapons and flew to earth. They fought a mighty battle with the army of King Pulagra, defeating it. The King went back to his kingdom and did not bother his neighbours again.

Then the gods went in search of Princess Scri and Prince Sedana.

"This matter must be resolved," they ordered. "A marraige must take place."

"But whose marriage and to whom?" asked the prince. "Would it be best for the peace of the land for Princess Scri to marry King Pulagra? Is it selfish for us to wish to marry each other? Would it be unwise for the princess to marry King Pulagra when she does not love him? Would her unhappiness make him unhappy and bring fury on our peoples? Would our happy marriage, bring forth a wise son, who would be the greatest blessing to the island? Is such an idea wishful thinking?"

The gods held up their hands.

"Do you wish to marry Princess Scri?" they asked.

"I wish to marry someone exactly like her," replied the prince, "but is it the will of fate that I should marry her? Who knows?"

The gods looked at the princess.

"Do you wish to marry Prince Sedana?" they asked.

"I wish to marry someone exactly like him," replied the princess, who was beginning to think like the prince, "but whether, in the judgement of eternity I should be selfish to insist on marrying this particular man, I do not know."

"We order you to marry each other," said the gods.

The marriage took place and peace reigned over the island.

186

The Bridge of Magpies

The mighty land of China, with its ancient civilisation and thronging population, covers nine million square miles. It stretches from the Pacific Ocean in the east to the far borders of Tibet in the west. Many Chinese merchants have journeyed to spend their lives in neighbouring countries. Here is one of the stories they brought with them to Malaya, Burma, Java, Hawaii and many other countries. A similar story is also told in Japan.

The children of men who raise their eyes to look towards the heavens may sometimes be favoured with the sight of a silver river. This is the River of Stars which divides the northern skies from the southern kingdom of the heavens.

Once, long ago, the King of the Land of the Stars had a beautiful daughter. This dutiful, hard-working maiden, sat every day at her loom weaving the clouds which floated across the skies. One day a prince from a neighbouring land rode near the palace of the King of the Land of the Stars. The prince was inspecting his many horses and cattle. As he rode amongst the bellowing herds, the prince looked towards the palace and saw the princess sitting at a window, weaving. Overcome by her loveliness, the prince asked for her hand in marriage.

The King of the Land of the Stars granted the request.

"It is right that my hard-working daughter should marry a fine prince with many cattle," he said, "and my happiness is the greater because the prince is a neighbour. Though she is married, I shall still be able to visit my daughter and she may continue to weave the fleecy clouds which float through my starry kingdom."

A magnificent wedding took place and the princess went to live with the prince in his own palace. Alas for the plans of the King of the Land of the Stars! Marriage changed both the young lovers for the worse.

The princess pushed her loom aside and wove no more clouds. She ran out into the sunshine and picked pretty flowers at the river's edge. She passed the hours away with brushing her hair into different styles to please her husband. She changed her clothes three times a day. She whispered and laughed with the dressmakers, seeking to be shown the prettiest new materials. She adorned her hands and neck with jewelry.

"I have worked enough," she laughed. "Life is for enjoyment. There will be plenty of time for duty when I am old and grey."

The behaviour of the prince was equally dismaying. He left the care of his lands and cattle to his servants. He laughed and danced with the princess, and they spent their time idling amongst the flowers by the side of the river. When he was not with his wife, the prince rode out with wasteful, chattering friends. He decked himself in extravagant clothes and gambled away his money.

"Why should I forever be burdened with the cares of cattle and rents and harvests?" he said. "I must enjoy myself whilst I am in my youth and strength. Tomorrow may be too late."

The King of the Land of the Stars was disappointed and angry. He needed clouds for his heavens. He did not want his daughter and his son-in-law reduced to poverty and dependent upon him. He was old and he had forgotten what it was like to be young.

The king sent for his daughter and her husband.

"You are not good for one another," he said. "You must be separated."

He ordered his son-in-law to be banished to the north side of the River of Stars with his servants and horses and cattle. The princess was ordered to stay on the south side of the river with her father and to resume weaving the clouds of the heavens.

The princess wept and the prince pleaded, but the King of the Land of the Stars would not relent. So the lovers were parted and they spent their days in sorrow and bitterness.

At last, seeing the great unhappiness of his daughter, the King of the Land of the Stars said, "You may not be reunited with your husband, but I will allow you to go to the bank of the great River of Stars and gaze across and talk to your wastrel prince."

The princess ran down to the river and, looking across the shimmering stars, she saw her beloved husband and called to him. He stood on the far bank and stretched out his hands towards his beautiful wife, but still the lovers were apart. So great was their unhappiness that their tears fell in a flood to the earth below. Fields and houses and trees were carried away by the torrents of tears.

Finally the birds met together to decide what should be done. After much twittering and chirping, the magpies offered to fly up into the heavens and form a bridge over the River of Stars.

"If the prince and princess are reunited and cease their weeping, then the earth will be saved," they said.

All the magpies of the world gathered together into a whirling flock. They circled seven times round the tops of the trees, then flew up to the River of Stars. They gathered close together, head to tail, wings spread, and formed a swaying bridge from one side of the river to the other. The prince and all his servants and horses and cattle crossed from the north to join the princess in the southern heavens. By the time they had reached the other side, the heads of the magpies had turned black with the mud of the travellers' feet. To this day, those who look will see that the heads of magpies are black.

The prince and princess laughed with happiness. Their tears stopped

flowing and the earth was saved. However, the King of the Land of Stars did not entirely forgive them.

"The magpies have taken pity on you," he said. "They may continue to help you. On the seventh day of the seventh month of every year, the magpies may fly up to the heavens and make a bridge across the River of Stars. Then you may spend one day together. For the rest of the year you must stay apart, the princess working at her loom and the prince tending his cattle and estate."

So it has been through all the centuries since the world was young. As the seventh day of the seventh month draws near, the prince and princess move to the banks of the River of Stars. On the seventh day of the seventh month every magpie disappears from the earth and flies up to the heavens to make the bridge over which the prince may travel to visit the princess.

During the remainder of the year, whenever rains fall heavily from the skies, the old people of China look up and say, "The princess is weeping with unhappiness."

On the seventh day of the seventh month, no rain falls because the prince and princess are together.

Australasia

AUSTRALASIA

How the Dingo Came to Australia   194

The Firemakers   198

Deereeree and the Rainbow   202

The Rainbow Serpent   203

Wirreenum the Rainmaker   207

How the Sun was Made   209

The Story of Maui   212

Kahukura and the Fishing Nets   216

How the Tongans first came to Fiji   220

The Giant with Teeth of Fire   226

The Great Shark God   228

How Coconuts Came to New Guinea   231

The Voyages of Shame   236

How the Dingo Came to Australia

The Australian Aborigines have lived in that vast country for longer than 40,000 years. Their legends and customs were handed down from generation to generation as an oral tradition. Most Aboriginal legends were concerned with the natural and physical world – the origin of the sun, the making of fire and the behaviour of birds and animals. The Dreamtime was the mystical time during which the Aborigines' ancestors established their world.

Long ago, in the Dreamtime, there was an old grasshopper woman called Eelgin. She travelled with a giant devil-dingo named Gaiya. Gaiya was as big as a horse and ferocious, but he did as grasshopper woman told him. The two of them hunted people and ate them for food.

One time Eelgin, the grasshopper woman, went to live in Cape York. She made camp and built a humpy, and thought she had come to a fine place. She thought so even more when she saw the Chooku-chooku boys walking by. They were butcher-bird brothers and they were well-fed.

"You are welcome to camp here for the night, boys," called Eelgin, the grasshopper woman, thinking that when the devil-dingo returned he would be able to slay the boys for her dinner.

The butcher-bird brothers glanced round uneasily. There was something about the camp they did not like, then they saw the footprints of the giant devil-dingo.

"We will keep on our way," they replied.

As soon as they were out of sight of Eelgin, the Chooku-chooku boys took to their heels and ran away fast. They were wise to do so. Some hours later, Gaiya returned to the camp of Eelgin, the old grasshopper woman.

"Trust you not to be here when I wanted you," screeched the old woman. "Two delicious looking boys walked by, when the sun was still high in the sky. They would have made a tasty dinner for both of us, but of course, you were hunting somewhere else."

Grasshopper woman looked in contempt at the devil-dingo, which had caught nothing.

"I will set you on their trail," she said. "You catch those boys and bring them back or you will be sorry."

Grasshopper woman pointed to the tracks left hours before by the butcher-bird brothers. The giant devil-dingo sniffed along close to the ground following in rapid pursuit.

Meanwhile the Chooku-chooku boys were still running away fast. At last the sound which they dreaded came eerily through the evening air, it was the howling of Gaiya, the giant devil-dingo. The boys ran and hid, ran and hid, day after day. They were fit and strong and they had a good start, but the dingo was big and hungry. At last the boys knew, without a doubt, that they would soon be overtaken.

"Our only chance is to lie in ambush and spear him before he can attack us," said one brother, and the other agreed.

They ran on until they found a pass through the hills near Barrow Point, where the sides were rocky and covered with scrub. The boys agreed that one should hide on the right of the pass while the other lay in wait on the left. Tired and breathless, the butcher-bird boys scrambled up the hillsides. Always behind them they could hear the terrifying howling of the giant devil-dingo, but now they could also feel the vibrations of his huge paws thudding on the ground. The boys fingered their spears and waited, wondering if these moments would be their last. A lolling red shape entered the valley.

"Here he is! Spear him quickly!" shouted the younger Chooku-chooku boy.

"That is his tongue. Spearing that will not kill him," replied his brother. "Wait!"

Then a huge, hairy, brown triangle with two glowing red slots in it came rising and falling between the rocks.

"Spear him now, before it is too late," screamed the younger boy.

"No! That is his head and those slits are his eyes. Wait for a better target!" shouted the elder brother.

Then the rippling, loping shoulders of the giant devil-dingo came into sight. The elder brother started to throw his spears, first one then another pierced the furry side of the fearsome pursuer. The dingo stumbled and fell. The younger brother moved forward and speared the dingo from the other side. At last the mighty Gaiya was dead.

All the while, grasshopper woman, old Eelgin, was hobbling along on the trail of her pet, hoping for a fine dinner.

Chooku-chooku, the butcher-bird brothers, were delighted with their kill and for the moment, they forgot their exhaustion. They called to all the people of their tribe to come and cut up the giant dingo and take what they wanted to eat.

Woodbarl, the medicine man, touched the elder Chooku-chooku boy on the arm.

"The spirit of the devil-dingo lives in the tail," he warned.

The boy struck the tail from the body with one slash of his knife.

"Now go back to meet grasshopper woman," he said to the spirit. "I hear her hobbedy-hobbling along on your trail. See what she thinks of your hunting today. Tell her to send no more devil-dingos to catch the butcher-bird brothers."

The spirit of Gaiya hurried back along the trail. Eelgin the grasshopper woman saw him coming.

"Did you catch those delicious boys?" she asked.

A ferocious growl was her only reply. Then Gaiya bit Eelgin on the nose.

"You deserve that for sending me after those two boys who killed me," he snarled.

When the Dreamtime had passed away and Eelgin and her descendants became true grasshoppers, the mark of Gaiya's bite was always to be seen on their noses.

One has only to look at a grasshopper's nose to see the truth of that.

Back by the carcass of Gaiya there was much happiness and feasting. The meat was being divided correctly according to custom. The medicine man took the kidneys and the head, as was his right.

"Give me also the bones and skin," he said. "The giant devil-dingo must walk the land no more, but a good dog would be a fine thing."

The medicine man went to the top of a high mountain. He rolled the kidneys and head and bones and skin together and made a male and female dingo. He made them a small size, so that they could not threaten man, then he blew into their mouths and breathed life into them. The two new creatures stood up and howled. It was not the baying, roaring howl of Gaiya, the giant devil-dingo, the terror of the land, it was the small howl of a brave little friend, who would follow at the heels of man.

When this was done, the Chooku-chooku brothers went in search of Eelgin, the old grasshopper woman. They found her sitting by the trail, clutching her bitten nose. They sharpened their spears and they killed her. They looked at her spirit as it came out of her body and said, "You stay at Barrow Point." And she did.

Later on, when the Dreamtime ended, Chooku-chooku, the butcher-bird boys turned into real butcher-birds. Anyone can see that this is true because the beaks of butcher-birds are long and sharp, like the spears with which the Chooku-chooku boys killed the giant devil-dingo.

The Firemakers

Long ago, soon after the days of the Dreamtime, the tribes did not know how to make fire. They had to eat their food raw or dry it in the heat of the sun.

In those days, Bootoolgah, the crane, was married to Goonur, the kangaroo rat. One day, Bootoolgah sat rubbing one stick against another. To and fro he rubbed the sticks, staring into the shimmering heat and thinking of nothing. Suddenly he noticed a smell of burning and saw a whiff of smoke. coming from the sticks. He called to Goonur.

"Look! Smoke!" he said. "Would it not be wonderful if we could make fire and cook our food!"

With the help of Goonur, Bootoolgah collected dried grass and bark. He continued to rub the sticks together. At last a spark fell on the grass and caught alight. The grass burned the bark and soon a fire was blazing.

Bootoolgah and Goonur were delighted. They cooked a fish that they had caught, and ate it. It was delicious, far tastier than the raw food to which they were accustomed.

The man and wife kept the fire in firesticks which they hid in the seeds of the Bingahwinguls. One firestick they always carried with them in a pouch of kangaroo skin. They told their secret to no one for they wished to keep the fire for themselves.

Whenever Bootoolgah and Goonur caught fish, or had meat to eat, they crept away into the bush and lit a fire and cooked it. Their meals were delicious, but still they did not share their secret with the other members of their tribe. Sometimes they took left-over food back into camp to eat later, until one day, one of their tribe noticed that their fish looked quite different.

"What have you done to that fish?" he asked.

"Oh, we let it dry in the sun," was the reply.

"Sun-dried fish never looked like that," replied the man, but Bootoolgah and Goonur would give him no other answer.

Everyone started talking about the way the mysterious pair kept sneaking away whenever it was time to eat. Obviously they had a secret which they did not wish to share. Boolooral, the night owl, and Quarrian, the parrot, were ordered to follow and spy on them.

Sure enough, next time fish were caught, Bootoolgah and Goonur took their portion and went away into the scrub. Boolooral, the night owl, and Quarrian, the parrot, followed them. The bush was thick and fearing that they would lose sight of their quarry, Boolooral and Quarrian flew into a tree. They saw Bootoolgah and Goonur stop in a little clearing. Boolooral and Quarrian watched the man and wife take their firestick from the kangaroo pouch and gather grass and bark and sticks. They saw them blow on the firestick and make a great fire. When the fire sank to embers, Bootoolgah and Goonur put their fish into the heat and cooked it. It was a finer meal than the rest of the tribe had eaten.

Boolooral and Quarrian hurried back and told the rest of the tribe. Everyone wanted to eat the delicious cooked food, however, it was obvious that Bootoolgah and Goonur had no intention of sharing their secret. The tribe debated how the fire could be stolen. At last it was decided to hold a great corroboree. Everyone hoped that Bootoolgah and Goonur would become so interested in watching that they would relax their guard on the pouch containing the firestick.

All the arrangements for the corroboree were made. At the last moment, Beeargah, the hawk, was told to pretend to be ill and to lie moaning, as if he was not interested in the corroboree, while, at the same time, keeping a watchful eye on the pouch.

All things went as planned. Bootoolgah and Goonur came into camp, with the kangaroo pouch carefully carried over Goonur's arm. They sat to watch the dancing and Beeargah, the hawk, lay near them. Beeargah curled up as if in pain and did not look at the dancing, but he never took his eyes from the kangaroo pouch. Several times the pouch slipped from the arm of Goonur but each time, as Beeargah was about to seize it, Goonur noticed that the pouch was loose and picked it up again.

At last the dancers of the Bralgah came forward. They were the most exciting and the funniest of all. Goonur rocked with laughter and forgot all about the precious pouch over her arm. As she clapped her hands and rocked in time with the dancing, she let the pouch fall and Beeargah seized his chance. He snatched the pouch and cut it open with one slash of his knife, took the firestick and ran. He set fire to as many bundles of grass and bark as he could before Goonur and Bootoolgah noticed what had happened.

Suddenly Goonur missed the pouch from her side. She cried with dismay and leaped to her feet. She and Bootoolgah ran after Beeargah, but he kept ahead of them, lighting fires wherever he went. Goonur and Bootoolgah looked around them and saw fires everywhere. What was the use of chasing Beeargah? Now fire was in the hands of everyone, they gave up the pursuit and said no more. From then on all the tribe had fire and everyone ate the delicious cooked food.

Deereeree and the Rainbow

Deereeree was a widow who lived in a lonely camp with her four daughters. One day, Bibbee came and made his camp nearby. Deereeree was afraid, for she was alone with four little girls. All night long she could not sleep. She lay awake listening for sounds from the camp of Bibbee. At the slightest noise, Deereeree wailed with fear.

"Wyah, wyah, Deereeree, Deereeree," she moaned all night long.

The sound disturbed Bibbee and in the morning he went to the camp of Deereeree to ask what was wrong.

"I am afraid," said Deereeree. "I thought I heard someone walking about in the night."

"I heard no one," replied Bibbee. "There is nothing to fear."

Bibbee returned to his camp. The next night he was disturbed in the same way. From the camp of Deereeree the wails of "Wyah, wyah, Deereeree, Deereeree," came all night long.

Night after night, Deereeree lay awake listening for sounds from the camp of Bibbee. If she heard a noise of any sort, she thought that danger was threatening and she would cry, "Wyah, wyah, Deereeree, Deereeree."

Bibbee again went to see her.

"If you are afraid," he said, "marry me. Come to live in my camp and I will protect you."

Deereeree did not want to marry again and she refused. So things continued, with Deereeree lying awake shaking with fear and crying out while Bibbee was disturbed in his sleep. Many times Bibbee asked Deereeree to marry him, but always she refused.

Bibbee decided to impress Deereeree with his power so that she would be obliged to marry him. He made a beautiful rainbow which he called Euloowiree. It stretched from one side of the earth to the other, and its colours were many and beautiful to behold. It was a pathway which stretched up to the stars. Bibbee made Euloowiree, then he sat in his camp and waited.

Deereeree awoke and saw the rainbow arching all across the sky. She had never seen such a thing before and was terrified. She seized her four girls and ran to the camp of Bibbee and asked for protection.

"There is no need to be afraid," said Bibbee. "I made Euloowiree the rainbow. It is beautiful and will do no harm. Now you see how powerful I am and you must marry me. If you do not marry me, instead of making lovely rainbows, I will make things which are terrible and cruel, and you will have cause to fear."

At once Deereeree changed her mind and agreed to marry Bibbee. She lived in his camp with her four daughters and he protected them.

When Deereeree died, she was changed into a willy wagtail which cried, "Deereeree, wyah, wyah, Deereeree."

The Rainbow Serpent

Long, long ago in the Dreamtime everything was different. The land was flat, there were no rivers or lakes, there were no animals, only people. There was the earth and the sky and the sun and the rain. Sometimes, after the rain, a great rainbow arched through the heavens and its colours were beautiful.

One time, the rainbow turned into a serpent and came slithering down to earth. He alighted in the south of Australia. "I must find my own people," thought the Rainbow Serpent. "I must find the people who speak the tongue I understand and who dance the steps which please me."

Rainbow Serpent twisted and slithered across to Cape York where he made a big red mountain and called it Narabullgan. He crept close to the camp fires and listened to the talk of the tribes, but he could not understand a word and the voices were harsh in his ears.

"These cannot be my people," he thought. "I must travel further north."

Rainbow Serpent was big and heavy and his weight made a deep gorge as he wriggled along. He journeyed for many days. Every now and then he would pause and raise his head and turn his ears to the wind. He would hear laughter and chatter blowing down the breeze, but he never heard a word that he could understand. Onwards went Rainbow Serpent, grooving out streams and valleys as he struggled along. He made two more mountains, one long and hard and formed of granite, the other was riddled with caves in which men and animals were later able to live.

By this time Rainbow Serpent had reached Fairview, but still he had not found his own people. He was losing weight and the ground was becoming harder, so that the valleys he made in his passing were not so deep. On and on travelled Rainbow Serpent until, to his delight, he heard the sound of singing and he understood the words and the rhythm swayed his body with delight.

"These must be my people," he thought.

Rainbow Serpent crept closer and closer to the friendly sounds. He saw a tribe holding a Bora and dancing and singing at a fine camp site by the meeting of two rivers.

For a while Rainbow Serpent lay and watched. Then he spoke to his people.

"I am Rainbow Serpent come out of the Dreamtime," he said. "You are my people."

The tribe welcomed Rainbow Serpent and he dwelt amongst them. Then Rainbow Serpent taught his people many things. He showed them how to dance more gracefully and he taught them how to paste up their hair with beeswax. He gave them feathers to put on their heads and bones for their noses and he painted white patterns on their bodies. Everyone was happy that Rainbow Serpent had slithered down from the sky to join them.

203

Then the sky filled with clouds and a great rainstorm threatened, so the people built humpies and crawled into them to shelter from the wet. Two boys, who had been out hunting and had not built a humpy, ran into camp as the storm started.

"Give us shelter!" they called. "Give us shelter!"

No one would let the boys in to share a humpy, not even Rainbow Serpent, who was tired and snoring. The rain fell harder and harder and the boys became desperate.

"Give us shelter, someone!" they yelled. "Make room for us somehow!"

At that Rainbow Serpent opened his mouth very wide and it looked like the entrance to a warm, red humpy.

"Come in here," said Rainbow Serpent. "You may shelter with me!"

Blinded by water running into their eyes, the boys ran into the mouth of Rainbow Serpent and he swallowed them.

Rainbow Serpent fell to thinking that the tribe would guess what had happened to the boys and that the people might not like him any more. He crept away north to the only mountain in that vast flat land.

Next morning the people were surprised to see that their fine, bright friend, Rainbow Serpent, had left them. Then they asked after the two boys.

"There was no room for them in my humpy," said one, "did they take shelter in yours?"

"No," was the reply. "My humpy was filled with me and my children. I could not squeeze the boys in."

When all the tribe had been questioned, the people guessed that the two boys had been eaten by Rainbow Serpent. The men picked up their spears and set off in pursuit. Easily they followed the track of Rainbow Serpent, whose stomach was heavy with his shameful meal. They found the serpent coiled round the top of Bora-bunara mountain. The Emu man, the Turkey brothers, Possum and many others all tried to climb up the mountain, but it was too steep for them. At last two Tree Goanna brothers walked by to see what was causing all the commotion.

"Rainbow Serpent has eaten two of our boys, but we cannot climb up to rescue them," said Emu.

The two Tree Goanna brothers fingered their knives of quartz and said, "We will climb up and save them for you."

For days and nights the two men climbed the mountain. Luckily for them Rainbow Serpent was deep asleep, tired after his long journey across Australia.

Closer and closer scrambled the Tree Goanna brothers, until they were at the side of the giant serpent then, with their sharp quartz knives, they slit through his skin and released the two boys. But the boys were no longer human, they had turned into lorikeets and were now coloured in the same lovely hues as the rainbow serpent. Flapping their wings, the boys flew down over their people and then soared away, glistening in the sunshine.

The Tree Goanna brothers came down from the mountain and told the tribe that the boys were saved but they had changed, into birds. Everyone was pleased and about to journey home, when there was a terrible stirring at the top of the mountain.

A cold wind had blown into the stomach of the Rainbow Serpent who had awakened and, looking down, had seen the wound in his side and realized that the two boys had escaped. Rainbow Serpent burned with fury. What ingratitude! He had done so much for his chosen tribe and they repaid him by injuring him and robbing him of his dinner.

The mighty serpent slashed from side to side with his great tail and flashed his forked tongue in and out of his huge mouth. He broke up the one huge mountain and sent pieces of it flying all over the countryside to make the many smaller mountains which can be seen today.

All the people were terrified. Some ran swiftly away and were safe. Others were so frightened that they turned into animals and crept into holes in the ground, or they turned into birds and flew away through the sky, or they turned into insects and hid under stones. They did anything to escape the wrath of Rainbow Serpent. On and on raged Rainbow Serpent, filling the air with thunder and flying boulders, until the whole of the high mountain was flattened. Hot and exhausted, he slid into the sea, where he lives to this day.

Behind him on the land, nothing was ever the same again. Now there were hills and valleys and lakes and rivers. There were fewer people, but many animals of all sorts and shapes and they had to learn to live together. Sometimes the people looked up into the sky and saw a bright shooting star.

"That is the eye of Rainbow Serpent flung up into the heavens to watch what we are doing," they would say.

A story from the Australian Aborigines

Wirreenum the Rainmaker

Once there was a terrible drought. No rain fell and the grass withered and blew away. The animals died and the people were hungry. The young men of the Noongahburrah looked at Wirreenum the rainmaker and muttered amongst themselves.

"If Wirreenum has the power to make rain, then why does he not do so?" they asked. " The earth is dry. The grass blows away and there is no seed to grind. The kangaroo and emu are dying, while the duck and the swan have flown away. Soon we shall all die. If Wirreenum has the power to change all this, why does he not do so?"

The glances they directed towards Wirreenum the rainmaker were angry. Wirreenum noticed all this, but he said nothing. Instead, all on his own, he went down to the waterhole. Into it he put a willgo willgo or long stick. The top of the stick was ornamented with white cockatoo feathers. Next to the willgo willgo he put two big, smooth stones. Usually he kept these stones hidden in a pouch, they were magic and had to be hidden from women. Three days running Wirreenum went to the waterhole and put in a willgo willgo ornamented with white cockatoo feathers.

On the third day he said to the young men, "Cut bark and build huts. Then take ant-beds and build them a foot high and put wood for fires on top of them."

The young men did as they were told.

Then Wirreenum called the whole tribe together and took them to the waterhole. He told everyone to plunge into the water and play there until they were shivering with cold. Wirreenum plunged into the water with the others and went round to all of the young men pretending to bite a cinder from the head of each of them. When he was shivering with cold Wirreenum leaped from the water. All the other members of the tribe leaped from the water with him. They were exhausted and the young people went to sleep in the huts which Wirreenum had ordered to be built. The old people stayed awake to watch for the storm, which they knew would come.

The black clouds rolled across the sky. Thunder shook the earth and lightning flashed. Everyone was terrified. The old people and the dogs crowded into the huts with the young folk. The men said nothing, the women wailed and the dogs whimpered.

207

Then Wirreenum went out and spoke to the storm. He sang to it and told it to keep away from the camp of his people. After that the thunder and lightning drifted away. A chill breeze shivered the trees and the first rain began to fall. The rain fell in torrents and Wirreenum hurried to the waterhole and took away the long sticks and the two stones, for they had done their work. The whole country became green again and the tribe was saved. The men were so happy that they decided to hold a big corroboree to celebrate the end of the drought.

Then Wirreenum wished to show even more of his power. He told the young men to invite the rainmaker from a neighbouring tribe to join them. When the man came, Wirreenum took him and all the men to Googoorewon, which was then a dry plain. The two rainmakers worked together and with their double power managed to fill the plain with water and turn it into a huge lake. The young men were amazed, but still Wirreenum was not satisfied.

"Fish in the lake," he said.

The young men laughed. "There are no fish in rainwater," they replied. "That lake has not been made by water from rivers. There are no fish to be caught."

"Fish in the lake," insisted Wirreenum.

In order to please the rainmaker, but with no thought of success, the young men fished. They caught goodoo, murree, tucki and bunmillah.

Then indeed they admired the powers of Wirreenum and he was satisfied.

"In such times of good fortune we should hold the Bora which turns the boys into young men," said the elders of the tribe.

A great Bora was held on a ridge of the mountains, far away from the women, and the tribe rejoiced in days of plenty.

A story from the Australian Aborigines

How the Sun was Made

L ong, long ago, in the Dreamtime, before there were men on earth, there was no sun in the sky. A dim light came from the moon and the stars, and the birds and animals down on earth had to creep about as best they could.

209

One day Dineewan the emu and Brolga were on a large plain near the Murrumbidgee River. They fell to quarrelling and fighting, for what cause no one knows, but they were in a great rage with each other. Suddenly Brolga ran to the nest of Dineewan and snatched one of the huge eggs. With all her strength she flung the egg high into the sky. Up and up it soared until it was far too high to fall down again. Then it burst, and the yolk landed on a heap of firewood and set a light to it. The fire blazed red and gold, and cast light on the plain below. The animals were amazed. Their eyes were dazzled and they were pleased, for the first time they could clearly see the world about them.

Up in the sky, a good spirit noticed what benefit the great light gave to the earth below. He decided that the fire should be kindled every day to light up the world and make the lives of the animals happier. All night long the spirit in the sky and his helpers collected wood and as the next day was due to begin, the spirit was ready to light the huge fire. However, he thought it best to warn the creatures on the earth below, in case they should be frightened. The spirit sent the morning star to shine and warn everyone on earth that the sun was about to blaze forth, but very few creatures were awake to notice the morning star gleaming in the sky. Most birds and animals slept on undisturbed.

The spirit turned to Gougourhgah, the Kookaburra.

"Your loud, braying laugh should rouse the soundest sleeper," said the spirit. "Will you wake every morning, as the morning star shines, but before the sun begins to burn? Will you call with the full strength of your voice? Will you screech, 'Gou-gour-gah-gah'?"

Gougourhgah, the Kookaburra agreed. He looked at the morning star shining in the sky. He looked at the huge fire waiting to be lit. He opened his big mouth and called, "Gou-gour-gah-gah!"

Every creature on the plain near the Murrumbidgee River awoke. The great fire in the sky was kindled. At first the light was faint, then the flames grew stronger and hotter. At midday, the sun was ablaze, sending light and heat on all below. Towards the end of the day, the blaze died away, until only embers remained to make the pink and yellow glow of sunset. Then the good spirit in the sky wrapped the embers of the fire in clouds and preserved them. The next morning he used the embers to light another fire and so he has continued from that day to this.

As for the Kookaburra, he continued to call, "Gou-gour-gah-gah," before each dawn. Children were forbidden to laugh at his big mouth and his strident cry.

"If you insult Gougourhgah, the Kookaburra, he might stop calling and the sun might not shine in the sky," the mothers told their children.

If children defied their mothers and ran behind Gougourhgah shouting, "Gou-gour-gah-gah," and laughing, then an extra tooth grew above their eye teeth. The children were disfigured and lost their beauty and everyone knew that they had laughed at Gougourhgah.

The Story of Maui

The Maori people live in New Zealand. They are believed to be of Polynesian origin and to have emigrated in their large canoes across the vast Southern Oceans from Hawaii, sometime during the twelfth century.

Many years ago, near the beginning of time, soon after the earth and the sky had been forced apart and the trees had found room to grow tall and the light had found space to shine, Maui was born. He was the fifth son of a beautiful woman named Taranga, but he arrived before his time and was weak and feeble. Taranga should have killed him, but she looked into his eyes and could not harm him. Instead, she cut off her long hair, wrapped it around the baby and cast the wailing bundle into the sea.

The baby rocked in the cradle of the waves and, as its wails turned to gurgles of contentment, the God of the Ocean took pity on it and cared for it as his own. With such a protector, Maui learned the secrets of the glittering waters and became half god himself.

When he had grown into a youth, Maui said goodbye to the God of the Ocean and leaving the cold depths of the sea, walked up through the warm shallows and onto the hot sand of the beach. There he met an old man called Tama, who took the boy home to live in his hut. Tama taught Maui the ways of men and the secrets of the animals. He chanted the spells of his people to the boy and revealed the magic of his tribe.

Now learned in the ways of the sea and the land, both half god and a man of magic, Maui said, "I must go to my own people."

Bidding goodbye to the old man, Tama, Maui walked across the sand dunes and for many a further footsore mile, until he reached a clearing where smoke was rising from a long house. Amongst the people walking about was a tall beautiful woman. It was Taranga.

Maui knew her at once and walking up to her said, "Mother, here am I, your son."

Taranga looked at him and, giving no thought to the weakly baby she had cast away so many years before, said, "I have four sons and you are not one of them."

"You have five sons," replied Maui. "I am the fifth, whom you wrapped in your hair and cast into the sea. I am Maui."

Then Taranga knew that this stranger was her son. She took him into her arms and loved him with all her heart, and Maui lived once more with the family of his blood.

The years went by. Maui and all his brothers married and had children, but Maui's wife was not content. She complained that her husband was lazy and did not catch enough fish.

212

"I am a magnificent fisherman," protested Maui, "did I not learn my skills from the God of the Ocean himself?"

"So you say," replied Maui's wife, emboldened, because she had the support of Maui's brothers, "but you do not practice your skills very often. You go fishing one day and bring back a magnificent catch, but then you lie in the sun for a week, while I and the children starve."

Maui's brothers, who had been jealous of him ever since his return from the sea with his grand stories of being half a god, agreed.

"You are lazy, Maui," they jeered. "We pity your wife and children. You say you are half a god. You are certainly only half a man!"

Stung by these insults, Maui was determined to show his brothers that he was the finest fisherman who had ever stepped into a canoe. Taking the jawbone of his grandmother, he sat in solitude and secretly fashioned it into a fishing hook with the skill taught to him by the God of the Ocean, and polished it with the magic secrets chanted to him by the old man, Tama.

Maui returned to his wife.

"Tomorrow I shall go fishing with my brothers," he announced.

She nodded and yawned, having heard such promises many times before.

Maui went to his brothers.

"Tomorrow we shall go fishing together," he said. "You may seek nothing more than to catch food to fill your bellies, but I shall haul up something which will dazzle your eyes with wonder."

His brothers laughed.

"Fine words do not fill cooking pots," they said. "Ask your children if they would rather have a father who brings home food or one who wastes his breath with boasting."

They went home grinning, but Maui hid his magical fishing hook in the folds of his clothes and smiled the smile of a man who knows the secrets of the gods.

The next day, Maui went fishing with his brothers and, to their dismay, he told them to paddle far from shore.

"It is dangerous and useless to go such a long way from land," they objected. "The sea currents will carry us away and besides, the fish like the warm shallows."

"Fish? Fish? Why should I, a half god, be content with catching fish?" laughed Maui. "Paddle further from the shore. Paddle towards the deep blue sea and let us seek to behold the mysteries of the gods."

At this the brothers of Maui were terrified, but such were his powers that they could not refuse to obey him. They paddled their canoe further over the swelling waves, until land was lost to their sight.

Then Maui took from amongst the folds of his clothes the fishing hook, made from the jaw of his grandmother, fashioned with the skill of the God of the Ocean, and polished with the magic secrets of the old man, Tama. He attached it to a line and cast it over the side of the canoe. As the fishing hook sank through the water, Maui's brothers huddled together and watched with terror-filled eyes. Maui felt no fear. He knew very well what was in the

depths below, for he had walked the valleys and hills of the land beneath the sea in the days of his youth.

At first, Maui felt a slight pull on the hook, but he did not haul in the line. "That is but a carved figure on a rooftop," he smiled.

He shook the hook free and let it float further until it caught firmly in a doorway. Maui knew that the hook was caught in the doorway of the house of the son of the God of the Ocean.

"Now I will haul up my catch," smiled Maui and chanting one of the magic songs taught to him by Tama, he hauled with all his strength. He hauled with the strength of a man and with the strength of a god and with the strength of worldly magic.

There was a heaving and a swirling. Brown mud filled the water round the canoe. Patches of grass came up to float on the waves and still Maui pulled and heaved at the fishing line. The foundations of the home of the son of the God of the Ocean were so firmly fixed, that as the house came up to the surface, it dragged the bed of the sea up with it. Up came the roof, up came the house, up came the land and looking round, Maui's brothers found that their canoe was out of the water and resting on grass. Their eyes were dazzled with wonder, as Maui had said they would be.

Maui and his brothers stepped from their canoe.

"Wait here while I seek the God of the Ocean to speak with him and make my peace," said Maui.

He left his brothers staring with amazement at the lovely land on which they so unexpectedly found themselves. No sooner was Maui out of sight than the four brothers began to quarrel as to who should be king over this new land. They shouted and fought and stamped. They threw rocks and clumps of grass at each other. Soon they had broken the land into two islands. The rocks they threw became mountains. The places where their feet stamped became lakes. The tufts of grass became little islands round the shore. By the time Maui returned, his brothers had made New Zealand into the shape it is today, with its two big islands, its mountains and lakes and the small islands around the coasts. For on that sunny, far-off day, it was New Zealand that Maui pulled up from beneath the waves.

Kahukura and the Fishing Nets

Kahukura, the great war chief, awoke in the night and rose to his feet and cried, "A vision has come to me. In my sleep the mists of time were pulled aside and my eyes looked into the bright future. I saw my tribe sleek and fat and rich. I saw my tribe greater than any other. As this vision of delight glittered before my gaze and made my heart warm with happiness, a great voice called to me. Such a voice of majesty could have come from the gods alone. It told me to go north to the land of the Rangiaowhia. It told me to go alone and in secret. It told me that if I obeyed this voice of my dreams, I should bring back a great blessing for my people."

The next day the war chief Kahukura prepared to set out alone for the land of the Rangiaowhia.

"You must not do this!" cried his warriors. "In the north are our enemies. Alone you will be captured and slaughtered. What then will become of us, your followers, when our leader, the source of our wisdom, lies bleeding in the dust?"

"I will go alone, but I will also go in secret, as the great voice told me," said Kahukura. "I will pass like a shadow at midnight and my enemies will not see me. I will walk as silent as the sun on a stone and my foes will not hear me. I shall be safe and I shall bring back a blessing to my tribe."

"Indeed and indeed, oh great Kahukura," said his warriors, but still they were afraid for his safety. They watched Kahukura day and night and if he attempted to slip away to travel north, small bands of men followed in his wake. The journey, therefore, was not as the gods wished and Kahukura returned home.

Kahukura stretched his arms out to the great world of nature all around him.

"Voice of my dreams. Voice of the gods," he cried. "I will obey you. I will obey. Keep the great blessing prepared and ready to be taken by my eager hands."

Kahukura waited until a night of great feasting. He waited until the warriors of his tribe were gathered together to dance the Haka, the throbbing dance of war. He stood with his long lines of warriors, brandishing his spear and stamping his feet. Kahukura chanted the Haka in his thrilling, deep voice and his warriors chanted with him. They swayed and stamped and shouted and saw nothing but visions of victory and the smiling faces of heroes from the past. They did not see Kahukura pull his cloak of feathers about him and slip away into the darkness.

Alone and in secret, Kahukura walked north towards the land of the Rangiaowhia.

In the dimness of sleepy sunset, when his enemies were going to their beds and in the half-light of dawn, before his foes had brushed sleep from their eyes, Kahukura travelled. He went unseen and unheard and, after many days, he reached the land of the Rangiaowhia.

One evening time, he stood amongst the trees and looked out at a long, curving beach, where the sea washed high and low across the sand. He heard a rustle and a scratching and yet no creature moved on the beach. He looked at the sea and saw that it was filled with thousands of fish coming in on the flowing tide. The noise was the sound of their scales brushing against each other. Their numbers were so great that they turned the sea silver.

Were these fish to be part of the blessing for the tribe of Kahukura?

He hid amongst the leaves of a flax bush and watched and waited.

After many hours, when the head of Kahukura was nodding with sleep, he heard the sound of beautiful music. Peering between the leaves of the flax bush, the weary man saw many small canoes drawn up on the beach. Stepping from the canoes were small fair people with golden hair. Kahukura had heard many times of the golden-haired people who came from the sea, but he had never seen them.

They ran about laughing and talking together while the young maidens set out food. Kahukura noticed that two groups of the grown men were hauling in something from the sea. They pulled with bent backs and great labour. Gradually a bag filled with holes flopped up onto the beach. Water spilled out of it, but hundreds of fish remained within. Kahukura was looking at a fishing net.

This, indeed, must be the blessing which would make his tribe fat and sleek and rich. If Kahukura could take one of these wonderful things to his people, the days of catching a few fish on a line would be gone for ever. Fish could be dragged ashore in their hundreds and hunger would be no more.

Still Kahukura sat watching from the midst of the flax bush. How could he gain possession of this blessing? How would he know how to use it or how to make another when it wore out?

He watched the men shake the fish from the net onto the beach. He saw the fish caught, killed and gutted and loaded into the canoes. He saw the men spread the nets along the sand and the women clean them of weeds and sticks. He heard a laugh and a squeal. One of the maidens, with a small basket in her hands, was running away from a group of the boys who had been teasing her. Straight towards Kahukura she scrambled and hid amongst some leaves a few paces away. She smiled and panted and peered out at the boys who were searching for her in vain. Her youth and loveliness was such that Kahukura fell in love with her at once. He glanced from the girl to the fishing nets which were spread out in the moonlight. He would take them as the blessing promised by the voice in his dream.

Rising to his feet, Kahukura gave a mighty shout and all the golden-haired folk turned to look at him. At once they fell into a panic, for as Kahukura well knew, they were terrified of human folk. The lovely girl rose, thinking to run to the canoes of her people. When she saw that she was too close to

Kahukura to escape his reach, she sank down again and sat shaking with fear.

Meanwhile, her companions were running hither and thither, trying to save their catch of fish, trying to pick up their nets, trying to save themselves. Finally, as Kahukura walked boldly towards them, with his broad shoulders and rippling muscles shining in the hard, white light of the moon, the golden-haired folk boarded their canoes and paddled away.

Left on the beach amongst the fish heads and the scales was the precious fishing net, and Kahukura, looking at the beautiful, golden-haired maiden.

In her turn, the maiden stared at the fine, strong figure of the war chief, Kahukura. He was so much bolder and braver than the men of her own race that she fell in love with him at once.

Hand in hand the couple returned to the land of Kahukura and with them they took the fishing net and the girl's basket in which were the implements for making new nets and mending the old.

"Indeed I have returned with the blessing foretold in my dream," cried Kahukura to his tribe, who had missed him sorely and waited in anguish for his return.

He held up the fishing net.

"This is the blessing which will make this tribe greater than any other," he smiled. He turned to the girl at his side. "And this is the blessing which will make me happier than any other man in the land," he said.

Kahukura and the maiden lived happily together for the rest of their lives and they had many children.

How the Tongans first came to Fiji

The Fiji Islands lie in the Pacific Ocean, north of the tip of New Zealand and east of the Great Barrier Reef. The Samoan Islands are to the northeast, while the Santa Cruz and the New Hebrides islands lie in a north south chain to the west. In spite of the distances between the islands, similar folk tales and legends, obviously from a common origin, are found all over the Pacific.

There was once a fisherman from Samoa, named Lekabai, who was carried far out to sea by a sudden storm. The wind blew relentlessly and the waves raced ever onward. The spray blinded Lekabai's eyes and swamped his boat. Finally, the unfortunate man felt the familiar boards of his canoe sink away from under him, and he was left struggling in the vast sea. Suddenly, his waving hands felt the comfort of solid rock. He pulled himself on to a ledge, climbing high out of reach of the stinging spray, then he rested.

Lekabai soon found that although he had been saved from drowning, he was by no means safe. He was on a narrow, barren rock, which stretched up towards the clouds. Believing that if he climbed high enough, he might find water and food, or even people, Lekabai began clambering up the steep rock face. He drank rain water from crevices, but he found no food.

He climbed to the clouds, and through them, and still the rock stretched upwards. After several days, Lekabai fainted. When he opened his eyes he found himself lying on soft turf, in a land of gentle breezes where food grew and birds sang. Lekabai was able to eat and regain his strength, even so he was not happy. Lekabai missed his home and family in Samoa, he sat and wept.

Now the land into which Lekabai had climbed was the realm of the Sky King. No weeping was ever heard in that perfect place, so the Sky King hurried to Lekabai and asked him what was wrong.

Lekabai realized that he was talking to a god. He spoke with respect and humility and explained that perfect though this kingdom was, he, a humble Samoan, could not help feeling homesick.

The Sky King smiled on Lekabai and said, "Weep no more. I will lend you a sacred turtle on which you may ride back to your home. Sit on the back of the turtle and cover your eyes. Whatever happens, do not look at anything until you feel the turtle crawl up the beach of your island in Samoa. If you open your eyes on the journey, that will be the end of you."

Lekabai thanked the Sky King and was climbing on to the back of the huge turtle, when the Sky King added, "If you wish to thank me, give the turtle a coconut and a mat woven of coconut leaves to bring back to me here in the sky. We have no coconuts and I have heard that they are delicious. Send me one and we will grow trees. Send me a mat and we will learn to weave our own, by copying yours."

Lekabai agreed willingly. He shut his eyes and covered them with his hands. He sat on the back of the turtle as it crawled towards the edge of the rocky pinnacle on which they all stood.

The turtle leaped from the rock and fell through the air like a stone. Lekabai was terrified, but he kept his hands over his eyes, gripping the shell of the turtle with his legs. They hit the sea with a mighty crash and plunged deep beneath its surface. The sharks swam around them and brushed against Lekabai with their rough skins.

"Open your eyes," they hissed. "These are dangerous waters. Surely you should look where you are going!"

Although he was shaking with fright, Lekabai remembered the words of the Sky King and kept his hands firmly over his eyes.

Up, up through the water they rose, until they broke into the air and the light. Now dolphins plunged through the waves at their side.

"What a foolish man to cover his eyes!" they laughed. "Open your eyes and look where you are going."

Still Lekabai kept his hands over his eyes and clung to the back of the turtle with his legs.

As the strange pair neared Samoa, the sea birds flocked around them.

"Here is Lekabai returned from the dead!" they screeched. "Open your eyes Lekabai. Look where you are going or the sea will take you away again."

Still Lekabai remembered the words of the Sky King and did not open his eyes. He waited until the turtle waddled on to the hot sand, only then did Lekabai take his hands from his eyes. He looked round and saw his home and his wife and his children and he was happy.

Everyone on the island was amazed at Lekabai's return. They thought he had been drowned weeks before. A great feast was made and there was laughing and dancing for the rest of the day.

Suddenly Lekabai remembered his promise to give a coconut and a mat of coconut leaves to the turtle. He hurried back to the beach, but the turtle was nowhere to be seen. It had grown tired of waiting and had swum out to the reef to eat seaweed. Lekabai hurried to a canoe and was paddling towards the turtle, when he saw a boat full of returning fishermen stopping by the reef. They speared the turtle, thinking that they had made a fine catch to complete a good day at sea.

How Lekabai wailed and wept. "The Sky King will never forgive me!" he groaned. "We shall all be punished for this terrible deed."

Everyone on the island was frightened. They decided to bury the body of the turtle so deep that the Sky King would never know what had happened.

All the men of the island joined together and dug for five days. They put a tall palm tree into the hole so that they could climb up and down its stem with the loads of earth. On the sixth day they put the turtle in the hole together with a coconut and a mat woven of coconut leaves. Then they covered everything over and hoped that all would be forgotten.

The Sky King did know what had happened, but for some reason his anger was not great. He did not punish Lekabai or the people of the island. Instead, he sent a bird to hover over the grave of the turtle. As the last of the earth was being thrown into the hole, the bird swooped down and gently touched a boy called Lavai-pani.

Nothing more happened.

The years went by and all seemed well. Lekabai grew old and died. His children grew old and died and their children grew old and died. The strange thing was that the boy, Lavai-pani, never grew old. He never grew up. He stayed a fresh faced child for year after year after year.

Many more years passed. One day the king of the Islands of Tonga heard the legend of the turtle of the Sky King which was buried deep on an island in Samoa.

"I should like the shell of that turtle. It would make many fish hooks," he said. He looked at a group of his young men. "Go to Samoa and fetch that turtle shell," he ordered.

The young men sailed in a large canoe to Samoa, but when they arrived and explained their mission, everyone laughed.

"We all tell that old legend," smiled the Samoans, "but it is only a legend. No one knows where the turtle was buried, or if there was a turtle at all!"

Back to Tonga sailed the young men and told their king that the shell of the great turtle could not be found. The king fell into a terrible rage.

"Go back to Samoa," he said, "and return here with the shell of the great turtle. If you come back empty handed for a second time, I will kill you."

The young men fell over each other in their haste to set sail. They reached Samoa and spoke to the oldest men in the villages.

"Surely you remember where the great turtle was buried," they said.

The grey-haired old men shook their heads and laughed.

"We cannot help you. It is an old story, nothing more."

The strange young boy, who had been young for as long as memory lasted, stepped forward. It was Lavai-pani, the boy who had been touched by the bird sent by the Sky King.

"Do not be distressed, men of Tonga," he said. "I will show you where the great turtle was buried. I was there when the deed was done."

He walked to a spot along the beach and pointed.

"The turtle was buried there," he said.

The Tongans could scarcely believe Lavai-pani's story. How could a boy so young have been present at the burial of the turtle? His was the only help they had, so they started to dig. They dug all day and found nothing. All the while the Samoan villagers stood at the edge of the hole looking down at the Tongans and laughing.

"Fancy believing the words of this crazy boy," they jeered. "You will never find anything."

The Tongans dug for another day and still they found nothing. They spoke angrily to Lavai-pani. They said their very lives depended on finding the

turtle shell, and if they had to sail home without the shell and so to their deaths, they would take Lavai-pani to die with them.

Then it was the turn of Lavai-pani to laugh and the Samoans stared at the boy, for they had never heard him laugh before.

"These Tongans have already sailed twice to and from Tonga, yet they complain at a little digging," chuckled Lavai-pani. "I tell you, dig for three more days and you will find the shell of the sacred turtle. Or give up and go home. I care not."

In desperation, the Tongans carried on with their digging. On the evening of the fifth day, they found the body of the turtle, but strange to say neither the coconut nor the mat was there. Perhaps they had found their way to the Sky King after all.

Filled with joy the Tongans took the turtle shell into their canoe and hurried home. On the way, they decided that after all their exertions, they deserved to keep some of the turtle shell for themselves. When they arrived in Tonga, they gave twelve pieces of turtle shell to the king and left the thirteenth piece hidden in their canoe. The king was not to be deceived so easily.

"All the shell is not here," he raged. "Where is the thirteenth piece?

The king in his fury was terrible to behold. Not one of the young men dared to tell him that they had kept back the piece of shell. Instead, one of them spoke up and said that it had been kept by the people of Samoa.

"In that case," roared the king, "go back and get it. I tell you, I am to be feared more than the people of Samoa."

Again the unfortunate young men climbed into their canoe and sailed out into the vast ocean. They did not want to go back to Samoa again and they were afraid and tired of their bullying king, so they let the wind blow them where it would.

After many weeks they came at last to Kadavu, which was then ruled by King Rewa. He was kind to the weary young men and gave them land on which to live. They built houses and took wives and were happy. So it came about that the first people from Tonga settled in the islands of Fiji.

The Giant with Teeth of Fire

Long, long ago, in a cave high up on the side of one of the mountains of Rotuma, there lived a giant. He was not an ordinary giant, he was fearsome and terrifying to behold for his teeth burned like coals of fire. Every time he opened his mouth, heat like a furnace blasted out before him. If he drew back his huge lips in one of his frightful smiles, the glare from his burning teeth outshone the sun.

Fortunately most of the time, the giant slept in his cave, but sometimes he roused himself and strode down the mountain. He'd open his mouth and breath out streams of heat and flame. He'd grin in all directions and singe the leaves of the trees with the glare of his blazing teeth.

The villagers, who lived on the lower slopes of the mountains by the sea, ran away whenever they saw the giant approaching. They dreaded his coming. They prayed that he would sleep forever in his cave.

Some of the brave young men looked with longing at the fire which streamed from the teeth of the giant. In those days the people of Rotuma did not know how to make fire.

"If only we could steal a little fire from the giant, how pleasant life would be," thought the young men. "Our women could cook delicious meals. We could have warmth and light in the chill of the dark nights."

So the bravest and most daring of the young men of Rotuma gathered together. They took bundles of dried coconut palm leaves and crept cautiously up the side of the mountain towards the cave of the giant. Outside the cave they stood and listened. There was no sound. Feeling very brave they crept into the cave.

There lay the giant sound asleep and breathing deeply. With every outward breath his huge, thick lips parted, letting out a glow of light from his burning teeth. With every puff of breath, tongues of flame bubbled out into the cave, only to be sucked back into that enormous mouth.

The brave young men crept forward, using the light from the giant's teeth to see the stones on the cave floor. They did not want to stumble or make a noise.

Closer and closer they crept. At last the young men were able to hold out the bundles of dried leaves so that the little flames dancing round the giant's mouth, reached them and set them alight. The young men then turned and ran down the mountain side.

They were not to escape so easily. In his excitement, one of the young men had let his hand quiver. The leaves had tickled the lips of the giant who stirred, and blinking his eyes caught sight of the light from the burning leaves, flickering away down the mountain side.

The giant rose to his feet in a rage.

"Who dares to steal my fire?" he roared and long flames darted from his burning teeth. "No one on this island but ME may have fire."

He shook himself and rubbing the sleep from his eyes, stamped down the mountain side after the brave young men.

Luckily the young men were slim and swift. Holding the precious burning coconut leaves, they ran into the cave where they lived and rolled a huge boulder across the entrance. Then the young men lit a wood fire from the burning leaves. At last they could eat cooked food and keep warm.

Meanwhile the giant stood outside the cave. He pushed at the rock. He stamped. He shouted. The rock did not move. The giant breathed fire over the rock, but it stayed in one piece.

Then the giant had an idea. He bent close to the rock and called in a sweet voice, "Let us be friends. Pull the rock aside so that I may sing to you."

The young men did not believe for a moment that the giant desired to be friends, but they did not wish to stay in their cave forever.

"Let us humour him and perhaps he will go away," they said.

The brave young men moved the rock, making a small gap at the entrance to their cave. At once the giant tried to push in his head, but it did not fit.

"That is not wide enough," he said. "You will never hear my lovely song through that narrow hole. Push the boulder further aside."

By this time the brave young man had thought of a plan.

"Very well," they called. They pushed the rock to one side so that the giant could easily thrust his head into the cave.

The giant drew in a deep breath and thrust his head forward, ready to open his mouth and breath out flames and heat from his burning teeth.

"Soon there will be nothing left of these impudent young men, but cinders," he thought.

But he was wrong.

The moment the giant's head was through the gap, the young men rolled the rock forward, crushing the giant's head flat. The giant was dead. His flaming teeth spluttered and grew cold and dark. The young men ran from the cave shouting and calling the people from all the villages around.

"We have killed the giant!" they laughed. "His teeth no longer burn with fire, but the fire is not lost. We have it. Now life will be pleasant for us all."

The brave and generous young men shared the flames with everyone on the island. Soon a fire blazed in every hut and the lovely smell of cooking yams and fish filled the air. Perhaps best of all, the islanders no longer lived in fear of the giant with teeth of fire.

The Great Shark God

The swelling waves of the Pacific Ocean heaved and rolled from island to island. Everything important in the world seemed to be above this bright, blue sea. Yet beneath the surface of this great ocean there lay another world. This was the realm ruled by the sharks.

The great god of the sharks was called Dakuwaqa. He was big and quarrelsome, a brawling fighter, always looking for trouble and usually finding it.

In those days, when the world was young, each island had its guardian. The guardian was usually a shark which lived beside the reef entrance to the island that was its home. Only friends and those willing to bow before the guardian and pay tribute were allowed to enter.

Dakuwaqa liked to think he was the greatest of the guardians. Many was the fight he had with other guardian sharks. He always won. Often the struggle was bitter and the thrashing bodies of the huge creatures sent tidal waves washing over the beaches and up the rivers of the islands, drowning many people and flooding their homes.

Dakuwaqa did not care. All he thought of was fighting and winning, and making all the other guardian sharks pay tribute to him. He was the god of the sharks and that was the way things were going to stay.

One day Dakuwaqa was swimming towards Beqa when he met an old friend called Masilaca. Masilaca was also a shark god, although not as powerful as Dakuwaqa, but he was a mischief maker. "I hear you have recently won a great fight at Lomaiviti," Masilaca greeted his friend.

"I did indeed," he agreed. "A fine monster they had living there. He thought he could challenge me. ME! What stupidity! He will be making no more challenges, I can tell you!"

"I am sure he will not," smiled Masilaca. "Truly you are a wonderful fighter, Dakuwaqa." After a pause, he added, "I notice you never swim to Kadavu Island. Of course it cannot be that you are frightened, not YOU! Perhaps in your wisdom, you are being cautious. After all, you have always won all your fights. Why go to an island where you might lose? Why risk your reputation? You are quite right to visit only islands where you are sure of finding guardians whom you can beat. Surely your wisdom equals your courage, oh mighty Dakuwaqa!"

Dakuwaqa lashed his tail in fury. "Do you dare say that I am afraid to swim to Kadavu Island," he bellowed. "I have not been there because I thought there was nothing there worth visiting. What is at Kadavu Island?"

Masilaca circled round, well out of the reach of Dakuwaqa. "They say that a mighty monster guards the land so that no one dares to go ashore," he called, "and they also say that the guardian of the reef is a creature such as has never been seen before. No one knows how to fight it. Everyone is frightened.

228

People are whispering that you are too. I said that you were frightened of nothing, but people ask, 'why does he not swim to Kadavu Island then?'"

Long before Masilaca had finished speaking, Dakuwaqa had beat his mighty tail from side to side and slid through the sea towards Kadavu. He could not bear that any creature in the sea could be thought mightier than he.

As Dakuwaqa neared the island, he heard a low throbbing voice calling to him from the shore. For the first time in his life, Dakuwaqa felt a cold shiver run down his back. It was fear. He swam on. The voice was strange and disturbing, and it came from the land. Nothing on the land could hurt Dakuwaqa, a god of the sea.

The voice called again, "I am Tui Vesi, the guardian of the Vesi tree. I know you have come to challenge the power of the gods of this island. How I long to fight you, but I cannot leave the land and you cannot rise out of the sea. Go my friend. Swim to the gap in the reef and there you will find a monster, such as you have never met before. He will fight on my behalf. He will teach you not to come to Kadavu Island with eyes bright with insolence."

By this time, Dakuwaqa was in a fury. He roared through the water towards the gap where the ocean boiled in and out through the razor sharp gap in the reef. His eyes darted to and fro, looking for the big shark which he expected to see. He saw nothing.

Dakuwaqa swam on. The next moment he was gasping and struggling as an arm lashed out from a cave and wrapped itself round his body. Another arm curled round his tail, stopping Dakuwaqa from moving. A third arm twined round the shark god's head, holding his jaws together, so that he could not bite. The guardian of Kadavu Island was a giant octopus and it held Dakuwaqa helpless in its grip.

Dakuwaqa had met his match at last. Tighter and tighter squeezed the arms of the mighty octopus. The strength left the body of Dakuwaqa. He was about to die. Though his teeth were clenched together by the pressure of the arms of the octopus, Dakuwaqa managed to squeeze out a few words. For the first time in his bullying life, he begged for mercy.

"Will you pay tribute to me?" asked the octopus.

"Yes," gasped Dakuwaqa.

"Will you pay tribute to my master Tui Vesi, the guardian of the Vesi tree?"

"Yes," groaned Dakuwaqa.

"Will you promise never to attack the fishermen of Kadavu Island and to guard them wherever they go?" asked the octopus.

"Yes," moaned Dakuwaqa, thinking his last moment had come.

"Then you may go free," said the octopus, releasing the god of the sharks to roll weakly to the sand on the ocean bed.

At last Dakuwaqa regained his strength and once more swam the waters of the Pacific. The other sharks were still afraid of him, but Dakuwaqa kept his promise to the guardian of Kadavu. So it is to this day, that while the men of other islands roam the sea, fearful of the dreadful sharks, the men of Kadavu ride happily in their canoes. They know that Dakuwaqa is protecting them and that no shark will dare to attack.

230

How Coconuts Came to New Guinea

All over the islands of New Guinea, there is a story – that the coconut tree first grew from a human head. Who owned the head and why the head was buried in strange circumstances, varies with each tale, but the linking of the growth of a coconut tree with a buried body, usually on the beach, remains the same. It is interesting that the story of the origin of Palm Beach in the United States of America is similar. In that story a Spanish ship, loaded with coconuts, was supposed to have been wrecked offshore in a storm. The coconuts were washed ashore, grew and so made Palm Beach.

Long ago, so people say, there were no coconuts on the island of Salimum. People ate taros and yams and bananas and tapioca and they caught fish, but they ate no coconuts.

Now, there was one man who worked diligently at fishing, but who did not like gardening. He fished from dawn till dusk and caught a fine haul, but he would not bend his back to plant and hoe and weed. This man had the habit of hawking his fish from hut to hut asking the other islanders to exchange vegetables and fruit for his fish. Being kind, his neighbours would give the fisherman some of their yams or bananas or a portion of tapioca, but eventually they grew impatient with his requests.

"We can catch all the fish we want for ourselves," they said. "Fish are plentiful. We work hard to grow food in our gardens, why should we give it to this lazy man, we do not need his fish. If he cannot bother to tend a garden, let him eat fish and fish only. If he grows bored with fish, that is his problem, not ours."

All the neighbours agreed that they would refuse to exchange any more fruit and vegetables for fish. The evening of the next day, the strange fisherman returned at sunset, much later than the other men because he had fished long hours in order to catch enough fish to exchange for other food. He was tired and scorched by the sun, which shone mercilessly down on the little fishing boats. Wearily the man went to a hut where a fire was lit and the delicious smell of cooking food filled the air. To his amazement he was ordered away, his fish were scorned and he was given no tasty vegetables. He went to the next hut and the next, but everywhere his treatment was the same. No one would take his fish and no one would give him vegetables or fruit.

If the man had been wise, he would have gone home to rest. Instead he took a bamboo stick and kindled it for a light. He was sick of fish, which he had been handling all day, and was longing for the taste of vegetables. By the light of the fire stick, the man searched for wild yams. They were not as

plump as the yams grown in the gardens, but they were better than nothing. He walked through the darkness away from the village and at last he found the food he sought. He blew up the fire to make a better light, then he tied the bamboo torch to his back and with his hands free, he bent over to dig.

Alas! So weary and hungry was the fisherman that he did not notice when the fire caught his hair and the flames spread to his clothes. He fell forward into the hole he was digging and there he died. The next day the man's neighbours found his body. They covered it over where it lay, for the man had no relatives who wished to mourn his death, and within a month the man was forgotten. He had been a nuisance and in their hearts, the islanders were glad to be rid of him.

To everyone's surprise, a strange plant started to grow up out of the grave of the fisherman.

"Perhaps the plant is magical. Perhaps it is sent by the spirits," said the beholders.

The plant was watered and tended. It grew tall and developed a thick trunk. After a while it bore green fruit which turned brown and fell to the ground. When the islanders cut it open, they found that it had a mouth and eyes, like a human face. Then they were sure that it had grown from the head of the strange fisherman. The fruit was a coconut.

On a neighbouring island, things were rather different. Here there was no strange fisherman. Instead there was a beautiful maiden named Ina, who loved to swim in a rock pool near her home.

One day, as the lovely Ina was bathing in the pool, she felt something brush against her leg. It was an enormous eel. The girl was terrified and scrambled out of the water and turning to look back into the depths, she saw the eel curled up at the bottom of the pool.

The next day, when Ina went to the pool, she could see neither quiver nor shimmer of the eel and as the day was hot, the girl slid into the cool water. At once she saw the enormous eel circling her as she swam. It looked at her with big gentle eyes and all her fear left her. Ina continued to swim and the eel did her no harm as they played together in the pool. For weeks the two unusual companions swam and circled together in the water. One day, when Ina was sitting on the rocks drying her hair, the eel climbed out beside her and, to the girl's amazement, it turned into a tall young man.

"I am Tuna, the god of the eels," he said. "It is my duty to swim in the streams and protect my subjects, but when I saw how beautiful you were as you swam in the pool, I left them. Now I can think only of you."

Tuna and Ina were married and lived happily together. While Tuna was with Ina, he had the appearance of a handsome young man. When she left him to work in her garden or visit her friends, he resumed the shape of an eel and swam in the pools and streams.

One day, Tuna slithered from the pool and stood in his human form before Ina.

"The gods are angry with me," he said. "They say I am neglecting my duty

234

and I may not stay with you. A flood is being sent as a punishment for our wickedness and there is only one way I can save you. Promise that you will do exactly as I tell you."

Ina was heartbroken that she was to be parted from her beloved, however, she had little choice but to obey him.

"The flood will surround your home," said Tuna. "The water will lap at your door, then an eel will swim up from the water and lay its head upon your threshold. You must cut off its head and bury the head near your house. You will be saved and you will also receive a parting gift of great value from me."

Tearfully Ina agreed, without realizing what a gruesome deed she was to perform. Tuna said goodbye and swam away through the shifting waters. Rain fell heavily all the night through and floods ran down from the hills. The next day Ina's house was surrounded by rising waters and she feared for her life, until she saw a rippling near her door. An eel lay its head on the threshold. With a quick blow from an axe, Ina severed the head, only to see it turn immediately into the head of Tuna. She screamed with horror, but still she was brave enough to do as her dear husband had asked. She looked around her and already the waters were receding, so the weeping girl buried the head near her hut.

A few weeks later, to her surprise a strange plant grew from the very spot where she had buried the head. Wondering if this might be the gift about which Tuna had spoken, Ina tended the new growth with all her love. The shoot grew into a tree. The tree sprouted leaves, then it bore fruit which ripened and fell to the ground. When Ina broke away the brown husk, she saw two eyes and a mouth looking at her from the fruit beneath. It seemed that Tuna was staring at her. Ina knew that this new fruit, which she called coconut, was the gift which Tuna had promised her. The food from the coconut has been a blessing to the islands ever since.

A third story tells of a boy who was exploring an uninhabited island with some companions. As evening approached, the other boys went home, but the first boy was too busy catching birds to hear their calls. When he finally went back to the beach, he found that his companions and the canoe had gone. Fearful of being alone on the island during the night, the boy rolled a tree-trunk into the water and tried to paddle his way home. Inevitably a shark found him. Fortunately the boy had with him the birds he had caught. One after the other the boy threw the birds to the shark and each time the shark ate the bird – and then returned.

Finally, the shark pulled at the boy himself. The great jaws snapped and only the boy's head was left to drift to his home shore where it was found and, with much sorrow, buried near the home of his grieving parents. After a while a tree began to sprout from the grave. It grew tall. Such a tree had never been seen on the island before. In due time the tree bore fruit. On the side of the fruit were eyes and a mouth and everyone knew that the coconut tree had grown from the head of the unlucky boy.

The Voyages of Shame

L ong ago on the island of Manihiki, there lived a skilled sailor named Here. Here was married to Muhu, a lovely and worthy woman, who had several brothers.

It was the custom of the people of Manihiki to live on their island while the food lasted. When the crops were gathered and eaten, the people would climb into their boats and sail to the island of Rakahanga, to eat the food which was growing there. When the food on Rakahanga was eaten, the people would return to Manihiki. Before they left either Rakahanga or Manihiki, the people would plant food which would grow during their absence.

So it had been for as long as anyone could remember.

The journey from Manihiki to Rakahanga was not easy. It had to be undertaken in the customary way if misfortune was to be avoided. The big double canoes had to be prepared and lashed together. No single canoes were permitted to make the voyage. The sails of the canoes had to be handwoven mats, strong and new. Ahead of the main fleet sailed the official canoes with the skilled sailors, the most important families and the wise men. This official party would lead the way over the long, rolling waves. They would land first on Rakahanga to inspect the sacred grounds and do everything that must be done to make the great gods happy. Then the wise men would declare Rakahanga safe and allow the rest of the people to land.

In spite of all these precautions, some canoes were always lost on the voyage. The vast sea was a dangerous place.

Here was a proud and ambitious man. He smiled at the important people and pushed himself forward until he was included in the official party which sailed first from Manihiki to Rakahanga. In truth he deserved to be amongst the important folk. He was a fine sailor. He could stand in a swaying canoe and feel the direction of the long regular swell which always came from the same direction. Then, still standing, sometimes with his eyes closed, he could feel the change in the rhythm of movement, which meant that the canoe was down-sea from an island that had broken the movement of the swell. He knew that birds flew out from islands to feed in the daytime and flew back to roost in the evening. He also knew that as evening fell, a canoe which followed the flight of the birds, though it was for many hours, would find an island on which to land.

Here was a useful man and indeed, deserved to travel with the important official party, but he did not take his wife with him in this honoured group.

"You have many brothers," he said to his wife. "Travel with them in their canoes." He did not want his wife bothering him while he was talking with important people.

236

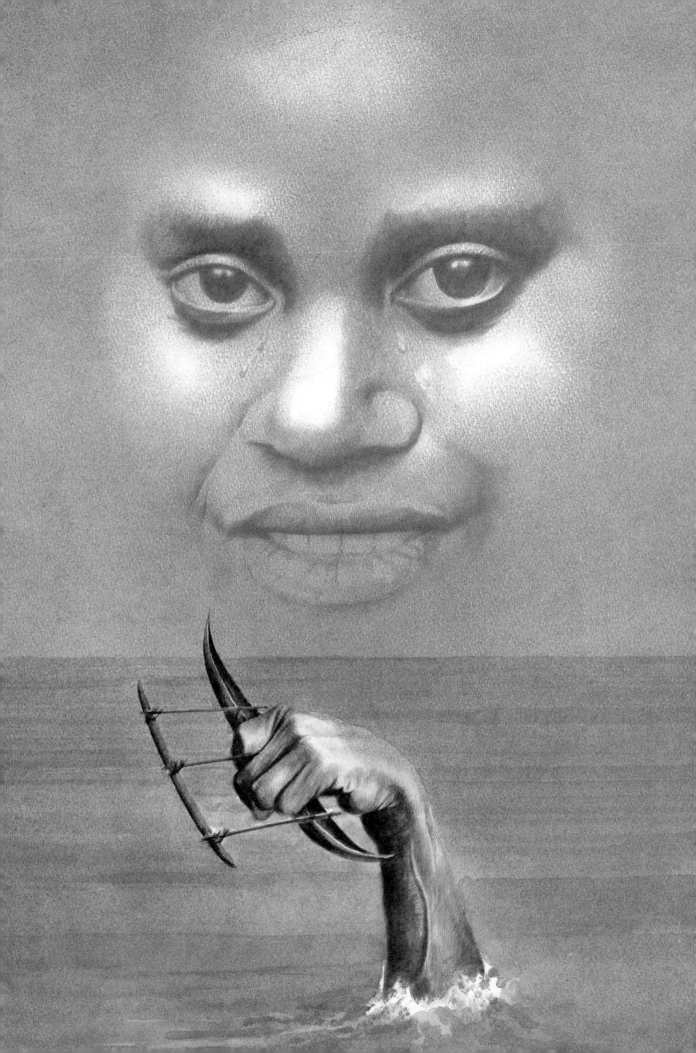

So on the first voyage after their marriage, Muhu stayed behind and travelled with her brothers. Here landed first on Rakahanga and visited the sacred grounds with the wise men, and took part in all the grand ceremonies. When they were over he went to the beach and waited for Muhu to arrive.

"Come along. Come along," he called, as she scrambled ashore. "Go to our house. There is work to be done."

Muhu went with her husband, but she felt ashamed that she had been left behind with her brothers, like a woman without a husband.

The same thing happened on the return journey. Here did not ask his wife to accompany him in the official canoes, as he could not be bothered with her. She travelled in shame with her brothers, a neglected wife.

For several seasons Muhu tried her best to please her husband, hoping that he would appreciate her merit and ask to include her with the great and the good in the official party. He did not.

As one voyage from Rakahanga to Manihiki was drawing to its close and Muhu and her brothers were within sight of shore, Muhu said to her brothers, "Untie my canoe from yours. From this short distance you can paddle safely to the island in one canoe. I would like to travel further on my own."

Her brothers knew that Muhu could bear the shame no longer. She wished to paddle into the vast ocean and end her life away from slights and jeers. Once a small canoe was caught by an ocean current, no one could ever paddle it back to the island. The brothers tried to dissuade their sister from such a course, but she had endured the shame of neglect for too long. She was certain that Here would never treat her with respect.

So the brothers unlashed the canoe. They reached Manihiki, but Muhu was carried on by the long swelling waves.

Here was waiting out on the reef.

"Where is Muhu?" he asked in surprise, at the sight of the single canoe.

The brothers were so distressed with grief and so angry at Here, that they could not reply. They turned their faces away and paddled to shore.

"Where is Muhu?" shouted Here, scrambling along the reef.

At last one of the brothers called, "Turn your eyes to where the sea meets the sky. There you will see Muhu."

Here looked out to sea and saw the lone canoe drifting swiftly away on the strong current. He flung himself into the sea and tried to swim after his wife, that he might bring her back to the island. He did not succeed. Hours later, he struggled exhausted onto the reef.

The other islanders stared at him in silence. Everyone blamed him for the death of a good woman.

Here wailed and moaned. He slashed his skin with coral to show his regret. Still no one spoke to him. He had treated his wife badly and this fate had come through his own fault.

So Here lived on alone, for no other woman would ever marry him.

238

The Americas

THE AMERICAS

The Crow and the Daylight   242

Paul Bunyan   246

Nanook, the White Bear   251

The Medicine Wolf   254

Pilotte – The Dog that saved a settlement   257

The Moon in the Millpond   260

Napi and the Buffalo-Stealer   264

The Legend of Johnny Appleseed   267

The Fate of Napoleon   272

The Earth Giants   276

The Jungle Spirits   280

The Great Flood   282

The Sun and the Moon   283

The Crow and the Daylight

This is a story told by the Inuit, or Eskimo, of Northern Canada. In those far northern lands of ice and snow, for half of the year the sun does not rise above the horizon and darkness covers the land. For the remaining months the sun does not sink and there is continuous daylight.

Many, many years ago, when the world began, there was no daylight in the lands where the Inuit lived. Day and night did not exist. The people lived as best they could by the glimmers of light from their seal-oil lamps. They did not know when they should get up, nor when they should go to bed. There was much trouble and quarrelling, as half the folk tried to sleep, while the other half were up and noisily going about their work.

At that time, living in one of the villages, was a very wise crow. He had learned to talk and was much respected by all the people. Sometimes, as the Inuit gathered together by the light of their tiny lamps, the crow would tell them stories of the wonders he had seen when he had flown on journeys to other lands. One evening he mentioned seeing a wonderful thing called daylight.

"What is daylight?" asked the Inuit.

"Where there is daylight," replied the crow, "folk can see all around them. They can see the whole countryside and animals approaching from afar."

The Inuit thought that daylight sounded a most desirable thing.

"How much easier hunting would be!" they said. "How much safer we could keep ourselves from the fearsome polar bears, if only we had daylight here in our land."

They gathered round the crow and begged him to fetch some daylight for them. At first the crow refused.

"It is a long flight to the land of daylight," he objected, "and if I reached there safely, no one would give me any."

The Inuit begged and beseeched and at last the crow felt so sorry for them, living in darkness as they did, that he agreed to go. After a rest and a meal, he flew up into the black sky and turned towards the east because daylight comes from the eastern lands.

After travelling for many days, the crow saw a dim light above the horizon. He flew further until he could see the ground beneath him. He flew but a few hours more and the sky was flooded with light. Thankfully, the exhausted crow settled on the branch of a tree to rest. Looking around him, he saw that he was near a village. In the centre of the village was a large snowhouse. This was the home of the village chief and from this house shone the daylight.

242

As the crow sat staring about him, he saw the beautiful daughter of the chief leave the large snowhouse and walk to the river to fetch water. The river was frozen over, but there was a hole in the ice through which the girl could haul water with a bucket made from seal skin. At once the crow slipped from the branch of the tree and crept to the doorway of the large snowhouse. He shook off his skin and turned himself into a tiny speck of dust, dancing in a beam of light. As the chief's daughter walked back with her burden of water, the speck of dust settled on her dress and went with her into the house which contained the daylight.

Inside the house was bright and warm. The chief sat watching a pretty baby crawling and playing on a rug made from the skin of a polar bear. The baby had toy dogs and foxes and walrus and boats (called kayaks), all carved from walrus ivory. He amused himself by putting the toys into an ivory box and then tipping them out over the curly hair of the rug.

When she had set down the water, the chief's daughter picked up the baby and as she did so, the speck of dust, which was the crow, drifted from the girl's dress into the baby's ear. The baby began to cry and the chief, who loved the child dearly, at once asked what was wrong.

"Ask to be given some daylight to play with," whispered the speck of dust in the baby's ear.

The baby asked for the daylight and the smiling chief told his daughter to untie the rawhide string, which secured his leather hunting bag, and take out the carved box which she would find within. The girl did so and for a few moments she and the baby were amused by looking at the pictures on the box, which told of all the brave things that the chief had done. Once again the baby began to cry for some daylight. The baby was the favourite of the chief and he could refuse it nothing. He told the girl to open the box and give the baby one of the shining balls, that were kept within.

The girl did so and for a long time the baby played on the polar bear rug with the glittering, shining ball. Once more the speck of dust whispered in the baby's ear.

"Ask for some string to tie around the ball," it said.

The baby did so and the string was given to it at once. The baby played happily, dangling the bright ball with the string. Then the chief and his daughter stepped outside their house, leaving the door open, so that the baby could call to them if it wished. This was the chance the crow had been seeking.

"Play near the doorway," the crow whispered to the baby.

The baby did so.

"Creep out into the air," whispered the crow. "Take the daylight with you and swing it in the breeze."

Again the baby did as it was told. As they passed the place where it had left its skin, the speck of dust, which was the crow, jumped from the baby's ear into the skin and was itself again. The crow snatched the string from the baby's hand and carried the string and the ball of daylight high into the sky and away to the west towards the land of the Inuit.

The baby screamed and cried at the loss of its pretty toy. The chief and his daughter came running. The whole village turned out and all the hunters tried to bring the crow down with their arrows, but they could not reach him.

Westward and ever westward flew the crow. He left the great light behind him, but the daylight from the swinging ball lit the ground below him. As he came to the land of the Inuit, the crow broke off a tiny piece of daylight and left it behind in each village. When he came to the village of the people, who were his friends, he dropped the ball so that it shattered and sent light shining into every house.

The people were delighted and crowded around the crow to thank him.

"If I had brought back the big daylight, there would never have been darkness here again," he explained. "There would have been light day and night, winter and summer, but the big daylight was too heavy for me to carry. This small ball of light will give you daylight for half of the year and darkness will return for the other half."

"That is wonderful," smiled the Inuit.

Since that day the Inuit have been true friends to the crow and never sought to kill him.

244

Paul Bunyan

In the eyes of history, the United States of America is a young country. It is a land freshly hewn from the wilderness by determined men eager to build a new nation. Paul Bunyan was one of those men.

The big forest was no place for small men. If roads were to reach into the wilderness, those trees had to be felled. If houses were to be built to shelter the new settlers, those trees had to be felled. If railroads were to join the East Coast to the West, those trees had to be felled. But those trees had hides tougher than buffalo and when they fell, the earth shook. It took a special breed of men to topple those giants of the forest.

If men were tall in Texas, they had to be tough in timber country.

Legend tells us that the toughest, strongest lumberjack who ever lifted an axe, was Paul Bunyan. Paul was remarkable from the day he was born. He was a big, strong, bonny baby and his folks were proud of him. Of course he was a mite of trouble. He was too big for the cradle which had fitted the other babies and his Pa had to set to and build a new one, and that was only the start. When Paul grew big enough to laugh and clap his hands, the vibration broke every pane of glass in the house. In the end Paul's Pa grew a-weary of replacing the glass and left the window frames empty for the breeze to blow in and out as it liked.

However, that was nothing to what happened when young Paul was big enough to run round the neighbourhood. Every time he sneezed or coughed, he blew the roofs off the neighbours' houses. After it had happened three or four times, some of the folks went to Paul's Pa and complained. Mighty mean, some people are!

Then, when Paul had grown into quite a lad, he decided it was time to learn to swim. He went down to the sea and jumped in, he made a splash so big that a tidal wave flooded the land for miles around.

"Pa!" said Paul's Mom. "If we don't watch out, that boy of ours will soon be getting difficult!"

Next spring, when the loggers went up into the forests, Paul's Pa, who was a logger, took Paul with him. Paul was taught which trees to fell for building houses, which trees were best for laying railroads and which trees were best for furniture-making. He was taught how to fell a tree, where to fell a tree, at what age to fell a tree and where to sell a tree. Paul's Pa was a good teacher and Paul was a good learner.

By the end of that first summer there was nothing about trees that Paul did not know. The next summer he set up a camp of his own. Paul swung his axe and felled trees, until the axe became red hot. Folks gathered round and warmed their hands at it. Paul Bunyan's name and fame spread all through the forest. Other tough lumberjacks came to join him, they wanted to see if they could outchop the famous Paul, but no one ever could. Paul was such a fine fellow and such a fair boss that all the good loggers stayed with him. His camp became the most successful in the forest and his men lived in the warmest cabins and ate the best food and made the most money. Paul was smart as well as tough.

Of course Paul did have his strange ways. Most loggers had a dog for a pet, if they had a pet. Not Paul. Paul Bunyan's pet was a blue ox!

One winter, so the story goes, some mighty strange snow fell over the forest. The snow was blue. Some folks said the blue of the sky had stuck to it as it came down. Others laughed and said the blue was the minerals washing up out of the rivers. Whichever way it was, as he was walking past a big blue snowdrift, Paul Bunyan saw a baby ox calf lost and half frozen. He picked him up and carried him home. No one knew if the little creature was blue from the snow or blue from the cold, but blue he was and blue he stayed for the rest of his life. Paul called him Babe and made him his pet. Babe was like his master. He was big. First he drank eighteen pints of milk a day. Soon he was drinking eighteen gallons. After that folk stopped counting. Babe grew well. To begin with he lived in the dog kennel. Then he moved to the wood shed. Next he had to find bigger quarters in the barn – and that was all on his first day!

Babe was happy in the barn for some time. Then one morning, Paul looked out of his bedroom window and saw that his barn had gone. He ran outdoors and looked across the fields. Feeding in one field was a huge blue ox. It was Babe.

"Babe is thriving well. I have a fine animal there!" smiled Paul. "But what is that strange sort of wooden saddle he seems to have on his back?"

He looked again and saw that the saddle was his barn. Babe had grown so big, he had walked away with the barn on his back.

After that Babe was taken to live at the logging camp. Worth his weight in gold he was. With his huge strength, the mighty animal dragged cut timber to the river and moved huts from one part of the mountain to the other.

Then one summer, Paul Bunyan had a real problem. There was a fine stand of special trees needed felling for a rich customer who would pay a top price. Cutting the trees was easy for Paul, but getting them down to the river was difficult. One twisty road ran from the mountain side to the valley. It was clear to everyone that those tall, fine trees would never get round the bends in that road.

"Babe!" said Paul. "It's time you earned those sugar-lumps I give you of a Saturday night!"

Then Paul put a harness round Babe's shoulders and hitched him to one end of that twisty road.

"Pull Babe!" ordered Paul and Babe pulled and heaved and pawed the ground. It was a tough task and that Babe sweated a tiny bit, but with one

last lunge forward, Babe pulled the whole road straight. After that Paul took the trees down to the valley with no trouble at all.

"Things are easy when you know how to set about them," he grinned.

Now Paul was not merely big and tough, he was smart.

One day he fell to thinking about the way he ran his lumber camp.

"I reckon as I'm a-wasting money up here," he said. "I'm spending money on things we don't need, that could be spent on good things like extra beans with our beef, and more syrup on our pancakes."

Paul spoke to his friend Johnny Inkslinger, who kept all the books for the buying and selling of the timber. By this time Paul's camp was so big and so successful that Johnny Inkslinger was using ink by the barrelful. He used so much that he had a hose fitted from the barrels to his pen, so that he did not have to get up each time his fountain pen needed refilling.

"Johnny," said Paul. "We are going to save money on ink."

"How can that be, with all the orders and bills and receipts I have to write?" asked Johnny.

"Well," replied Paul. "From now on, stop dotting 'i's and crossing 't's. It isn't necessary. Everyone will still understand what you mean."

"Darn me, if you may not be right!" agreed Johnny Inkslinger.

He stopped dotting 'i's and crossing 't's and in a few weeks, he had saved six barrels of ink. The money gained was put to good use and all the loggers said what a fine thing it was to work for a smart boss.

The stories about Paul Bunyan are endless. They could fill a book on their own, but here our tale must end. Some folk say that Paul is still out there in the distant hills felling trees. That may not be true. It sounds like rather a tall story, and telling a tall story would never do!

Nanook, the White Bear

The Inuit of Northern Canada still remember the stories which were told in the igloos during the long winters of the olden days. In those days they regarded the birth of twins as being unlucky. This tale was related to a Frenchman, who had visited their icy encampments during the early years of this century.

Long, long ago, a young mother gave birth to two boy babies, she was filled with grief and she bemoaned her fate. The woman's husband tried to comfort her.

"They are strong, healthy boys," he said. "Forget the stories about twins being unlucky. Our babies will grow into good hunters."

The young woman would not be comforted.

"Ill-luck will follow us while these children are with us," she said. "I have brought sorrow to our family."

The strange thing about the two growing babies was that they were very hairy. As they crawled across the fur rugs of the igloo, they could hardly be seen, except for their gleaming, bright eyes. The young mother became more and more distressed, her health was affected and she could no longer give milk to feed the babies.

One day she took them out and abandoned them in the snow.

Many old heads nodded at her wisdom, this should have been done when the babies were first born. The tribal group moved on and, in the course of time, new people came into the district.

The babies did not die. Their strength and hairy skins saved them. One twin crawled towards the sea with its great icebergs and became Nanook, the white bear. The other baby struggled towards the moss and bogs of the tundra and became Nanook, the black bear. Meanwhile, anyone who had ever known about the twins, soon forgot them.

One day, a hunter named Uluksak, journeyed across the frozen sea. Suddenly to his terror, the unfortunate man heard the sound of cracking ice as the sea thaw had set in early. Long, widening gaps opened up between Uluksak and the distant shore. He looked desperately around, but there was no path back to land, he was trapped on an ice floe and carried out to sea.

For days the hunter crouched on the swaying ice. The cold sapped his strength, and as he had eaten all his food, he pulled off his leather mocassins and started to chew them. The ice floe tipped alarmingly and looking around, Uluksak saw a white bear crawling out of the sea to join him. He lowered the mocassin from his lips, his heart sinking now, for sure, he would be killed.

To his astonishment, the white bear gave a growl, more like a throaty purr, than a snarl of attack. Then it spoke.

"Do not be afraid," it said. "I wish to help you. I am a cousin of man, not his enemy."

Seeing that Uluksak was starving, the white bear went hunting for fish. It returned with food, and while the man ate, the bear lay at his side and warmed him with its fur and body heat. For several days, these two unlikely friends shared the ice floe. With the food and warmth supplied by the white bear, Uluksak regained his strength. One morning, the wind changed and the ice floe was blown back from the open sea, towards the very part of the shore where the igloos of Uluksak's tribe were standing.

As the ice bumped against the beach, Uluksak spoke to his saviour.

"I should like to tell my family about you," he said, "but who will believe me? Can you give me something to show the other Inuit?"

Nanook, the white bear, nodded, "As true as Williwaws, the icy wind, blows from the north, what you say is right," he agreed.

The bear thought for a moment, then he plucked the hairs from the great clumps of fur which grew like boots all around his feet, and twisted them into a lace.

"Show this to your friends," he said. "No man has ever made a lace like this. Only Nanook, the white bear, and cousin to man could have made such a lace."

The great white bear dived into the sea.

"Goodbye Uluksak," he called.

"Goodbye Nanook," replied Uluksak.

He ran thankfully ashore to rejoin his family.

The hunter's family were amazed and delighted to see him home and safe, but they did not believe his story.

"Your hardships have turned your head," they said. "Hunger made you see visions."

Uluksak held out the lace, woven in a strange fashion from fur from the foot of the white bear. No one had ever seen such a thing before, and they could not tell how it had been made. The family of Uluksak believed him and his tribe believed him. More people examined the strange lace and could discover no way in which it could have been made. At last the whole of the great frozen Northland came to believe in the existence of Nanook, the white bear, cousin of man.

252

The Medicine Wolf

Before the arrival of the white man, North America was populated by Red Indian tribes, believed to be of Asiatic origin. They were mostly hunter-gatherers and they lived very close to nature. Legends of the Blackfoot tribe were collected from oral sources at the end of the nineteenth century and, like many Red Indian legends, they concern mystic relationships with animals.

At one time, the Blackfoot Indians were moving camp. They travelled in a slow-moving, straggling line, with warriors at the front and the rear. In the centre were the women, the children and the old folk, together with such possessions as they had, dragged along by horses or on dog carts.

Suddenly a band of Crow warriors, who had been lying in ambush, rushed out and attacked the centre of the line. Swiftly they killed and robbed and took the stronger, young women to be their slaves. Before the Blackfoot braves could reach the scene of the struggle, the attackers were away and could not be overtaken.

The Crow camp on the Yellowstone River was far, far from the scene of the ambush and it was many days of travel before the triumphant war party reached home with their exhausted prisoners.

One of the Blackfoot captives was a young woman called Sits-by-the-door. She was forced to work as a drudge from dawn till dusk and beaten if she refused. At night, the brave who had captured her tied her feet together and put another rope round her waist, this one he gave to his wife. The wife was not an unkind woman and felt pity for the Blackfoot girl. Although their languages were different, she managed to speak a few words to the prisoner and while her husband was out of camp, did her best to make life a little easier for the unfortunate slave.

One day, the wife told Sits-by-the-door that the braves were talking of killing her.

"You must escape tonight," she said, "or you will never see another sunset. I will help you."

That night, the wife waited until her husband's breathing told her that he was asleep. She crept over to Sits-by-the-door and freed her from her bonds. She gave her a new pair of moccasins, a flint and a small bag of pemmican, which was a sort of dried meat.

"Travel as far as you can before morning," said the wife, "for when my husband and his friends find you gone, they will surely follow you and if they find you, they will kill you."

254

Scarcely needing such advice, Sits-by-the-door hurried from the tepee and half walked and half ran until the sun was well above the horizon, and she knew that the Crow braves would be astir. Creeping into the thickest part of the undergrowth, she lay shivering with fear and hoping that her efforts to walk on stony ground and leave no trail had succeeded.

Fortune smiled upon the girl, for her captor and his friends searched and raged to and fro for several hours, but as they found no tracks they gave up and went home and bothered with the affair no more.

For four nights Sits-by-the-door journeyed towards the land of the Blackfoot. During the day she hid and rested, for she still feared that the Crow braves might be searching for her. She shivered with the cold. Her moccasins wore out on the rough ground. She ate up all her pemmican, but worst of all, she saw that she was being trailed by a large wolf. Desperately Sits-by-the-door tried to hurry her pace, but she was too weak and was only able to stumble along.

Closer and closer padded the wolf, until one night he came and lay down at her side. Sits-by-the-door could scarcely breath for terror, expecting at any moment to feel the wolf's sharp yellow teeth tearing at her throat. To her amazement, the wolf did not harm her, but lay close and kept her warm.

In the morning she said to him, "I am faint for lack of food. If you cannot help me, I shall surely die before I reach my home."

The wolf looked at her with his sharp eyes and trotted away. Quite quickly he returned and laid a freshly killed buffalo calf at her feet. Gratefully Sits-by-the-door cooked some of the meat over a fire which she had made with the flint given to her by the Crow woman. The food and the warmth revived the desperate girl and soon she was strong enough to continue the long walk home. Now she travelled by daylight with the wolf trotting a few paces behind her. By night she slept with the wolf at her side. When she was hungry, Sits-by-the-door rested in the undergrowth, while the wolf hunted. Then they both ate.

At long, long last Sits-by-the-door walked into the camp of Blackfoot Indians. How pleased they were to see her and how amazed they were to see a huge wolf walking at her heels. The children would have driven it out of the camp with sticks and stones, but Sits-by-the-door stopped them.

"He is my friend. He saved my life. There is powerful medicine between us," she said.

As the Indians believed in medicine or magic between humans and animals, the wolf was accepted into the camp and no harm was done to him. For many months the wolf lived with Sits-by-the-door and fed in her lodge.

However, Sits-by-the-door fell ill and the village dogs drove the wolf out of the camp. Every evening the wolf would come to a hill and look down at the lodge where Sits-by-the-door lay sick. Her friends went out and threw food to him. Every evening the wolf came, until Sits-by-the-door breathed her last. Then, although the girl's friends went on throwing out food for him, the wolf was seen no more.

Pilotte, the dog that saved a settlement

Canada is the icy crown to the North American continent. It stretches from the snow of the Arctic Circle down to the lush market gardens next to the border with the United States of America. Many immigrants have come to this vast land. This story concerns some men and women who made the long journey from France, and a dog which came to their rescue.

Immigrants to a new land will always look for the lushest pastures and the richest hunting grounds in which to settle. Alas! When these people smile at their sunny new homelands, they do not always realize that if the location is so good, someone else may have found it before them.

So it was with the small band of French settlers who arrived on the Island of Montreal over three hundred years ago. Men and women looked at the sweet river water, the forests offering a free larder of game and the unfailing grass on which to feed their domestic animals. To European eyes, accustomed to the tamed and densely populated landscapes of their old homes, the new country seemed empty of people.

It was not.

The Iroquois Indians were already hunting across that landscape and they saw no reason why they should make room for newcomers.

The sun shone on the innocent hopefuls as they felled trees and built a sturdy fort and a hospital. They put up an altar before which Father Vimont, their priest, prayed that their little settlement would one day grow to be a fine city.

A few weeks after their arrival most of the men were down by the river, clearing land and cutting more timber. Suddenly a screeching war-whoop tore through the mumble of idle chatter. The Iroquois had arrived to wipe out their unwanted visitors. Immediately the men ran for the shelter of the fort. None of them reached it. The lucky ones were killed in the fighting. No one cared to think about the lingering deaths of the others.

Those within the fort were safe. They did not leave their new homes, carried on trading and farming and welcoming newcomers from France to swell their numbers. There was never a moment of relaxation, watches had to be kept day and night. Anyone thoughtless enough to step aside and become separated from his companions was usually found dead. Animals and implements were constantly stolen, as if by the very shadows. The Iroquois harried and robbed, until the settlers started to discuss leaving the island.

Paul de Chomedy, one of the original settlers, did not wish to leave, it seemed disloyal to those who had died. Instead, he had the idea of sending back to Paris for a supply of dogs.

257

"The right dogs could save this settlement," he thought. "The right dogs would be able to tell the difference between Iroquois and other men, they could be trained to patrol the forest and give us warning of an attack."

So a request for dogs was sent to France. To the agents in Paris, this commission to supply canines to a village on an island half a world away, seemed less than pressing.

Other, more lucrative, orders were attended to. Shortly before the next supply ship was due to sail, they remembered the order for the dogs. Hastily a batch of strays were rounded up from the streets of Paris, old and young, big and small, if they were dogs with no apparent owners, they were suitable.

The rough Atlantic journey in the rolling, wooden sailing ship was accomplished and thankfully, the sailors unloaded the rowdy dogs into small boats for the journey to the Island of Montreal. Eagerly Paul de Chomedy welcomed the dogs ashore, but they were not to fulfil his highest hopes. Some were sick and died, others had lived the wild life for too long to be trained and many had vicious natures, which was why they had been turned out on the streets in the first place. Others were not intelligent and could not learn the difference between the scents of an Iroquois, a Frenchman or a friendly Indian.

There was one noble dog amongst this motley pack. She was a female with a fine sense of smell and a faithful nature. She was given the name of Pilotte.

Pilotte could pick up the scent of the Iroquois and confuse it with nothing else. She learned to patrol the edges of the forest and cross the trails of Frenchmen and friendly Indians with no fuss, but let her pad across the tracks of an Iroquois, or glimpse one flitting between the trees, and Pilotte would rush barking to the fort and the alarm would be raised.

So the Iroquois found that picking off settlers and stealing from the encampment became more and more difficult.

Pilotte bore several litters of pups and trained them in her own good ways. Soon relays of fine dogs were available to guard the forest tracks.

In 1648, a man named Lambert Closse was sent to Montreal. It was his task to transform the defences of the hopeful little settlement into a properly organized force.

Pilotte came forward to snuffle a greeting to the new defender of her territory. From that first moment she and Lambert Closse were friends. Pilotte walked watchfully at Lambert's heels as he surveyed the forest approaches and made his plans. Soon Indian attacks ceased and before much longer, they were a fading memory. So, from a tragic beginning, the settlement on Montreal Island grew into a lovely city.

The modern citizens, living in their warm houses and rolling along smooth roads in comfortable motor cars, have not forgotten the desperate struggles of days gone by. They have raised a fine monument in the Place d'Armes as a tribute to the city's founding fathers, and on the base of the monument, there is the figure of a dog. It is Pilotte.

The Moon in the Millpond

The adventures of Brer Rabbit and his rascally friends were first written down by an American journalist named Joel Chandler Harris, born in 1848. As a boy in Georgia, Harris used to visit the negro cabins and listen to the stories being told by the old men sitting by the firesides. Later, when he was writing a daily column for a newspaper in Atlanta, Harris remembered his boyhood days and retold one of the stories he had heard about Brer Rabbit. It was an immediate success. From then on, stories about the doings of Brer Rabbit and his friends, recounted by an old character named Uncle Remus, were a regular feature in the newspaper. They have been popular ever since.

Many years ago a little boy used to visit an old man named Uncle Remus to listen to the tales he told about that scamp, Brer Rabbit, and all the other folks and animals who lived in the olden days.

One day, the little boy found Uncle Remus sitting in his usual chair and talking about a time when all the animals had been at peace with each other.

"Tell me all about that," said the little boy.

So Uncle Remus settled himself back into his chair and began:

There was a time when there had been no trouble for weeks and weeks. All the creatures were chatting and talking together, as if there had never been any falling out.

Now, that Brer Rabbit, he began to feel bored. He lay in the sun and kicked at the gnats, then he nibbled at the grass and finally, he wallowed in the sand.

Then he fell in with Brer Terrapin and after they had shaken hands, they sat down by the side of the road and chatted about old times. By and by Brer Rabbit ventured to say that he thought it was time to stop being peaceful and have some fun.

"Brer Rabbit," said Brer Terrapin, "you're just the fellow I've been looking for."

"Well then," said Brer Rabbit, "we'll tell Brer Fox and Brer Wolf and Brer Bear, that tomorrow night we'll meet them down by the millpond, to do a little fishing." Brer Rabbit paused for just a moment. "I'll do all the talking. All you have to do is sit back and say, 'Yes. That's right, Brer Rabbit'." With that Brer Rabbit ran off home and went to bed.

Now Brer Terrapin, he was rather slow at getting about, so he set off for the millpond, to make sure that he would be there on time.

Next day, Brer Rabbit sent word to all the other creatures about going fishing in the millpond that night.

"How wonderful," they all said. "Why didn't we think of that?"

Brer Fox invited Miss Meadows and Miss Motts to come and

watch how clever he was at fishing. In those days animals dressed in clothes and talked to human beings.

Sure enough, when the time came, everyone was at the mill-pond. Brer Bear brought a hook and line. Brer Wolf brought a hook and line. Brer Fox brought a dip net and, not to be outdone, Brer Terrapin brought the bait.

Miss Meadows and Miss Motts didn't bring anything. They stood well back from the edge of the pond and squealed every time Brer Terrapin shook the bait box at them.

Brer Bear said he was going to fish for mud cats. Brer Wolf said he was going to fish for horney-heads. Brer Fox said he was going to fish for perch for the ladies. Brer Terrapin said he was going to fish for minnows. Brer Rabbit winked at Brer Terrapin and said he was going to fish for suckers.

They all got ready and Brer Rabbit marched up to the pond and made to throw his line into the water. Suddenly, it seemed as if he saw something. The other creatures, they stopped and watched.

Brer Rabbit dropped his fishing rod. He stood there scratching his head and looking down into the water.

The girls began to feel uneasy and Miss Meadows, she shouted out, "Land sakes, Brer Rabbit. What in the name of goodness is the matter in there?"

But Brer Rabbit, he scratched his head and looked in the water.

Miss Motts, she hitched up her skirts and said she was monstrous feared of snakes and she surely hoped there were no snakes about.

Brer Rabbit, he kept on scratching his head and looking into that millpond. "Ladies and gentlemen," he said, "we might as well make tracks for home. There is going to be no fishing in this pond."

With that Brer Terrapin, he scrambled up to the edge of the pond and looked over. He shook his head and said, "Yes. That's right, Brer Rabbit."

Then Brer Rabbit called out to the girls, "Don't worry ladies. We will take care of you. There's nothing much the matter except that the Moon has dropped into the water.

With that they all went to the bank and looked in. Sure enough, there lay the Moon, a-swinging and a-swaying at the bottom of the pond.

Brer Fox, he looked in and said, "Well, well, well!"

Brer Wolf, he looked in and said, "Mighty bad! Mighty bad!"

Brer Bear, he looked in and said, "Tum, tum, tum!"

The ladies looked in and Miss Meadows, she squealed out, "Well, I never did!"

Brer Rabbit spoke up, "Ladies and gentlemen, whatever you say, unless we get that Moon out of the pond, there will be no fish caught this night. If you ask Brer Terrapin, he will tell you the same."

And Brer Terrapin, he said, "Yes. That's right, Brer Rabbit."

Then the other animals asked how they could get the Moon out of the millpond.

Now Brer Rabbit, he looked at Brer Terrapin and said, "I reckon the best way out of this little difficulty is to send round to your old uncle, Mr Mud-Turtle. We'll borrow his big net with the handles and drag that old Moon out of the millpond."

And Brer Terrapin, he said, "Yes. That's right, Brer Rabbit."

All the animals agreed that Brer Rabbit should go and borrow the net from Uncle Mud-Turtle. While he was gone Brer Terrapin said that he had heard tell, time and again, that anyone who pulled the Moon from the water pulled a pot of money out with it.

This made Brer Fox and Brer Wolf and Brer Bear feel mighty good, and they said that as Brer Rabbit had been so kind as to fetch the net, they would do the fishing for the Moon.

When Brer Rabbit got back with the net, he made as if he wanted to go into the water. He pulled off his coat and was just unbuttoning his waistcoat, when the other animals said they wouldn't dream of letting Brer Rabbit go into the water.

So Brer Fox, he took hold of one handle of the net and Brer Wolf, he took hold of the other handle and Brer Bear, he waded along behind them to lift the big net clear of logs and snags.

They made one haul, but they didn't get the Moon.

They made another haul – still no Moon.

By and by, they got further out from the bank. Water ran into Brer Fox's ear. He shook his head. Water ran into Brer Wolf's ear. He shook his head. Water ran into Brer Bear's ear. He shook his head. And while they were a-shaking of their heads and before they knew what was happening, they came to where the bottom of the pond shelved down fast.

Brer Fox, he stepped into deep water. Brer Wolf, he stepped into deep water. Brer Bear, he stepped into deep water. And, goodness gracious, they kicked and splattered so much it seemed as if they were going to splash all the water out of the pond.

When they finally scrambled out, the girls were a-sniggering and a-giggling and no wonder, for look where you might, you would never see three sillier looking creatures than Brer Wolf, Brer Fox and Brer Bear.

Brer Rabbit, he shouted out, "I expect you gentlemen will want to go home and put on dry clothes." He grinned, "Better luck next time. I do hear say that the Moon will bite at a hook if you have fools for bait."

So, Brer Fox and Brer Wolf and Brer Bear went dripping away. Brer Rabbit and Brer Terrapin went off for a party with the girls.

Uncle Remus looked at the boy, "Time for you to go home too," he said.

Napi and the Buffalo-Stealer

One year there was a great famine amongst the Blackfoot. The buffalo did not appear on the plain. The hunters hunted in vain and there was no meat for the cooking pots. First the old and sick died, then the weak and the very young. When even the braves in their manly strength started to fall, the chief prayed to Napi, the great creator, for help. Napi was far away in the south, painting the colours on the bright birds of the sunny lands, but he heard their pleas and hastened to the Blackfoot.

The chief explained that the buffalo had not come grazing across the grasslands as they usually did and that his people were starving.

"Fear no longer," smiled Napi. "I will find game for your hunters and also the cause of your troubles."

Taking with him the son of the chief, Napi set off westwards in search of the buffalo. The two men travelled a long, weary journey, but on the other side of the green grass hills, they saw a small lodge at the side of a river. Napi stood and stared and let his eyes see the meaning of everything before him.

"Here is the cause of your trouble," he said to the son of the chief. "Living in that lodge is a buffalo-stealer, who has taken all the buffalo from the plain for himself and left none to give food to others."

Then Napi turned himself into a pretty little dog and his companion into a fine strong stick. Soon the chief's son realized why. A little boy came running along the river side.

"Oh, what a dear little dog," he exclaimed. "Let me keep it."

The boy's mother, who loved his every look, agreed at once and picking up the stick said, "Indeed we are in luck. This stick is exactly what I need for digging up roots."

Together they walked to the lodge of the buffalo-stealer, for they were his wife and son. Towards the end of the day, the buffalo-stealer returned home with buffalo meat for the pot. He glared at the little dog.

"I don't want that creature in the lodge," he said. "I don't like it. It has an evil look about it. It will do us no good."

The little boy cried and said he loved the dog. The mother begged that the boy should not be upset and at last the buffalo-stealer agreed that the dog could stay. So the dog and the stick stayed within the lodge, while the meat was cooked for the evening meal and the family ate and then went to sleep. When all was still. Napi and the chief's son resumed their normal shapes and ate well from the cooked meat.

"This man has taken more buffalo than he can ever need. He is the cause of your troubles," Napi said. "In the morning you will see that I am right."

In the morning, the buffalo-stealer was furious that the meat had been eaten.

"It was that dog. He is evil. I want him to go," he said.

Once more the little boy cried and the woman pleaded, and the dog was allowed to stay. Presently the buffalo-stealer went out and, a little later, the woman took up the stick and called the boy to follow her out amongst the bushes to look for roots and berries.

For half the morning, the woman dug for roots and the boy collected berries, with the dog frisking round about them. Then the woman sat down to rest and put the stick, which was really the son of the chief of the Blackfoot, on the ground at her side. At once the stick heard the little dog yipping to it from a good distance away in a thicket of bushes. Wriggling like a snake, the stick joined the dog, which was really Napi the great creator.

The dog had found a cavern, almost concealed by branches and brambles. Inside the cavern were buffalo, herds and herds of buffalo. This was where the buffalo-stealer had hidden the animals which he had driven from the plains. The little dog ran in amongst the huge creatures and drove them out into the light. With the help of the stick, the little dog began to drive the herds back towards the land of the Blackfoot.

Suddenly the wife and son of the buffalo-stealer realized that the stick and the little dog were missing. Their shouts brought back the buffalo-stealer.

"Where are my buffalo?" he shouted in a rage.

"We know nothing of your buffalo," cried his wife and son, "but our stick and dog are also gone."

"I knew that dog was evil," roared the buffalo-stealer. "He has taken the buffalo. I will find him and kill him and break the stick in two."

Hearing these words from a great distance, Napi, still in the form of the dog, hid amongst the long mane of one of the buffalo and the stick crept in with him. Although the buffalo-stealer raced to and fro, he could not see the dog nor the stick and nothing he could do would make the buffalo return to his cave. So after several days, feeling safe from attack, Napi turned the stick back into the son of the chief and assumed his own form.

The joy of the Blackfoot people was great when they saw the buffalo being driven towards them across the plain. They prepared an enclosure into which some of the animals could be driven, to keep them close to the village, however, a great grey bird persisted in perching on the fence of the enclosure and frightening the buffalo away. The actions of the bird were so unusual, that Napi became convinced that it was really the buffalo-stealer.

Turning himself into an otter, Napi lay down near the grey bird and pretended to be dead. At once the bird swooped down to make an easy meal, as it thought, but Napi seized the greedy creature by a leg. Resuming his normal shape, Napi tied the great grey bird over the smoke-hole of a wigwam, where his feathers turned black and he coughed and choked and at last begged for mercy.

"I confess I am the buffalo-stealer," he cried, "but release me or my wife and child will starve without me to hunt for them."

Napi's heart was moved to pity and he let the buffalo-stealer go.

"Hunt only what you need for your family," he warned, "for if you take more, I shall surely seek you out and destroy you."

The bird flew away and the Blackfoot had trouble with the buffalo no more, but from that day on, the feathers of the raven have been black and not grey.

The Legend of Johnny Appleseed

The first European settlers in North America established themselves on the east coast. As their numbers grew, their eyes turned westwards to where a whole continent awaited. Into this unploughed, unknown land, rolled covered wagons, filled with people convinced that by hard work and with the help of the Lord, they could make the wilderness blossom. They believed that in this new land, they would live a life of freedom.

Johnny Appleseed first saw the light of day at about the same time as the United States of America themselves – and that was quite a while ago. He lived over in the east, as did most of the folks in those times. Good folks they were too. They worked hard and read the Good Book and feared the Lord. They had built themselves some smart little towns, where the children could grow up decent and outside the towns were plenty of real fine farms.

There were stories about forests and rivers and endless plains on the other side of the mountains to the west, but boys like Johnny Appleseed did not pay too much heed to that. Those wild places were for trappers and mountain men, not for family folk.

Johnny grew up to be an apple farmer. Row after row of apple trees he owned and they glowed with pink blossom in the springtime and were bowed down with shiny apples at summer's end. Proud of his apple trees Johnny was, and everyone for miles around said that sure enough, no one could raise apples like Johnny could.

Then one day, when he was not quite as young as he used to be, Johnny heard a rumbling and a creaking and a chattering and a clattering of hooves. He looked over his fence and saw a long line of covered waggons rolling along the track.

"Where might all you folks be going?" asked Johnny.

"We're going West," was the reply. "We're going West where the forests are full of game and the rivers are full of fish and the land is black and rich and ready for the plough, and where folks can make a new life and have room to grow."

"Sounds mighty nice," replied Johnny, "but are there any apple trees out West?"

"Reckon not," laughed the people in the waggons.

267

"In that case I'm staying put right here," grinned Johnny and went back to picking his apples.

On along the track rumbled waggon after waggon, throwing up so much dust that Johnny had to have a good cough. He looked over his fence once more.

"Land sakes! How many more of them are there?" he thought.

Then he saw that in one of the waggons was a gal he had been to school with, and clustered round her were her four rosy-cheeked little ones.

"Mary-Lou," gasped Johnny. "You surely aren't going to take those innocent children to a place where there aren't any apples! No apple pie! No apple dumplings! No crunchy apples to slip into their pockets when they sneak off a-fishin'! What are you thinking of, Mary-Lou?"

Mary-Lou smiled at Johnny.

"We shall miss your apples, that is for sure, Johnny," she said, "but the West is the place for youngsters. It is the place where they can walk tall and free."

"Don't see much fun in walking tall and free without an apple in your pocket," muttered Johnny.

Mary-Lou called back to him, as she rolled away round the bend of the track, "Fill your pockets with apple seeds, Johnny, and come West and plant apple trees for us. Then I can go on baking Momma's apple pie for the little ones."

Johnny slipped down from the fence and sat in the orchard looking at his beloved apple trees. He did not what to leave his farm, but he felt real troubled about those fine folk setting off to start a new life in a land without apples.

It was the end of a hot day and Johnny had been working hard. He dozed in the shade and with the buzzing of the insects and the distant rumbling of the waggon wheels, it seemed to him that an angel rustled out from amongst the leaves.

"Now look here, Johnny," said the angel, "that isn't the only waggon train heading West, you know, there's hundreds of them going. Now, how can you sit still and let all those good folks long for an apple, year in year out, without so much as a sniff of one. You take your crop of apples and put all the seeds into a bag and head West. You plant apple seeds everywhere that looks a likely spot and you surely will be doing the work of the Lord."

"Darn me, but I believe you're right," said Johnny and with that the angel disappeared.

But Johnny, he did not forget and come the right time, which Johnny knew being a good apple farmer, he filled a bag with apple seeds and started walking West. On his head was a cooking pot, which doubled as a hat and his cloak was made of an old coffee bag. In his jacket pockets were ribbons and little fancies to please the mothers and the children, and tucked in his inmost pocket, where it was safe from the rain, was the Bible, the Good Book itself.

"We all need the words of the Lord to guide us," thought Johnny.

Johnny did not carry a gun and he was not afraid.

"I'm not a-going to hurt no one and no one ain't a-going to hurt me," he smiled.

So Johnny walked West and he walked West and he walked West, until the towns and the apple orchards were left far behind him. Sometimes he slept under the stars, wrapped in his cloak. Sometimes he snuggled down amongst the dried leaves and undergrowth in the forests. Nothing ever harmed him, neither bear, nor snake, nor wolf, nor mountain lion. The wild creatures knew a good man when they saw one.

Wherever Johnny found a fertile spot of land where an apple tree could grow real good, he planted some of his apple seeds. He dug the soil over to make it easy for the little young roots to wriggle downwards. He watered the new shoot and he built a fence around it to protect it until it was strong enough to look after itself. Then Johnny went marching on.

Sometimes, as darkness fell, Johnny would see the lights of a cabin where some of the folks from the waggon trains had liked the look of the land and dropped off to make a garden in the wilderness. Then Johnny would go a-knocking at the door and ask if there was a mite of supper to spare, if all the family had already eaten their fill. Then while the good lady of the family was filling a plate for him, Johnny would take out a pretty ribbon and give it to the little girl of the house. And mighty pleased she would be, as it was probably the first pretty ribbon she had ever seen in her life. When he had eaten his supper and said his thank yous, Johnny would take out his Bible and ask the folks if they would like him to read to them from the Good Book.

"Can you read?" they would gasp, for there wasn't much schooling about in an empty wilderness and folks who could read was thin on the ground.

"Sure can," Johnny would grin and he would sit and read all evening to the family, who gathered round real grateful for the children to hear such fine words.

Then before he left next morning, Johnny would plant a little orchard of apples trees at the side of the farm, and tell the folks how to care for the growing trees.

"This is a job for you," he would say to the little boys. "You tend these trees real good, like I'm telling you and before you can look round, you will be carrying apples in to your ma and asking her to bake you deep-plate apple pies, just like Grandma used to make."

"Thank you, Johnny. We'll do as you say," the little boys would reply.

And the little fellows were as good as their words. Everywhere that Johnny had visited, everywhere that he had stopped in the forest, apple trees sprang up. In the springtime, as folks looked out across a valley or over the plain, they would see a path of apple blossom.

"That's the way Johnny Appleseed walked," they would smile. "Good old Johnny Appleseed."

The years went by and apple trees were everywhere. Now there was not so much need for Johnny and his apple seeds, but still he walked the trails, stopping at a farm here and calling at an apple festival there. He was always welcome. In fact he was more than welcome. As soon as people saw who he was, Johnny Appleseed was made the guest of honour. At harvest time, when neighbours gathered to help each other with the apple picking and enjoy a picnic and dancing, Johnny Appleseed would be sat at the top of the table and given a plate piled with food.

"Without Johnny Appleseed there would be no apples," laughed the farmers. "Good luck to Johnny, who gave us our apple pies and apple dumplings and toffee apples."

Then Johnny would smile and eat a little of the food, for he never ate a lot, and go on his way. One year, Johnny lay down to rest in a forest and suddenly there was a rustling of leaves and that same angel, who had spoken to him so many years ago in the old apple orchard, came and stood before him.

"Time for you to come with me, Johnny," the angel said. "The Good Lord is waiting for you."

"I can't go yet," gasped Johnny. "I've still a few apple seeds to plant."

"Well, you can't plant them down here," said the angel, "but I tell you what, there's a corner in the garden of the Lord where we could do with some new trees."

"In that case, I don't mind going with you," said Johnny and putting his hand into that of the angel, he left worldly cares behind.

The Fate of Napoleon

Many immigrants have shaped the history of Canada. In this tale Russians, Frenchmen and Squamish Indians, come together to influence the history of Europe – or so it is claimed. This strange story was told by Chief Capilano, who visited London in 1906. Although in places the story would appear to have gained in the telling, parts of it have a pathetic ring of truth, particularly the account of the French captives. It certainly shows how news can travel the world in unexpected ways.

During the late eighteenth century, the Pacific Coast of Canada was very remote from Europe. How unlikely it seems that any of the Indian tribes then living there would have heard of Napoleon Bonaparte, but they had. 'The Great French Fighter' they called him and the tribes appear to have taken a close interest in the fate of this valiant French commander.

The hunters and explorers, who trod the lonely reaches of the wild north, were not surprised that Indian tribes living near Quebec should have a knowledge of French affairs because it was an area of French settlement. However, when they reached the far shores of the Pacific, the hunters were puzzled to find quite a knowledge of French affairs there also, and a demand for the latest news about Napoleon.

"You have had other travellers here from Quebec?" asked the hunters. "They told you about France?"

"No! No!" was the reply. "Our news came from the west."

The west was the Pacific Ocean, so the hunters were mystified.

Later, in the days of Edward VII of England, Chief Capilano of the Squamish Indians, journeyed to London to promise loyalty to the English king. While he was there, he related the story of 'The Lost Talisman' which, he claimed, had sealed the fate of Napoleon, the 'Great French Fighter'.

In earlier day, the warriors of the Squamish tribe liked to carry a talisman or charm. This was always a joint from the backbone of a sea-serpent. The bigger and more magical the sea-serpent had been in life, the more powerful was the talisman.

Sea-serpents were rare and terrifying creatures. Anyone who approached them was seized with fits of the palsy, they shook and their bones became disjointed, while their minds wandered. They were bewitched. Only a warrior of complete and absolute purity could overcome a sea-serpent, because the power of the creature could not defeat perfect goodness.

When a backbone of one of the fearsome monsters fell into human hands, it had to be treated with great caution. The medicine men of the tribes used to throw the power of their magic over each vertebra, so that it did not harm its wearer. The charms would continue to affect the enemies of the wearers with the same dreadful seizures that had tormented the beholders of the serpent.

Now it so happened that one of these vertebra talisman had been for many years the treasured possession of a mighty Squamish warrior, the hero of many battles. At last the day came for this man to die, but he had no close male relative to whom he could pass the powerful talisman. The family gathered round his deathbed were all women – sisters, daughters, grand-daughters, but no men.

This greatly distressed the old man, for he knew the talisman must not be kept by a woman. It was such a wonderful and powerful charm that the old man wished it to go to help another mighty warrior, such as he had been himself. He spoke to the women gathered weeping about him and made them promise to send the talisman to the 'Great French Fighter called Napoleon Bonaparte'. Then the warrior died.

The old women of the family said it was impossible to send the charm to Napoleon and that it should be buried with the dead man, but the younger women would not agree. They said that somehow they would fulfill the last wishes of the fine old warrior, so they kept the talisman safe and turned their eyes towards the sea. The very next day, a sealing vessel approached and anchored in the inlet. It was a Russian ship and it was from visitors such as its crew that the Indians gained their knowledge of Europe.

The sailors came ashore and spoke with another white man, who happened to be in the district. He was a trapper down from Hudson's Bay. The Indian women spoke to the trapper, whom they knew, and asked if the crew of this ship might have any knowledge of Napoleon.

"You are in luck," replied the trapper. "Did you notice those two men, who are not like the others in appearance? Those two, thinner, taller men who do not mix with the others?"

The Indian women had noticed the men, who had been badly treated by the rest of the crew and appeared to be little better than slaves.

"They are Frenchmen," explained the trapper. "They are captives and are being forced to work for the Russians. Perhaps they can give you news of Napoleon."

The women waited for an opportunity, then spoke to the two Frenchmen. They asked them if they would take the vertebra of the serpent to the 'Great French Fighter'.

At first the two men were reluctant.

"How do we know we will ever return to France?" they asked. "And if this talisman is so powerful, will it not have a bad effect on us? We are not of your tribe."

The women assured the two men that no harm would befall them through the talisman.

"The medicine man has put a great power on it," they said. "If we give it to you freely, it will not harm you, it will bring trouble only to your enemies."

At last, through little more than politeness, the Frenchmen took the talisman. When the sealing vessel was watered and restocked, it pushed out into midstream and headed for the open sea. The Squamish women stood on the banks of the inlet to watch it leave. Then they saw a strange sight. All the Russians on deck started to fall about and clutch their heads, they were being stricken by fits of the palsy, only the two Frenchmen were unaffected. By the time the ship reached the open sea, the Frenchmen were in charge. Then the vessel was lost to sight. In later years other ships brought back messages of what had happened.

Now that they were the owners of a fine little ship, the Frenchmen were able to make their way back to their homeland. There, out of gratitude for the good luck given to them by the talisman of the Squamish tribe, they took the trouble to go to Napoleon and give him the vertebra of the serpent. From that moment even greater victories were his. His enemies fell away before him, confused and helpless. This continued until one terrible day, Napoleon mislaid the talisman.

Chief Capilano looked round at his spellbound listeners.

"It happened when the great emperor was on the way to do battle with people of your tribe." he said. "He was about to fight the English."

"What was the name of the battle, do you know?" asked one of the listeners.

"Yes, yes," said Chief Capilano. "It was a hard name for an Indian to say and in my land, we had almost forgotten it, but since I have been in London, I have heard the name several times. You have given the same name to a railway station. The name we heard from visiting sailors over on the Pacific coast was Waterloo, they said Napoleon had fought a great battle with the English at Waterloo and that he had been defeated. Defeated because he had lost the charm sent to him by the Squamish people."

Thus does news of great events travel to the remote parts of the world in the strangest ways.

The Earth Giants

The central American countries of Mexico and Guatemala are subject to earthquakes and this is reflected in their folk lore. The Mayan people were very powerful in these lands before Columbus arrived. Their book, POPOL VUH (or Book of Leaves), tells us how they thought the world began and who caused the earthquakes. The POPOL VUH was lost for many years and then re-discovered in 1854, in the University of San Carlos, in Guatemala.

Hurakan, the mighty wind, blew through the universe and created the earth. He made mother and father gods. He made animals. Then he created man. However, man became irreverent and insolent to the gods, who determined to destroy him. They sent torrents of rain and a surging flood to sweep across the earth. They caused the animals to turn upon man and torment him. When men climbed upon the roofs of houses to escape, the gods caused the houses to crumble. If men scrambled to the tops of trees, the gods cast the trees down. Not even in the mountains could men find shelter, for the caves clanged shut against them. So all men were destroyed, leaving only their little cousins, the monkeys in the trees.

For many years, the earth struggled to recover from this devastation and a few bands of men were once more sent to tame the wilderness. Before the task of making the world again a pleasant place was completed, two giants came to live amongst the mountains of Mexico. They were called Zipacna and Cabrakan. Every day Zipacna piled up mountains and every day his brother, Cabrakan, shook them with earthquakes. The brothers were boastful and proud and the gods did not like them. Hun-Apu and Xbalanque, the heavenly twins, were sent down to earth, with orders to humble the destructive giants.

First Hun-Apu and Xbalanque conspired with a band of young men to tame the giant Zipacna. The band of young men, four hundred strong, went to a part of the forest through which Zipacna always walked on his way to the mountains. The young men cut down a huge tree and waited for the giant to pass by.

"Why have you cut down that tree?" he asked in his huge booming voice, as soon as he saw the band of men.

"We wish to use it as the roof tree of a house we are building, your highness," replied the young men respectfully, for Zipacna was huge and powerful.

"And can you not lift it, you miserable little creatures?" thundered the mighty voice of the giant.

"No indeed, your highness, we cannot, not being strong and mighty like your excellency," said the young men, bowing low.

Glad to find an opportunity to show off his strength, Zipacna lifted the huge tree on to his shoulder.

"Show me where you wish to build your house," he said to the men, "and I will take the tree there."

He strode through the forest at the heels of the scampering youths, until they came to a place where the men had previously dug a deep ditch. Telling Zipacna that this ditch was to take the foundations of their house, they persuaded him to crawl into it. When the creature was on his hands and knees, the men cast tree trunks and boulders over him, thinking to kill him. Zipacna heard the missiles descending and took shelter in a side tunnel, which the men had intended to use as a cellar beneath their house. Seeing no movement beneath the trees and boulders, the men thought they had overcome the giant and they began to sing and dance with triumph.

To convince them all the more that he was dead, Zipacna pulled several hairs from his head and gave them to some ants to take up to the surface of the earth.

"Tell the men you took these from my dead body," said the giant and the ants obeyed him.

Now completely sure that the giant Zipacna had perished, the band of men built a great house over the ditch. They took food and drink into the new building and held a merry party. For hours the house rang with singing and laughter. However, all that long time, the giant Zipacna had been lying in the cellar, building up his strength and brooding on revenge.

Suddenly he rose up and cast the house and all the people in it high into the air. The building was destroyed and the young men were thrown so far into the sky that they never came down, but remained in the heavens as the stars called the Pleiades.

The heavenly twins, Hun-Apu and Xbalanque, were much dismayed at the defeat of the band of men and determined that they themselves must destroy the giant Zipacna. They watched their victim for several days and saw that he had a fondness for eating crabs, which he collected from a river at the foot of a certain mountain. The heavenly twins made a model of a large, succulent looking crab, such as would tempt the appetite of a giant. They set it in the river at the foot of the mountain, they hollowed out the mountain, and they waited.

Presently Zipacna came wandering along the riverside.

"What are you seeking?" called out Hun-Apu.

"If it is any of your business," thundered Zipacna, "I am looking for crabs and fish to eat for my dinner."

"Then look down there," advised Xbalanque, the other heavenly twin, pointing to the deepest ravine of the river. "Only a few moments ago, I saw a crab big enough even for a giant like you."

Greedily Zipacna splashed down into the depths of the river and at once Hun-Apu and Xbalanque cast the shell of the mountain upon him. Such was the strength of Zipacna, that even with so many tons of earth on his back, it seemed that he might break free. The heavenly twins looked at the earth heaving and tumbling and swiftly used their magic powers to turn Zipacna into stone.

Thus, at the foot of Mount Meahuan, near Vera Paz, lies a mighty stone which is the giant Zipacna.

Yet the task of the heavenly twins was not completed. Cabrakan, the giant brother of Zipacna, still walked the earth and shouted and boasted and shook the mountains, to the terror of all who lived on them.

Hun-Apu and Xbalanque set out to meet him.

"Good morrow," they smiled, as they confronted the giant. "Who are you and what do you do?"

"I am the mighty Giant Cabrakan," boomed the huge creature, "and I can pick up and throw down any mountain you care to mention. Let me show you."

"Oh yes, indeed," agreed the heavenly twins, "but surely you need a meal to build up your strength before you perform such wondrous deeds. May we assist you by hunting some birds with our blow pipes and preparing them for your dinner?"

"If you wish," agreed the giant and watched while Hun-Apu and Xbalanque shot two birds out of the sky. He would have snatched them up and eaten them raw, but the heavenly twins insisted on covering them with clay and roasting them over a fire.

"They taste so much better cooked this way," insisted the heavenly twins, but they put poison into the clay and it soaked into the skins of the birds.

When the birds were cooked through and smelled delicious, the twins handed them to Cabrakan, who swallowed them in huge, vulgar gulps.

"Now I will show you how to topple a mountain," he boasted, but as he stood up, the poison ran through his veins.

He rubbed his hand across his eyes.

"I cannot see so well today," he sighed.

He took a step towards the mountains and fell to his knees.

"Where has my strength gone?" he asked.

Then he felt cold … and he shivered … and he died.

So perished the last of the Earth Giants and Hun-Apu and Xbalanque, the heavenly twins, returned to live with the gods.

The Jungle Spirits

As all the Indians knew, the jungle was full of spirits. Most of the spirits were evil and needed to be treated with respect and caution, or best of all, avoided. Curupir was the owner of the jungle and a powerful spirit. His feet were turned back to front, so that his footprints were deceptive. Those who thought they were running away from Curupir were actually running towards him and could easily be captured. Curupir was a great friend to the tortoises and anyone who went tortoise hunting did well to beware.

One day, a hunter went into the jungle after tortoise. He was successful and caught several of the creatures, made camp, lit a fire and cooked a tortoise for his supper. All seemed to be going well, but as the hunter settled down to sleep he heard a noise approaching from afar.

Te-wo-yi! Te-wo-yi! TE-WO-YI!

The noise came closer, becoming louder. The hunter leapt to his feet terrified. Limping towards him through the trees, he saw a tall creature with swollen knees. Round either leg was tied a calabash and it was the clashing of the calabashes that made the eerie te-wo-yi noise. Around the figure's neck hung some more calabashes and these gave out a weird green light. The hunter knew at once who his visitor was. It was Timakana, the friend of Curupir.

The hunter screamed in fear.

"Go away!" he shouted. "Go away and leave me alone."

Still the figure stood in the bushes near the fire, staring at the hunter with burning red eyes, but saying nothing.

Now, all the Indians knew that to see a ghost or a spirit of the jungle was nearly always a sign of approaching death.

"Go away!" screamed the hunter to Timakana. "Go away or I will shoot you."

Seizing his bow, the hunter shot arrow after arrow into the bushes towards Timakana, but his hands were shaking so much that he missed every time. In desperation he snatched up a burning log from the fire and rushed at the staring creature. At last the hunter seemed to be making some impression on his tormentor. The spirit turned and limped away into the forest. The hunter chased it, brandishing the burning wood. Satisfied that he had driven Timakana away, the hunter returned to his fire, only to find Timakana sitting there waiting for him.

"Oh woe is me! What are you that you have such powers!" moaned the unfortunate tortoise hunter.

The jungle spirit rose to its feet and clashed its swollen knees together. The rattling calabashes sent the sound TE-WO-YI echoing around the forest.

By now, cold with fear, the hunter took a branch from the palm tree. He held it in the fire, till it blazed up with a dozen tongues of flame. He rushed at

Timakana and this time drove him far away into the forest. The limping figure swayed and rattled out of sight. Sighing with relief and thinking he had driven the spirit away at last, the hunter once more returned to his fireside. There was Timakana sitting waiting for him, smiling a thin joyless smile and staring with unblinking red eyes.

The hunter did not dare to sit by his fire. Least of all did he try to go to sleep, instead he stood amongst the bushes until dawn. As the sun rose Timakana stood up and walked a few paces from the fireside. He looked at the hunter and smiled again and went away.

The sun rose above the horizon. The hunter took up his bow and his hammock and stumbled back to his home.

"What is the matter with you?" asked his wife.

"Timakana was with me all night and he has eaten my soul," said the hunter. He fell down and lay for five days without eating or drinking and then he died.

As every Indian knows, the hunter need not have died. He had done two very foolish things. He spoke rudely to Timakana, who was the friend of Curupir and very powerful. Anyone who meets Timakana should speak to him politely, then he will do no harm. However, the hunter's second mistake was the worst. He told his wife that he had seen a spirit. Anyone who sees a spirit and talks about it, will die for sure. Spirits are secret creatures and do not like to be gossiped about.

A tale from South America

The Great Flood

Every Indian from the south to the north of the continent knows that, long ago, there was a great flood. Before the flood, there were Indians who lived in fine stone cities linked by good roads. The roads were guarded and safe. People had to pay to travel along them, but they knew they would not be robbed.

There were also other Indians who lived as savages on the plains, hunting and gathering vegetables, and they were homeless.

One day, an old man married a beautiful young wife. The wife was discontented and she stood on the banks of a great river.

"Overflow! Overflow!" she begged the river. "Cover the whole land."

So the river overflowed and many people were drowned, but the beautiful young wife fled up into the sky to live with the moon.

Away in the valley, a peasant was tethering his llama to graze, but the llama was restless and kept tugging at the rope.

282

"What is the matter with you?" asked the peasant. "Why will you not let me tether you?"

"I do not wish to be tethered here," replied the llama, "soon a mighty flood will come and we shall be drowned."

The peasant was naturally greatly alarmed and asked the llama what he should do.

"Collect food for five days, take this with your family and me to a high mountain," replied the llama.

Up into the mountains went the peasant, his family and the llama. They saw the waters of the river flood the plain. They saw the waves of the sea rise up and wash over the land. For five days the floods rose, until they were lapping round the peasants and the llama as they stood on the highest mountain range. All the animals were driven up to the mountains with them. Gradually the waters abated, the sea rolled back from the land, and the river lay once more in its bed. Almost everyone on earth was drowned. The man and his family and the llama came down from the mountains. From that family are descended all the people now living in South America.

A tale from South America

The Sun and the Moon

Before the Europeans came to South America there was no writing of folk tales. Records, if any, were kept by knotting variously coloured pieces of string. Legends were a spoken tradition. Any folk tales which remain from the early days, are those which Europeans happened to record after their arrival. The explorers of the late nineteenth and early twentieth centuries, when writing accounts of their adventures, also sometimes mentioned the legends of the tribes they were visiting.

Back in the time when the world was young, Mair was the god of the sun. Every day he travelled across the sky from east to west. Every night he travelled under the earth and came up again on the other side. Sometimes Mair took the form of a jaguar. Sometimes he took the form of a snake. Jaguars and snakes were always his helpers and travelled with him through the underworld. While Mair was in the underworld there was no light because, in those days, there was no moon.

One day a man of the Urubu tribe became the father of a son. He held a feast for his relatives, in order that a name should be chosen for the boy, and he could then be offered as a servant to Mair, the sun god. The feast began at sunset with much eating and drinking. It was hoped that by dawn all present would have agreed upon a name for the newborn.

However, one man and one woman would not stay and pay proper attention to the serious business of choosing a name. They ran away into a hut and the woman painted the man's face. She put big black circles round his eyes, a black line down his nose and a black mark across his mouth. They talked and giggled and took no heed of the other members of the family who were searching for them.

At last, as dawn came, the man and woman remembered their duty and went out into the light of day to help choose the name for the new baby. The man suddenly remembered the marks which the woman had painted on his face. He tried to wash them off before the other Indians saw them, but no matter how much he rinsed his face, the black marks would not go. His relatives jeered at him, when they saw the ridiculous marks.

Neither the man with the marks on his face, nor the woman who had painted them, were allowed to join in the final ceremonies for choosing the name of the baby, and they were turned away from the remainder of the feasting.

Suddenly the man snatched up an armful of arrows and a bow and ran to a big clearing. The woman ran after him. The man pulled the bow string back as far as he could and shot an arrow high into the sky. It flew so high that it could not fall down. The man shot another arrow which hit the butt of the first one and it also stayed in the sky. The man shot another and another. At last he had shot so many arrows that they stretched down to earth like a ladder. He threw away his bow and climbed up the ladder of arrows, wishing to go away and hide his black-marked face. The woman, fearing to be left on earth, and blamed by her relatives for the trouble she had caused, climbed the ladder of arrows after the man. They disappeared into the sky and were lost to their family forever.

Three days later, the Indians saw a pale light in the night sky. It was not bright and burning like the blaze of Mair in the daytime. It was silver and faint. The Indians were looking for the first time at the moon. It was a crescent new moon, but as the month wore on, it grew full and round. On its face the watching Indians saw the same black marks around the eyes, the nose and the mouth, as had been on the face of their relative, who had climbed up the ladder of arrows.

"There is our brother, who has become the moon," they said. "There is his face, as it was painted here on earth."

They noticed a bright star which followed the moon in its travels over the sky.

"There is the woman who followed our brother," said the Indians. "She has been turned into a star and is forever following the moon, seeking to wipe the black marks from his face."

From that time on, Mair the sun travelled across the sky by day. At night the darkness was lit by the moon with its black-marked face and the bright star which followed it.

284

Bibliography

In order to choose the stories included in *Folk Tales and Fables of the World,* I read many books. I was looking not only for interesting and contrasting tales, but also seeking to understand the historical and social backgrounds to the stories. For years I have struggled round crowded book fairs (trying to avoid being trodden underfoot by international dealers) and grubbed round tiny secondhand bookshops in unlikely backstreets, looking for books of fairy stories, folk lore, myths and legends. Some of the most rewarding shops have been in military towns, like Aldershot in England, where soldiers sell off books that they bought for their children when the family accompanied them to some distant foreign country.

Many of the embassies and high commissions in London have beautiful libraries of their national books and these were helpful and informative.

The following is a list of books which I read and researched, in order to write the tales I have chosen, in a manner I believe to be sympathetic to the outlook of the people who originally told them.

EUROPE

Gods and Myths of Northern Europe, by H.R. Ellis Davidson, published 1964 by Penguin Books, Harmondsworth

Myths of the Norsemen, by H.A. Guerber, published 1908 by George G. Harrap, London

Hero Tales and Legends of the Rhine, by Lewis Spence, published 1915 by George G. Harrap, London

Legends of the Rhine, by Wilhelm Ruland, written 1906, published by Koln am Rhein, Verlag von Hoursch & Bechstedt

The Children of Odin, by Padraic Colum, published 1920 by George G. Harrap, London

The Domesday Book, compiled in England in 1086

The Anglo-Saxon Chronicles, written in England from the ninth to the twelfth centuries. Modern version translated by Anne Savage, published 1983 by Book Club Associates, London

Stories of Legendary Heroes, published by Waverley Book Company, London

Hero Myths and Legends of the British Race, by L.I. Ebbutt, published 1912 by George G. Harrap, London

Le Morte d'Arthur, by Sir Thomas Malory, written 1469, as published by the Medici Society, Boston

British Folk Tales and Legends, by Katharine M. Briggs, published 1977 by Paladin Books, London

The Golden Fairy Book, published sometime before 1898 by Hutchinson & Co., London

English Fables and Fairy Stories, by James Reeves, published 1954 by Oxford University Press, London

English Fairy Tales, collected by Joseph Jacobs, published 1890 by David Butt, London

More English Fairy Tales, collected by Joseph Jacobs, published 1894 by David Nutt, London

English Fairy Tales, selected by Edwin Sidney Hartland, published by The Walter Scott Publishing Co., New York

Fairy Gold, Old English Fairy Tales, chosen by Ernest Rhys, published 1906 by J.M. Dent and Sons, London

The Old, Old Fairy Tales, collected by Mrs. Valentine, published 1889 by Frederick Warne and Co., London

The Book of Celtic Stories, by Elizabeth E. Grierson, published 1908 by A. and C. Black, London

Celtic Myth & Legend, Poetry & Romance, by Charles Squire, published by The Gresham Publishing Company, London

Myths and Legends of the Celtic Race, by T.W. Rolleston, published 1916 by George G. Harrap, London

Fairy Legends of Ireland, by T. Crofton Croker, published 1888 by George Allen and Co., London

Irish Fairy Tales, by James Stephens, published 1924 by Macmillan & Co., London.

Scottish Folk Tales and Legends, by Barbara Ker Wilson, published 1954 by Oxford University Press, London

Twenty Scottish Tales and Legends, edited by Cyril Swinson, published 1940 by A. & C. Black, London

The Welsh Fairy Book, by W. Jenkyn Thomas, published sometime before 1907 by Fisher Unwin, London

Welsh Legends and Folk Tales, by Gwyn Jones, published 1955 by Oxford University Press, London

Les Contes de Perrault, de Madame Leprince de Beaumont et de Madame d'Aulnoy, published by Fernand Nathan

French Legends, Tales and Fairy Stories, by Barbara Leonie Picard, published by Oxford University Press, London

Pictures and Legends from Normandy and Brittany by Thomas and Katharine Macquoid, published 1879 by Chatto and Windus, London

A Treasury of French Tales, by Henri Pourrat, published 1953 by George Allen & Unwin, London

Legends and Stories of Italy, by Amy Steedman, published circa 1909 by T.C. & E.C. Jack, London

Aesop's Fables, translated by V.S. Vernon-Jones, published 1912 by William Heinemann, London

A Classical and Biblical Reference Book, by H.A. Treble, published 1948 by John Murray, London

Classic Myth and Legend, by A.R. Hope Moncrieff, published by The Gresham Publishing Company, London

Greek Myths, by Robert Graves, published 1981 by Cassell and Company, London

The Myths and Legends and Ancient Greece and Rome, by E.M. Berens, published 1892 by Blackie and Son, London

Heroic Legends, retold by Agnes Grozier Herbertson, published by Blackie and Son, London

Romance & Legend of Chivalry, by A.R. Hope Moncrieff, published by The Gresham Publishing Company, London

Spanish Fairy Tales, translated by Vera Gissing, published 1973 by The Hamlyn Publishing Group, Feltham

THE MIDDLE EAST AND ASIA

The Arabian Nights, edited by Gordon Home, published 1918 by Blackie, London

The Arabian Nights' Entertainments, published by W. Nicholson & Sons, London

Myths and Legends of Babylonia and Assyria, by Lewis Spence, published 1916 by George G. Harrap, London

The Myths and Ancient Egypt, by Lewis Spence, published 1915 by George G. Harrap, London

The Holy Bible

Folk-Lore in the Old Testament, by Sir James George Frazer, published 1923 by Macmillan and Co., London

Myths of China and Japan, by Donald A. Mackenzie, published by The Gresham Publishing Company, London

Fairy Tales from Far Japan, translated by Susan Ballard, published 1908 by The Religious Tract Society, London

Tales of Old Japan, by A.B. Mitford, published 1891 by Macmillan and Co., London

Bengal Fairy Tales, by F.B. Bradley-Birt, published 1920 by John Lane, The Bodley Head, London

Children's Stories from Indian Legends, by Dorothy Belgrave and Hilda Hart, published by Raphael Tuck and Son Ltd., London

Hindu Fairy Tales, by Florence Griswold, published 1919 by George G. Harrapm, London

Old Deccan Days or Hindoo Fairy Legends, collected by Mary Frere, published 1898 by John Murray, London

Folk Tales of Pakistan, compiled by Zainab Ghulam Abbas, published 1957 by Pakistan Publications, Karachi

Hindu Mythology, by W.J. Wilkins, published 1913 by Thacker, Spink and Co., London

Indian Myth and Legend, by Donald Mackenzie, published by The Gresham Publishing Company, London

Myths of the Hindus and Buddhists, by Sister Nivedita and Ananda K. Coomarasswamy, published 1914 by George G. Harrap, London

The Worlds Best Fairy Stories, edited by Belle Decker Sideman, published 1967 by Reader's Digest, New York

Russian Fairy Tales, translated by Norbert Guterman, published by George Routledge & Sons, London

Russian Folk-Tales, by W.R.S. Ralston, published 1873 by Smith, Elder & Co., London

Pacala and Tandala, and other Rumanian Folk Tales, translated by Jean Ure, published 1960 by Methuen and Company, London

Ukrainian Folk Tales, translated by Irina Zheleznova, published by Foreign Languages Publishing House, Moscow

Skazki – Tales and Legends of Old Russia, told by Ida Zeitlin, published 1926 by George H. Doran Company, New York

Vasilisa the Beautiful, Russian Fairy Tales, edited by Irina Zheleznova, published 1974 by Progress Publishers, Moscow

Folk Lore and Legends – Russian and Polish, published 1890 by W.W. Gibbings, London

AFRICA

Folk Tales of all Nations, edited by F.H. Lee, published 1930 by Tudor Publishing Company, New York

Native Fairy Tales of South Africa, by Ethel L. McPherson, published 1919 by George G. Harrap, London

Stories from the Early World, by R.M. Fleming, published 1922 by Ernest Benn, London

AUSTRALASIA

Australian Fairy Tales, by Atha Westbury, published 1897 by Ward, Lock & Co., London

The Aborigines of South Eastern Australia As They Were, by Aldo Massola, published 1971 by William Heineman, Melbourne

The Giant Devil Dingo, by Dick Roughsey, published 1973 by William Collins, Sydney

The Rainbow Serpent, by Dick Roughsey, published 1975 by William Collins, Sydney

Australian Legendary Tales, by Mrs A. Langloh Parker, published 1896 by The Bodley Head, London

Myths and Legends of Many Lands, by Evelyn Smith, published 1930 by Thomas Nelson and Sons, London

Legends and Mysteries of the Maori, by Charles A. Wilson, published 1932 by George G. Harrap, London

Stories of the Birds from Myth and Fable, by M.C. Carey, published 1924 by George G. Harrap, London

Folk Lore and Legends – Oriental, published 1892 by W.W. Gibbings, London

Myths and Legends of Fiji, by A.W. Reed and Inez Hames, published 1967 by A.H. & W. Reed, Wellington

Tales of Manihiki and *Legends of the Atollas,* published by University of South Pacific, Suva

Heaven's Breath, by Lyall Watson, published 1984 by Hodder and Stoughton, Sevenoaks

Legends of the South Sea, by Antony Alpers, published 1970 by John Murray, London

New Guinea Folk Tales, by Brenda Hughes, published 1959 by George G. Harrap, London

When the Moon was Big, by Ulli Beier, published 1972 by William Collins, Sydney

Round the World Fairy Tales, by Annabel Williams-Ellis, published 1963 by Blackie and Son, London

THE AMERICAS

Canadian Wonder Tales, by Cyrus Macmillan, published 1918 by John Lane, The Bodley Head, London

Legends of Vancouver, by E. Pauline Johnson, (Tekahionwake), published 1922 by McClelland and Stewart, Toronto

Les Contes de L'Igloo, adopte par Louise Weiss, published by France Illustration – Le Mond Illustre, Paris

Legends of French Canada, by Edward C. Woodley, published 1931 by Arno Press, New York

The Complete Tales of Uncle Remus, by Joel Chandler Harris, published 1955 by Houghton Mifflin, Boston

Myths of the North American Indians, by Lewis Spence, published 1914 by George G. Harrap, London

The Crooked Tree – Indian Legends of Northern Michigan, by John C. Wright 1917

A Treasury of American Folklore, edited by B.A. Botkin, published 1944 by Crown Publishers, New York

American Folklore, by Walt Disney, published by Whitman Publishing Company, Wisconsin

Fantasy on Parade, by Walt Disney, published 1970 by Golden Press, New York

Folktales of Mexico, edited and translated by Americo Paredes, published 1970 by University of Chicago Press, Chicago

Myths of Mexico and Peru, by Lewis Spence, published 1913 by George G. Harrap, London

Affable Savages, by Francis Huxley, published by the Travel Book Club, London

Exploration Fawcett, by Lt. Col. P.H. Fawcett, published 1953 by Hutchinson, London

South America, Observations and Impressions, by James Bryce, published 1912 by Macmillan and Co., New York

New Larousse Encyclopedia of Mythology, published 1959 by Auge, Gillon, Hollier-Larousse, Moreau et Cie, the Librairie Larousse, Paris